"Levinson, Adkins and Forbes do a great job of pulling back the curtain to reveal the essence of successful marketing for nonprofits. They eliminate the mystery and provide very practical tools and insights to help an organization of any size maximize its mission."

—Ken Winter, Vice President, Church and Partner Services,
International Mission Board, Southern Baptist Convention

"Finally, a book on how nonprofits can benefit from the guerrilla marketing mind-set! This strategic approach, with 250 specific tactics, is custom-made to give nonprofits an edge—even with small budgets and no dedicated marketing staff. Whether you are focused on fundraising, member services, or changing the world, the tips in this book will help you succeed!"

—Nedra Kline Weinreich, President, Weinreich Communications and
author of *Hands-On Social Marketing: A Step-by-Step Guide*

"At long last, nonprofits have access to guerrilla marketing thinking, strategies, and tactics! This book has everything a nonprofit needs to market itself so that it doesn't just survive—it thrives—in today's incredibly competitive and stressed marketplace."

—Sandra Beckwith, author of *Publicity for Nonprofits: Generating Media Exposure That
Leads to Awareness, Growth, and Contributions*, nonprofitpublicity.com

"I'm surprised by how many nonprofit professionals see 'marketing' as a bad word, a practice that is beneath them. For years, I've tried to be an 'interpreter,' communicating marketing principles in ways nonprofits could understand and accept. Now I can just tell people to get *Guerrilla Marketing for Nonprofits*! It is packed with useful ideas, detailed strategies, and helpful tips from experienced professionals. *Guerrilla Marketing for Nonprofits* clearly communicates ways to market your nonprofit and conduct effective fundraising initiatives. Read it yourself or buy a copy to give to your favorite cause."

—Marc A. Pitman, CFCC, FundraisingCoach.com

"Within the first two chapters the authors have identified critical issues for nonprofits and 'guerrilla methods'of approaching them that will peak the interest of any nonprofit leader."

—Gayle Farley Community Programs & Grants,
Oklahoma City Community Foundation

"Think you don't have time, money, or skills for marketing? Think again. *Guerrilla Marketing for Nonprofits* will thrill you with how easy it can be. Devour *Guerrilla Marketing for Nonprofits* and you'll never be hungry for creative marketing ideas for your good cause again!"

—Kivi Leroux Miller, founder of Nonprofit Marketing Guide.com and
author of *The Nonprofit Marketing Guide: High-Impact,
Low-Cost Ways to Build Support for Your Good Cause*

"Yay, and double yay! Finally, the definitive how-to, resource, and idea book for guerrilla nonprofit marketers. It's all here: everything one needs to practice guerrilla nonprofit marketing—a resource you'll want to keep nearby for regular reference. I found myself applauding internally with every page turn. Nonprofits that adopt even a fraction of the guerrilla marketing ideas and principles here will be further ahead."

—Elaine Fogel, President and CMO, Solutions Marketing & Consulting LLC Chair,
American Marketing Association, Nonprofit Special Interest Group

"Buy this book immediately if you are on a mission to do good in this world. It's jam-packed with concrete ways to effect great changes—even if you have tiny staffs and itty-bitty budgets. *Guerrilla Marketing for Nonprofits* is a godsend to nonprofits and do-gooders everywhere."

—Katya Andresen, COO, Network for Good and author of
Robin Hood Marketing: Stealing Corporate Savvy to Sell Just Causes

GUERRILLA MARKETING FOR NONPROFITS

250 TACTICS TO PROMOTE, RECRUIT, MOTIVATE, AND RAISE MORE MONEY

Jay Conrad Levinson, Frank Adkins, and Chris Forbes

Entrepreneur Press

Jere L. Calmes, Publisher
Cover Design: Andrew Welyczko
Production and Composition: Eliot House Productions

This publication is designed to provide accurate and authoritative information in regard to the subject matter covered. It is sold with the understanding that the publisher is not engaged in rendering legal, accounting or other professional services. If legal advice or other expert assistance is required, the services of a competent professional person should be sought.

Library of Congress Cataloging-in-Publication Data

Levinson, Jay Conrad.
    Guerrilla marketing for nonprofits/by Jay Conrad Levinson, Chris Forbes, and Frank Adkins.
        p.   cm.
    ISBN-13: 978-1-59918-374-9 (alk. paper)
        ISBN-10: 1-59918-374-9
        1. Nonprofit organizations__Marketing. I. Adkins, Frank. II. Forbes, Chris. III. Title.
    HF5415.L47635 2009
    658.8—dc22   2009042334

Printed in Canada

14 13 12 11 10   10 9 8 7 6 5 4 3 2 1

Contents

CHAPTER 20

Launching and Maintaining Your Marketing Attack. **317**

Jay Conrad Levinson
Acknowledgments and Dedication

Acknowledgments

I feel privileged to owe acknowledgments to three extraordinary people. The first is Jere Calmes of Entrepreneur Press, who saw the vision of the book and added much of the spirit. Without Jere's enlightened attitude, you'd be holding blank paper in your hand.

I owe endless acknowledgments to Frank Adkins, who conceived of the book, then shepherded it from his mind to your hands. He worked tirelessly to make this a timeless book, though he was also working tirelessly on his teaching, coaching, parenting, and barbequing. I am blessed that he was a co-author, and so are you.

Chris Forbes is the third person deserving of the highest praise. He was introduced to us by my daughter, Amy Levinson, who masterminds many things guerrilla. Chris fit right into our team and worked painstakingly and brilliantly to make this book worthy of being a guerrilla book and worthy of the time you'll take to read it. If you like it, be sure to tip your hat to Chris.

Truly, this is a national book. Jere lives in California, Frank in Florida, Chris in Oklahoma, and I also live in Florida when I'm not traveling in our RV. This is also an international book because it contains insights that cross all boundaries and can help all nonprofit organizations. We hope it will help yours.

It's a joy to be able to acknowledge such remarkable people.

Dedication

I dedicate this book to wife Jeannie Levinson, daughter Amy Levinson, puppy Monroe, and to everyone who will benefit from the efforts of the nonprofit organizations which practice what we preach. The world will be a better place if they do.

Frank Adkins Acknowledgments and Dedication

Acknowlegments

First and foremost, I owe a great deal of gratitude to Jay and Jeannie Levinson. Your mentoring, support, and insights have taught me more than I could ever imagine. You both knew there was a need for this book and somehow put the pieces of the puzzle together to make it a reality. Thank you for having intelligent minds, kind hearts, and giving hands. You both are a shining example of the kindness that drives humans to help one another.

To my co-author Jay Levinson: You have been like a father to me; a teacher like Obi- Wan Kenobi was to Luke Skywalker. You have guided me along a path that was right there in front of me, yet I never stepped foot on. You gave me the confidence to walk, then run. This opportunity came about because you believed in me, and for that I am forever grateful.

I want to acknowledge my other co-author, Chris Forbes. You were the David Banner and Incredible Hulk who did so much of the heavy lifting on this project. I knew it was not by accident or chance that we worked together. Your valuable contributions have far surpassed my expectations, and I hope that this is the first of many collaborations with you. Indeed you have become a friend and brother.

Jere Calmes went out on a limb allowing two rookies to work alongside a Hall of Famer. I could not have asked for a more professional, organized, and pleasant experience from you and your staff at E.P. Jere, like Jay, knew the importance of this book and realized what was needed to meet the demands of countless nonprofits. Like a true guerrilla he took action and got the ball rolling.

Amy Levinson was the behind-the- scenes director and had a vision for nonprofit guerrilla marketing many years before its conception. Her soft steps made this book a reality.

The following list is an acknowledgment of those who somehow impacted my life or have used time, energy, and imagination to help an organization and the people they serve.

Ginger Adkins, Jason Laviolette, Jeremy Huffman, Carmen Nease, Eric Laviolette, Christy Huffman, Stevie Nease, Josh Huffman, Stan and Chris Beller, Dave and Barbara Toler, Billy and Maria Galdorise, Dr. Joel Hunter, Dr. Marc Rummler, Rob Bixler, Dr. William Gordon II, Frank Huffman, Ginger Stevens, Custer Whiteside, Jim Taylor, Kenny Bonnet Jr., Jason Crain, Hector Deida, Don Lipari, Steve Ruff, and Adam Dickson.

Each guerrillas in their own way.

I would like to acknowledge one of my favorite nonprofit groups: the 2009 C.F.Y.F.L. University Giants—Mitey Mite and Junior Pee Wee football players, cheerleaders, and coaches. They were my stress relief while working on this book. I am proud of their hard work during the season which resulted in bringing home multiple championships.

Finally, I would like to acknowledge the many nonprofit organizations who recruited me as a volunteer or donor. They used many of these guerrilla principles long before it became a book. Your dedication to your causes not only helped our society, but also gave me valuable knowledge and wisdom to pass along. Keep the spirit of helping alive while you battle in the trenches:

American Heart Association, American Cancer Society, Habitat for Humanity, Central Florida Council Cub Scouts Pack 219, University of Central Florida, The Track Shack Foundation, Ronald McDonald House Charities, Winter Park Health Foundation, Central Florida Youth Football League (C.F.Y.F.L.), Orange County Public Schools, East Lake Elementary, Killarney Elementary, Forest High School (Ocala), All Pro Dads, Northland A Church Distributed, River Run Community Church, and Teen Missions International.

Dedication

This book is dedicated to my entire family for always loving, supporting, and believing in me.

To my children, Austin, Blake, and Cali, for showing me what unconditional love meant the moment you appeared on this earth. You have changed my life more than you will ever know, and I pray that you will grasp everything that you reach for in life.

To my wife, Ginger Adkins, who has been my blessing and my best friend for over 18 years. You are my soul mate, and I say that with pride. My life is full of bliss because I have you as my companion in this journey. My dedications to you started off long ago with Teen Missions letters and Cedar River signs and have finally led to the print on this page. I love you.

To my mom, Diane Adkins Nease, and grandmother Rose DiMasi for making personal sacrifices in your lives so that I might have a better life of my own. You deserve the best this world and the next has to offer.

To my great-grandparents, Pasquale DiMasi and Filomena DiMasi, for setting an example of love and devotion to each other for over 75 years of marriage. You set the bar high.

To my other parents, Jay and Jeannie Levinson, for setting the foundation of guerrilla marketing, and allowing me the opportunity to add luster to the brand.

To my Dad, Frank Adkins Jr., and Grandfather Enrico Anthony Aprea, I hope that you have finally found that perfect peace in God's arms that eluded you on earth. I will cherish the memories of the little time that you were in my life while you were here.

Last, but certainly not least, I dedicate this book to my Lord and Savior Jesus Christ. For without Him, none of this would be possible. He carefully orchestrated the events in my life that would eventually lead to this book. It is my prayer that the concepts within these pages will assist organizations to help others on a grander scale and eventually lead people to Him.

Chris Forbes Acknowledgments and Dedication

Acknowledgments

I am in debt to so many people for the development of this book. Jay Conrad Levinson has been a marketing mentor to me since the days when I first picked up and read his original *Guerrilla Marketing* book back in 1999. Writing this book with him has been like playing baseball with Willie Mays, or shooting hoops with Michael Jordan—the thrill of a lifetime to have the opportunity to work with your hero. Working with Jay has raised the bar for me, deepened my appreciation for his insights, and inspired me to concentrate even more on mastering guerrilla marketing. Also, I appreciate Jeannie Levinson's guiding hand in helping shape the manuscript and coaching the writing process. Frank Adkins is not only a fellow writer on this project, but has also become a true friend and an encouraging brother. I hope to be working together again with him soon. Thanks to Jere Calmes and the staff at Entrepreneur Press for including me in this great project; every moment working with them has been a pleasure. Amy Levinson had the original vision for contextualizing *Guerrilla Marketing for Nonprofits*. We have been talking about it together since 2005. It is such a joy to finally see the book coming to fruition. I had the rare privilege to pursue my guerrilla coaching certification one-on-one with Mitch Meyerson. If I grasp guerrilla marketing at all, it is because he made the guerrilla mind-set more clearly understood to me.

Many marketing leaders and communication strategists in the social sector have helped me understand nonprofit marketing. But you can find no finer people than the ones that have helped shaped this book with their influence: Nedra Kline Weinreich, Katya Andresen, Marc Pitman, Elaine Fogel, Kivi Leroux Miller, Nancy Schwartz, and Sandra Beckwith. Thanks also to them for contributing comments to the book and for believing in the project and supporting it in their networks.

Like everyone else in the world, I am in debt to Dr. Philip Kotler, Dr. Alan R. Andreasen, and Dr. Peter Drucker for their deep insights and understanding about nonprofit work. No one has benefited social sector communications and management as much as they.

Dedication

This book is dedicated to those who have shaped me and encouraged me in life. Praise God, from whom all blessings flow. Thanks to my godly and loving wife Angela, and my three inspiring daughters, Hannah, Sarah, and Rebekah. They lovingly put up with me working a lot of late nights at the office. Thanks to my mother, Mary Gregory, who is the original master marketing expert in my life. I dedicate this book to John

Brimacombe for his consistent friendship and brotherly love since our days as college roommates at the University of Central Oklahoma and as study partners at Southwestern Baptist Theological Seminary.

Finally, I dedicate this book to the people who trained me and who still serve as proof that strategic communication can put people and relationships before programs: Mark Snowden, Steve Evans, Don Martin, Robert Devargas, Mark Kelly, Ginger Sinsabaugh-MacDonald, Cory Miller, Alan Muehlenweg, and Kerry Bural. Also to my supervisors in the past who have allowed me to experiment with new approaches to ministry communications: Jon Walker, Kathy Sharp, Alan Quigley, Jimmy Kinnaird, Randy Adams, and Anthony Jordan.

Preface

MARKETING HAS CHANGED SO MUCH SINCE I WROTE the original *Guerrilla Marketing* in 1984 that now there are 60 guerrilla marketing titles in 63 languages and more than 20 million copies of the books in print. All their revelations are in this book. That means you've come to the right place to learn how to benefit from state-of-the-moment marketing for your organization and gain the most possible from your efforts.

All too often, in the life of a nonprofit organization, all the hard work goes for naught because the group fails to understand how marketing works in the 21st century. It's a lot different these days than it used to be. The way it is today is clearly explained in these pages. To begin with, the book starts out by being about you—because marketing is all about people. No matter how much you may know about marketing, you've got to remember than nonprofit marketing is different than traditional marketing and guerrilla marketing is different still.

You'll become an expert in both as you read this book. You'll be brought up-to-date on the social media, on publicity, on the internet, on the free weapons of guerrilla marketing, and on recruiting volunteers. That's just a sampling.

You'll also be brought up to speed on your own organization and how it fits into the world of marketing today. We've tried to leave no epiphany unexplored as we've strived to give you the knowledge for your organization to achieve, then surpass its goals. Most of all, we've given you all the bare-bones, hard-nosed facts about marketing, while steering you clear of the pit-falls. There are many to avoid.

Guerrilla marketing is merely the truth made fascinating, completely different from the marketing approaches of the past, which weren't always true and were rarely fascinating. Marketing is also a process and not an event. For a process to be successful requires a plan and patience. This book takes you by the hand and guides you through the development of both—the plan and the patience.

No matter what cause or movement a person is involved in, that person is also and always in the marketing business. I'm talking about you. This book has been written for you.

If you get as much out of this book as we've put into it, the world will be a better place.

—Jay Conrad Levinson, DeBary, Florida

CHAPTER 1

What Nonprofits Need Is Better Marketing

SO YOU WANT TO REVOLUTIONIZE THE WORLD and make it a better place? We have some good news that will help you turn your great ideas into the powerful results you are dreaming about. You are at the starting point of a journey in which we hope to change your thinking in ways that will help you take your organization to the next level. We want to take you on a guided tour of what guerrilla marketing can do for your nonprofit. Right now you are at the beginning of your quest. Soon you will take charge yourself bringing your marketing plans to life. As your momentum builds, your voyage will get easier, but your marketing trek never ends until you completely accomplish your organization's mission. So let's get started.

Guerrilla marketing books have helped people all over the world turn their time, energy, and imagination into profitable results. With more than 60 titles and 20 million books sold in 63 languages, we know a thing or two about getting results. We want to help put the power of guerrilla marketing into the hands of you, the nonprofit leader. Guerrilla marketing isn't designed for people who want to know everything about marketing. It is designed for people who want to grow their organization and get results. Though organizations of all sizes can benefit from guerrilla marketing, it is designed with the smaller nonprofit in mind. You may already have in mind what you think guerrilla marketing is all about. But take a second look. There's more to it than a few attention-getting promotional tactics.

If you're like most nonprofit leaders, you started your plans for changing the world with an ideal vision of how things ought to be. At first you may not have realized your decision to change the planet is also a marketing decision. If you are a leader in a small nonprofit, you are already wearing a lot of hats. It may not be encouraging to know that you also need to learn about marketing. Few nonprofit executives realize that marketing is not merely a promotions program. It is a process that can turn around a flagging nonprofit's results. Marketing is people smart, and it can make your organization a more efficient and friendly place, too.

So even though your thoughts are crowded with all kinds of other pressing needs that demand your attention besides marketing, take the time to master guerrilla marketing. Marketing is everybody's job in a small nonprofit, but someone in your organization needs to take the reins and coordinate the messages, programs, and strategies into a cohesive brand. Your nonprofit needs a guerrilla who can lead the charge into the marketplace with a strategy for getting lasting results. Take charge now, so you can make your organization the best it can be. We are going to show you how adopting a marketing mindset can help you improve your organization's ability to influence others, expand awareness, increase recruitment, mobilize volunteers, enable advocates, and raise more money.

Why Nonprofits Should Embrace Marketing

Changing the world comes with a lot of communication decisions. How will you get the word out about your ideas? How will you change the way people think, act, and believe? What can you do to attract more people to help you in your cause? How can you persuade people to part with their hard-earned cash to support you financially in your quest? All kinds of questions are swirling around your head demanding answers. In addition, you are not making your decision to get the world's attention in a vacuum. There are hundreds of thousands of other organizations and businesses right now making their move to attract the eyes and ears of the people on planet earth, too. For-profit companies spend an average of $895 per year per capita on advertising to get the attention of the same people you want to reach. There is no way your organization can keep up with their spending. And, despite how you may feel about it, the people you want to reach are those same people that companies spend billions to market to.

The nonprofit sector has entered a new phase in the past decade. Nonprofits have increased so rapidly in recent years, that a new term has emerged to define the segment of the economy that is nongovernmental and not-for-profit social sector.

With a 65 percent growth rate in the number of nonprofits in the United States, the proliferation of new organizations has created more competition for attention. Social sector observers report that today, the greatest challenge facing nonprofit organizations is finding a way to compete in a complex and rapidly changing marketplace. There is a constant struggle today for a share of charitable dollars in a financial market that has not expanded as rapidly as the nonprofit sector has grown. Worse yet, economic problems have reduced the number of dollars people have and raised the stakes for convincing them to part with what cash they do have in the form of donations.

> All organizations have to market themselves if they want to impact their communities for the greater good.

Nonprofits continually search for ways to recruit and mobilize a rapidly changing and fickle pool of volunteers. There are more organizations in the social sector trying to find workers at the same time your organization is seeking community-minded people to help you accomplish your mission. Some volunteers move from organization to organization in a search for new and more interesting experiences.

Many nonprofits have turned to revenue-generating models such as selling products and services that put them in direct competition with big-budget for-profit companies. Add to that the fact that many for-profit companies are discovering cause marketing, and you will appreciate how much the typical nonprofit has to maneuver to remain viable and competitive today. All these factors point out the need for nonprofit leaders to get a little more marketing savvy—and fast! With so much competition and media clutter in the environment into which you want to take your message, you would be foolish to enter without a

FROM THE FRONT LINES

NAME: Katya Andresen

WEBSITE: NonprofitMarketingBlog.com

BOOK: *Robin Hood Marketing* (Jossey Bass, 2006)

"Many of us may wish marketing were not necessary and that people would pay our prices without expecting anything in return. 'Why should we have to do this when our cause is so worthy?' is a common refrain I hear from do-gooders. 'If people would only listen, they'd see that (fill in the blank) is the right thing to do.' We continue to operate under the assumption, conscious or not, that if people took the time to listen to us wax poetic about the urgent problems we are tackling—or if they just had more information—they would change their perspectives, embrace our world view, and take action. In our haste to pour our hearts into what we say, we forget to use our minds. We can't market as missionaries—we must be marketers with a mission. And we do that by focusing on our audience and showing people how our cause aligns with the values they hold now."

strategy, especially if you don't have a lot of money. If you are reading this, there is a good chance that you are aware of your challenge. This book is dedicated to helping you make the most impact with your ideas by presenting to you the proven principles of guerrilla marketing.

It's Not Just Propaganda

Marketing is a discipline, not a program for your nonprofit. All organizations have to market themselves if they want to impact their communities for the greater good. But many nonprofit leaders have mixed emotions when it comes to thinking about marketing. Some nonprofit organizations treat marketing as something that is beneath their dignity or even against their core values. But a greater understanding of marketing is really what they need most. If there is even the tiniest part of you that is still unable to embrace the idea of the benefit of marketing for your organization, we hope to help you get over it. You need to understand and apply good marketing to accomplish your goals.

If you have studied marketing at all, you know about the famous "Four P's" of the marketing mix: product, price, place, and promotion. These are the basic elements of marketing strategy. Get the right mix of the elements and you have a great hit. Get it wrong and . . . well, you know. Marketers dream of developing and promoting the right product at the right price, making it available through convenient distribution systems. Look at all the break-through products you personally like and you will see all these elements in place and firing on all cylinders.

What many people mean when they talk about marketing is promotion. But as you see from the "Four P's," promotion is only about one-fourth of the total marketing strategy picture. And considering promotion closely, you will find that advertising is just a small subset of the promotional picture. It's no wonder many nonprofit marketing efforts fail; they are too limited in scope. If you are over-focused on the promotional side of marketing (as many nonprofit marketers are), you are doomed to fail. Some nonprofits treat marketing as merely putting your organization's message spin into media channels and repeating that message as much as you can afford. That's not marketing, that's propaganda.

The reason social sector marketing flops so often is because most nonprofit marketers function only as promotional people. Often the bulk of the typical nonprofit organization's marketing activities center on promoting its program. In some cases, organizations spend more time planning the promotion than they do in developing the program to make it more appealing to the intended audience. There are many ways to make your organization the topic of word-of-mouth buzz besides grabbing their attention using some form of promotional media. If your program really scratches people where they itch, if it really benefits them, they can't help but tell their friends about it. Much of what is done in nonprofit guerrilla marketing will never make it to the nonprofit organization promotional calendar and it won't cost any promotion budget money.

As we think about nonprofit marketing, we need to think about more than program promotion. We need to have the full marketing mix, price, place, and product, too. Working with nonprofits, we have noticed them reading marketing books intended for the for-profit sector and scratching their heads wondering what all the good ideas mean for their work. You may be wondering how the "Four P's fit into the social sector. Is marketing compatible with the nonprofit world?

What Do You Mean by Product?

You are not merely product marketers in nonprofit work. Of course, you do have goods and services you exchange at times through your organization. For example, some organizations offer materials, books, supplies, and resources that help people. Some nonprofits provide low-cost meals, sell previously worn clothes, or offer various services. There are a lot of products in nonprofit organizations. But how can the intangible things non-profits do to help people and the world become appealing "products" in nonprofit work?

Nonprofit marketers step in with a different take on marketing than traditional marketers do. They have a new spin on the marketing mix. First, they expand the thinking of the marketing concept about products from being focused on goods and services only to include intangible things, too. In nonprofit marketing a "product" can be a good or a service, an idea, a behavior, a belief. Thinking this way, consider how many products your organization has. Your organization's real products usually relate to one of the following:

- Programs
- Services
- Classes
- Relationships
- Sense of belonging
- Behaviors
- Actions
- Beliefs
- Attitudes
- Outcomes

How often do the programs of your organization ultimately point toward an expected behavior? Isn't the awareness campaign you have truly about beliefs? When people visit your facility, what are they coming for? What is the outreach from your advocacy really doing? What is the ultimate product? Aren't many of the things your organization does actually promotional tools to get people to adopt an idea as their own?

A training course about infant care for parents, for example, isn't only about methods for caring for kids. It is ultimately about healthy and safe children. What are the core beliefs you expect a member of your association to articulate? When you have that down and you know what the products of your organization really are, then the programs, services, classes all will be designed toward the goal of getting your target audience to adopt your nonprofit's vision. Imagine everything you are doing working toward fulfilling your mission. Nonprofit programming ideas start to unfold as you thoughtfully engage the community in an educational campaign program with a clear purpose. Now you will no longer be tempted to treat your major community events as the products. They are a means to the end: to make your product appealing to the people

> Products, besides being the services and goods produced, can also be understood as behaviors and outcomes.

QUESTIONS TO ASK FOR NONPROFIT PRODUCT DESIGN

- What do you want people to know at each stage of your program?

- What are the beliefs you need to persuade people to hold if your plans are to succeed?

- What are the behaviors that lead toward the results your organization intends?

- What resources people need to use if your goals are to be met?

you want to reach so they will move in the direction toward the change you are looking for.

Questions to ask for nonprofit product design:

- What do you want people to know at each stage of your program?
- What are the beliefs you need to persuade people to hold if your plans are to succeed?
- What are the behaviors that lead toward the results your organization intends?
- What resources do people need to use if your goals are to be met?

> Price can be more than the exchange of money. Many kinds of values are exchanged in nonprofit marketing, and cost could also be considered part of what people have to give up to adopt new ways of thinking.

Don't pull out the marketing calendar yet. We hope to show you more about nonprofit marketing price, place, and promotion. Then we will unpack the rest of guerrilla marketing for nonprofits. You are already making progress!

Adding Price to the Mix

The second element in the mix is "price." We are not just talking about donating money or paying a fee for a service or program. Price can be anything from what other activity a person must give up to attend a free event to finding a stamp to mail a donation or making time for volunteering. Think of the ways people pay a price when they relate with your organization. What are the obstacles they have to overcome both physically and metaphorically to get involved? Below are a few ideas. This is not an exhaustive description, but these questions will get you started thinking about the role price plays in your nonprofit work.

Clients

Even the people who receive free services from your nonprofit pay a price for them in some way. What do they have to do or quit doing to participate? Do they have to give up or adopt a habit? Will they be embarrassed? How much bus fare or gas money will they have to spend to get to your facility to use your "free" services? Some people can't afford even minimal transportation costs. Is a paid service from a for-profit company a better deal for them? What is the typical work schedule of the target audience? Will they have to miss earning some money at work to participate?

Community Awareness

Costs may include overcoming whatever the prejudices may be about the central message or core values of your nonprofit organization. What are the community issues that impede acceptance? Does it take too much of people's attention to grasp your message? Do you make it easy for people who cannot read? In some places in the United States 18 percent of the populace is illiterate. What are the other cultural and linguistic issues in your community that keep people from understanding your organization? Does your major event cause traffic problems and force them to drive out of their way to get home from work?

Donors

Price for donors isn't always about money. Is it easy and convenient to give money to your organization? Is it clear how they can make an impact on your cause if they give to your nonprofit? Are brochures or website too slick and make donors feel you are wasting their monetary gifts? On the other hand, do your organization's materials look too cheap and shoddy to donors so that they think giving to you is an unwise investment? Will another organization allow them to have more control of the money they donate?

Volunteers

Volunteers give up more than time and energy when they work for your organization. What are the negatives volunteers experience by being identified with your cause? What does it feel like to be a new volunteer for your nonprofit? How much time does it take to take part in your program? Do the people believe they have the ability to do what you ask them to do? What will people have to give up to be involved? What training commitments do you expect from people who volunteer? Are the expectations so low there is very little perceived value in their commitment to volunteer for your nonprofit?

Questions about the price people pay to participate are often not considered closely enough by nonprofit organizations. Many nonprofits develop programs (and other products) without spending any time investigating what their intended audience thinks about what it takes for them to accept their offer. The more you get to know your audience, the better you will know how they perceive the costs of "doing business" with you.

Place Is More than Location

In general marketing place refers not only to where a product or service is performed, but also how it is made available to customers through distribution channels. Companies have developed complex supply chain solutions to make their products available rapidly and at a lower cost. These have included creative solutions like drive-through windows, home delivery systems, in-home demonstration parties, online shopping, and more. All these solutions have the same purpose, to give the company an advantage over its competition.

Your organization needs to find creative ways to get your message, goods, services, and programs to the people you want to reach. Place is more than the location where you have your offices; it includes any place where your organization makes contact with people. Even how clean your restrooms are can have an impact. The places you meet can have an effect on how your organization relates to people. Think of all the places your organization has, or can have, contact with people. Are you making most of the distribution channels available to you?

> Place fits well with organizations that have locations where they perform their services, but place also refers to where people adopt their new behavior.

The Role of Promotion

Promotion is anything you do to get the word out about your organization's programs, products, or services. Promotion can include advertising, word-of-mouth, or publicity. We have already said nonprofits can be over-focused on the promotional side of their marketing. It is easy to get out of balance, especially if you have been given all the accountability for directing the communication for your organization and none of the authority to participate in the designing of the products being offered to the public. Nonprofit organizations tend to practice all the elements of the marketing mix separately. They do not integrate programming into their marketing planning. They make programming (product) plans without taking measures to understand price and turn to making promotion strategies with only a slight glance toward place. Add to this the fact that hardly anybody in the organization has any idea about what is on the marketing calendar and you can see why it is hard to build momentum in nonprofit marketing.

> Promotion is the area most obviously informed by guerrilla marketing. Nonprofits need to become effective reaching out to their communities, connecting with stakeholders, and communicating with volunteers.

Unfortunately, many nonprofit marketing people are not allowed to participate in the strategic planning of their nonprofits— they are simply asked to develop the media for whatever plans have been decided for the organization by the executives and board members. Often these people have little or no understanding of marketing. Sadly, very often the people who will evaluate the nonprofit communication leader's marketing plans will use almost any other criteria except marketing to do so. By including the marketing mind-set in strategic planning, good plans can become better and communication can become more natural for the organization.

How can you pull off a stunning marketing promotional victory if you are not involved in how the products are designed, priced, or distributed? If you are not an executive leader in your nonprofit organization, you can help educate others in your organization about how much more effective promotion can be if the marketing plans are made considering the organization more holistically. This also puts a lot of responsibility on the communication leader to understand their organization at every level so they can know how to get the most impact out of how the organization relates to people.

Everybody Wins with Precise Marketing

Everyone knows increasing donations, attracting volunteers, and creating demand for programs, services, and products can turn an organization around. But hardly anyone in the nonprofit world seems to realize the process to make that happen is found in marketing. Traditional marketing complicates the process. In guerrilla marketing, we take the mystique out of marketing and put it in the hands of energetic people who crave more impact for their organization. Organizations that become more intentional with their marketing find that not only are they communicating better, they are also becoming more efficient in their

What They Say about Guerrilla Marketing	What Guerrilla Marketing Really Is About
The tactics are too aggressive	Not aggression, but consistent action
There is too much time or energy wasted	When you don't have a lot of money, what you have left at your disposal is time, energy, information, and imagination
We can't afford to spend money on marketing	There are 200 marketing tools in the guerrilla marketing arsenal; many of them are free
Segments people into stereotypes	Guerrillas are sensitive to the real lifestyles of the people they want to reach
Gets people to buy things they don't need	Guerrillas link their message to the real solutions people need
Intrudes into people's lives	Guerrillas use permission marketing
Adds to the clutter of advertising out in the marketplace	Guerrilla marketing isn't just about advertising; it's a mind-set that leads to results
Manipulates people into doing things they don't want to do	Guerrillas meet people's needs so well, they willingly give them referrals and spread the word

work and creating more demand for their programs and services. Guerrilla marketing can help you improve program quality, make it easier for people to access services, reduce barriers to adopting new behaviors, attract more donations—even make your board happier and more cooperative. Imagine that!

We have interviewed nonprofit leaders in preparation for this book and found some communication people who say they don't use guerrilla marketing. Knowing what we know about the benefits of going Guerrilla, it's hard to understand why anyone would resist the secrets that have helped so many. Apparently, some nonprofits fear they will lose some credibility if they use guerrilla marketing. The folks who feel this way tend to have a cartoon image of what guerrilla marketing is all about. Guerrilla marketing isn't all about in-your-face media tactics. It is more about having an acute focus on excellence. Guerrillas don't find a single marketing tactic and use it rudely to grab people's attention unexpectedly. It's about marketing combinations that work together for greater results.

Below are the answers to some common objections you may encounter to guerrilla marketing.

Marketing finds ways to link the message of the nonprofit to life solutions that attract their target audience.

Guerrilla marketing won't lead you astray. If you stay focused on your original vision and stay grounded in your values, you can make the best use of marketing. Frankly, you don't have much choice anyway. The marketplace is going to do what it does and it's up to you and your organization to make yourself relevant if you're going to maintain (or better yet, increase) your share. You can't change people's perceptions and behaviors if you don't understand and use the one tool that serves you in getting your message out in the public forum.

Know Your Customers

Guerrillas know that the intense competition in the nonprofit world means organizations need to become customer driven. Competition isn't always a bad thing. It helps you to become aware of your market and forces continual improvement in your nonprofit. Organizations should stay mission focused, but the increase in competition doesn't allow much room for error in knowing who your customers are. Though it may fly in the face of how you have been trained to think in your nonprofit work, if you can learn to be customer oriented, you can become more effective.

What Customers Want	How Customers Help Your Organization
Consumers want value	Shows you how to meet needs in ways that make people's lives better
Consumers are fickle and change their minds often	Makes you understand the psychology and emotions of people better
Consumers want what they want and they want it now	Forces your organization to become more humble and service minded
Customers want service	Focuses your nonprofit on maintaining good relationships and valuing people
Customers can leave you and change to the competition	Helps you make your organization as appealing and innovative as it can be
Customers want benefits	Leads you to obsess about creating value-added programs, products, and services
Customers demand to use current technology	Causes you to get your message into new media expanding to a global scale
Customers comparison shop	Teaches you more about your community and competition and where you stand in the marketplace of ideas

BENEFITS OF GUERRILLA MARKETING

- Makes individuals partners in developing products, programs, and services

- Gives people more variety and personal choices

- Builds trust because guerrilla marketing focuses on fair exchange of values

- Enhances communication and uses communication networks efficiently

- Puts focus on meeting needs of niche markets that would otherwise go unserved

- Effectively disseminates information, services, products, and programs more broadly

The marketplace is changing. People today have a consumer mentality that makes them very tough to convince. You may feel that this consumeristic attitude is a negative development for society. Perhaps in some ways it is. But on the other hand, what idea isn't made better when competing in a free marketplace? If you want to get your ideas out into the public forum, you are yourself trying to encourage consumption of your products, programs, or ideas. And even if you wanted to help people become less materialistic and consumption driven (that is a nonprofit product itself), at least it helps for you to understand the prevailing public attitudes about consumption. You can't lose learning about your customers, even when the thought of calling them customers concerns you.

For example, you may dislike the conspicuous consumption of the wealthy, but not realize that as a nonprofit leader you are a purveyor of the ultimate luxury item—philanthropy. As a fundraiser, you may have more in common with the Lexus dealer than you know. Some people are more comfortable with expressing disdain for the wealthy, but guerrillas know the truth that can help them raise more support and improve the life perspective of these donors who might otherwise have a shallow and selfish outlook on life if not confronted with human and environmental needs. Understanding consumers is a big part of what you do as a nonprofit marketer.

There are no promises that we can make you more effective in everything you do. But think of the countless nonguerrilla nonprofits functioning without a clue about marketing. They continue without the proper tools for evaluating their effectiveness and are continuing programs that are ineffective and wasteful. Waste of communication and program dollars is a bigger financial drain in the nonprofit sector than all the guerrilla marketing tactics combined.

> Guerrilla marketing is not considered intrusive to people, it is rather anticipated and expected by the clients of the nonprofit who give their permission to be marketed by the organization.

That's the problem with nonprofit work. Since effectiveness is not always measured by money or response, there is no standard metric you can use to tell if something is working or not. Guerrilla marketing can help you because it trains you to become more responsive to the people you want to reach. If you do guerrilla marketing right, you can build a stronger position for your organization without breaking your bank account, or your back. You can ensure a brighter future like the one your organization is dreaming of.

> Most people give up just before their marketing
> has a chance to work.

CHAPTER 2

Getting to Know Nonprofit Guerrilla Marketing

MARKETING IS EVERY CONTACT YOUR ORGANIZATION has with the public. Think for a minute what that means. Your organization has all kinds of points of public contact. Everything you do that touches people is part of your marketing effort, starting with the name of your organization and ending with the most seemingly unimportant e-mail. We are not trying to be dramatic and overwhelm you with concern about how your marketing might break down. Instead, we want to point out the tremendous potential your organization has to improve your marketing. With just a few positive changes, you could be marketing better right away.

Think of a few examples. You already know it is important to select a name that reflects your goals and objectives. You realize the way people in your organization relate to those you want to reach makes a big difference in the success of your organization. Of course you also know that marketing includes all the brochures, business cards, websites, and social media profiles you post on the web. But often overlooked is that marketing also includes how you answer the phone, how clean you keep your facilities, and even how long it takes you to return an e-mail.

Your marketing includes:

- The name of your organization
- Your mission statement
- The people serving on your board of directors
- Your monthly and annual reports
- Awards and recognitions
- Services, programs, and products you offer
- Sponsoring individuals and groups
- The methods you use in developing programs, services, and products
- The use of color, shapes, and sizes in your materials
- How you package your products and programs
- The location of the facilities in your organization
- Advertising
- Public relations
- Training of staff and volunteers
- How you answer the phone
- What problems your organization solves
- Your long-range planning
- How your organization gets referrals for donations or clients

■ How you follow up with contacts

■ And more

Marketing isn't simply a matter of getting the website up or dreaming up a great slogan. It is a complex process that requires your focused attention. Think of marketing as a circle that starts with your vision for making an impact in your community and completes itself when you have mobilized a loyal group of repeat donors, volunteers, and clients. Marketing is not a campaign you do once a year to generate donors or clients; it is an ever-present part of your organization's daily routine.

Investing Your Resources for Maximum Impact

If you are a nonprofit starting out in guerrilla marketing, you may not have much money for promoting your organization. What do you do when you don't have the ability to spend money in a seemingly endless manner like larger nonprofit organizations apparently do? Well, market smarter of course. Your way of thinking, your mind-set, makes all the difference in the world when you are marketing on a shoestring. You don't have the money to waste— you need all the marketing oars in your organization's boat rowing in the same direction. Guerrilla marketing helps you reframe the issues you face in getting the word out about your organization in ways that make the most of your resources. It shows you the keys to marketing success that are hidden in the sometimes most obscure places.

Guerrilla marketing is designed ideally for smaller nonprofits and startups that

> Guerrilla marketing helps nonprofits invest time, energy, and imagination so that they make a greater impact on their community.

don't have a huge bankroll to back them up. But even if you do have money in the bank, the guerrilla mind-set can help you save money and improve your organization's outreach. Even the largest organization can take advantage of guerrilla marketing. Think about it. If you don't have a lot of money, what do you have that will replace the power of cold hard cash? Time, energy, imagination, and information are all resources that you can invest in an effective ongoing guerrilla marketing effort. The best form of stewardship of your organization's resources is to maximize your use of these things that don't cost money. Make the most of them!

What Is a Guerrilla Anyway?

The word "guerrilla" comes from a Spanish word for a warrior with conventional goals that uses unconventional means to achieve them. We are all peace-loving people and maybe using an analogy from war is a little uncomfortable for some. But we can learn a lot from people who use creative strategies to compensate for being outnumbered. Many nonprofit marketers we know feel intimidated by the other organizations competing for donors. The attitudes in society that seem to exacerbate the problems nonprofits want to solve can discourage you. Nonprofits ask, "What can I really do to make a difference?" Rather than throwing in the towel, you can become a David to the Goliath problems you face in your outreach. You don't have to have a fancy advertising strategy or a lot of money to throw at the problem, but if you can find the smooth stones and sling them in the right direction, you can make a huge impact for the better.

You Say You Want Revolution?

A guerrilla marketer isn't concerned about big budgets and big plans—she is concerned with big impact. It's not the number of hits on her website or the number of people signed up for her programs that make a guerrilla's heart sing. Instead of looking at the organization and thinking how much better it is than last year, a guerrilla is looking for impact. There are a lot of organizations doing what appear to be a lot of good things, but when evaluations are made, no significant change has happened. Guerrillas ask, "What is it going to take to get the job done?" Conventional warriors try to impress others with their armaments and their massive strategies. Guerrillas are focused on achieving their goals and achieving their objectives! Don't be distracted by the things that don't really make a difference. Keep your eye on end results. If you gear all your efforts toward the outcomes you are looking for, you won't have your attention diverted when it is time to make the right decisions. There are many other groups that may be able to show their glossy brochures and huge-budget balance sheets. You can show your donors results. You can recruit people to something bigger, something that is making a real impact. You can make your community better and achieve your organization's vision.

A guerrilla wants a positive revolution that changes the status quo for the better. They want many donors and sponsors, but they would rather have true believers. They'd rather have people join them financially who understand and can see the outcomes before they even happen. This kind of supporter will be the most loyal and ardent advocate of the cause. They will give more than money: They will give of themselves in ways that will positively impact the organization. Here's how a guerrilla sees things:

- Instead of just getting donations and sponsors—he recruits partners to the cause.
- Employees are not just volunteers and workers—they become advocates who care and know their stuff.
- The work is about more than programs and products—it's about changing behaviors.

Guerrillas Know the Way People Think

Ultimately, the success of your mission depends on how well you master and use your understanding of people. A guerrilla doesn't just read books about the people he wants to reach, he writes one. Good guerrillas understand and use psychology in ways that help them connect with people. This helps them get more than only participation from people; they also gain the impact of their influence. One way to do this is to stop lecturing people to change their perspective or behaviors. Instead, by walking in their shoes, the guerrilla understands how people feel when they are considering making a donation. They know what it feels like for a prospect to walk into their facilities for the first time. They have a grasp of how the volunteers involved in their cause benefit from being a part of sustaining change in their community.

Don't be satisfied with the superficial things people say about why they like your organization or participate in your programs. Really get an understanding of them; know them better than they know themselves. It's not as hard as it may seem. Since you will likely be thinking more about your topic than anyone else, you can also train yourself to think outside your field and view your organization from the perspective of those you are trying to reach.

Increased Share of Your Network

The more you are fascinated with people, the better for your organization. A guerrilla marketer is not message focused, or program focused, he is people focused. Your success really comes from the network of relationships you establish in your work. Don't try to amplify the number of things your organization does in ways that put a strain on your ability to cultivate great relationships. Improve the excellence in your relationships, not the amount of stuff you do! You don't need to increase the share you have of the market you are working in as much as you need to increase the share of the response you get from the people in your network. Translated, that means you may already know the people who can take your organization to the next level. Scores of nonprofits are concerned about getting that next "Person X" out there into their database; meanwhile these same organizations are ignoring the people they already know. Where is the bounty? It is within your network. You can grow your organization and improve your effectiveness by focusing on the relationship exchanges in your network. Even if your organization is primarily concerned with helping the environment, your success or failure depends on your relationships. If you are over-focused on your cause and not known for your love of people, you risk the potential of coming off like a fanatic to them. Take a deeper look at what you do. Are there ways to make your interactions with people better? Here are some ideas.

- Expand how you relate to sponsors
- Improve your ability to read and use your databases
- Ask volunteers to help you innovate your processes
- Add value to existing services and products you offer the public
- Ask for repeat clients by booking the next session as you finish the present one
- Renovate or clean an existing facility to make it more appealing
- Interview your best and worst donors and find out what makes them tick
- Say "thank you" more often

Your success as a guerrilla depends on knowing the people you want to reach, learning their needs, and offering meaningful solutions to those needs. Stay in touch with your clients. Never get too busy to walk the floor of your facilities. Get to the front lines more. Every month or every quarter, your stakeholders need to hear from you. The people you want to help need to see you in the community making things better. When people respond and make a connection with your organization, for whatever reason, for the first time, it is a very special moment. This is your opportunity to build a foundation for a long-term relationship that will lead to the changes you believe in. Honor the moment and respect the people you reach.

Why is it so important to focus on relationships? Because every person you know knows someone else, who knows someone else, and so on. Every person you make contact with is connected to a network of other people. You want the people you meet thinking about you when they contact others. You need top-of-mind awareness in the people you reach so they will talk about you in positive ways to others.

Chances are high your donors will be talking to other potential benefactors as they go about their work this month. This week the people who are pumped up about your cause will be in conversations when they are not with you. This is the perfect opportunity to change public perceptions about the problems in your community. For all you know, that inspiring case study in life change who becomes your organization's greatest evangelist could be the next person walking into your facilities today. Will they talk about their experiences to their friends tomorrow? You want to be top on the list of things the people in your network think about when they think about anything related to your goals. Your present network is an endless supply of contacts, donations, volunteers, and clients just waiting for you. But you have to ask for them. You need to ask for referrals. Make sure you take names and keep up with the people you make contact with regularly. Your success depends on it.

The Geometry of Guerrilla Marketing

You don't have to be a whiz to understand that there is more than one dimension to nonprofit marketing. You have so many audiences you need to connect with, from the public and stakeholders to clients and volunteers—the list goes on. We know you feel like you are going in several directions at once. But did you know you could benefit from growing in different ways at once, too? Most organizations are focused on getting from Point A to Point B. They are growing in a linear fashion. It's good to keep the ball moving forward on the field, but it won't be enough to ensure the success of your operation. You need to grow geometrically. You need more *profitable* relationship exchanges, more *regular* relationship exchanges, and more *referral* relationship exchanges all while you are expanding in the right direction. Guerrilla marketing is designed to get you growing in more than one way so you can succeed beyond your wildest imagination. The habits you learn from guerrilla marketing will have lasting results on the bottom line of achieving your outcomes.

Three Keys to Your Amazing Success: Follow-Up, Follow-Up, Follow-Up

We need to reframe how we think about follow-up. What if you could change your perspective and make sure your follow-up is people-savvy and relationship-friendly? Could there be any tools that could help you have good growing relationships with the various publics you serve? And if you automated part of this with technology, would that make the relationships less organic? You can be network-smart and benefit from technology at the same time. Think of the loving grandmother who keeps a calendar (read database) of all her grandchildren's birthdays so she can send them a card with a $20 bill inside on their special day. Is she being less loving to her grandkids by having such a calendar? Or is she being relationship-smart? You can use technology in relationships if you think more like people than you think like a machine.

Guerrilla marketing is all about follow-up. Why should you work so hard to make all those connections if you are just going to ignore the people you make contact with anyway? Think of all the missed opportunity for making positive change resting in the network of people in your databases. If you can learn to value the people in the databases (like a grandmother does her grandchildren), you can unleash all the human passion, money, and energy potential your organization will ever need. In the business world 68 percent of potential sales are lost due to customers being ignored after the sale. As a guerrilla marketer you know follow-up is not just being nice to people, it's the lifeblood of your organization. If you have been collecting e-mails for some time now, ask yourself, why do you have them?

> Your follow up must be both consistent and rich with useable content.

Do you have business cards of people you have collected this year? What did you intend to do with them? Did you hear a sponsor of yours or one of your donors talk about a good friend of his who also cares about your subject? Well, did you ask for that person's contact information so you could talk to them over coffee? There is no reason for a person to contact your organization to not get a follow-up e-mail or phone call. Technology is available to send out personalized letters instead of cold form letters. Nonguerrillas take the easiest and least personable route when communicating with their publics. Don't stuff generic messages in envelopes to people you make contact with; make a real connection with something more personal.

In the course of operating your nonprofit, the temptation to go through the motions can get in the way of your best intentions.

Too many organizations are floundering with little results because they take a transactional approach to how they relate to people. You give me money, I send you the newsletter. You volunteer for my program, I take you and your service for granted. You put a sign in your yard, or sticker on your car, I watch you drive away. Where is the passion in that? Nonguerrillas think marketing is over once an exchange has been made. Their work is done. It's time to chalk it up to the annual report. But guerrillas know that that moment is the beginning of a long-term relationship that will go several steps further. Some nonprofits take donations on their websites. Others use their websites to develop relationships. When someone makes a donation, they get an automatic e-mail thanking them for their generosity. But they also get personalized information for other ways to get involved. A little later they might get a phone call or invitation to a social networking event.

Take an inventory of the organizations and businesses in your community. Do any of the ones you know of have this emphasis on follow-up? Most of them won't. You can easily see how much your organization will stand out from the crowd right away in the minds of the people you want to reach. But chances are you will see a few that do follow up well. It is very likely that these are the most successful organizations and businesses in your community. These will become your peers (and potentially partners) as you change your way of operating your nonprofit.

Fusion Marketing

Most nonprofits understand the benefits of working with sponsors. It just makes sense that the clients of other organizations and businesses in your community could become people you reach with your nonprofit. But it also makes good sense for the other business owners and leaders too. They know people like companies that care about the community. Guerrilla marketers in the business world will be your most ardent supporters and donors. Since you as a guerrilla have a curiosity about people and passion for networking, take a walk down your street and notice all the businesses there. Which ones are doing business with the largest number of people you also want to reach? Which ones have the most compatibility with your organization's message? Which one is most likely to want to reach the people you are already reaching? If you get to know the owners and workers in their businesses, you might find yourself trading information, e-mails, and contacts. It could be the people you need to help you with some legal or financial matters in your organization could be working there. Maybe there is a club the owners of these businesses attend that would enjoy inviting you to so you can make contact with new donors. Networking works at the business-to-business level, too. You may even run into the mother of the editor of your town's newspaper. For the fusion to work in your fusion marketing, both parties need to benefit. To avoid wasting time, don't continue a long-term relationship with a fusion partner if your organization is not being helped as much as you are helping others.

> Nonprofits who share a different vision, yet want to reach the same people become great fusion partners in guerrilla marketing.

Me Marketing vs. You Marketing

Many organizations put together their marketing materials with the worst approach for getting attention from the people they want to reach. They send their messages out with "Me Marketing." Me Marketing is the kind of communication that centers on the organization. When I pick up your brochure as a prospect, I am learning about you and what you want to do. You are talking about you. You are telling your side of the story. You Marketing is just the opposite of Me Marketing. Most people are tuned in to what matters to them. They tune in to the messages that speak to their needs from their perspective. If I pick up your brochure and it is talking about me, I'm more likely to pay attention. People are far more interested in what benefits them. This approach forces you to find the benefits and life application of what you are offering.

Now go back and look at your website or brochures. Do you tell about your mission, your great staff, your awards, your programs? Is it all about me, me, me? How can you change the copy to reflect more "You Marketing"? Nonprofits are sometimes the worst offenders when it comes to Me Marketing. It's not hard to find examples in the "About Us" sections of their websites. It's true nonprofits need to be passionate about their mission. But it is important to understand that people visiting your site will have their own perceptions. Don't just talk about yourself. Help the person who is reading your website or printed materials put themselves in the story line. Put the people you want to reach into the picture and they will pay much closer attention to you. Every sentence needs to be about the reader and how their involvement will make a difference in your community. As you write your first draft of the copy on your website or brochure, start all your sentences with the word you. The result will be a very compelling message that resonates with your readers.

While you are at it, take all the things you do in your organization that way. Put yourself in the shoes of the people accessing your organization at every level. Think about the decision-making process they are going through. People are at different stages in awareness and adoption of your ideas. The more you understand about how new ideas are adopted or how decisions are transacted in people's minds, the better you will be able to anticipate the things that will make them the most responsive. When a person enters your facility, what do they need to know? When they click a link on your site, what are their questions about the decision they just made to click there? Think about when you go through the airport on a trip. Don't you appreciate the people who went before you, walking in your steps and putting the signage in just the right places to help you get to where you need to go? Aren't you frustrated when you can't get the directions you need when and where you need them?

Marketing Combinations

In guerrilla marketing we hear people make the mistake of looking for the silver bullet to solve their marketing problems. You hear them say, "We tried direct mail and it doesn't work" or "Advertising in the newspaper is a waste of money!" While we agree direct mail can be ineffective and advertising certainly can be deployed in wasteful ways, the real problems nonprofits face come because they think in terms of looking for marketing magic from a single medium, instead of thinking in terms of marketing combinations. The strategy you need to improve your organization's marketing is not found in the use of a single tool; it is found in a combination of many tools. There are 200 marketing weapons you can use in your marketing attack; you need to be aware of all of them as a guerrilla marketer. We will discuss all 200 of them in other chapters.

> The days of single-weapon marketing are gone. Today and tomorrow marketing combinations are the wave of the future.

There is no "one-hit wonder" medium you can use to reach all people anymore. In the past when the number of media channels were fewer and the audience more homogenous, perhaps you could get away with using a single media tool for your outreach. But those days are far gone now. The proliferation of media channels and the advent of desktop publishing have made anyone with an internet connection and a computer a marketing force. New media channels are cropping up all the time. As a guerrilla, you can't let yourself become time-locked into ways of doing things that may have worked in the past. For example, many nonprofits are unaware of the tremendous opportunity to reach people using social media like Facebook, MySpace, and Twitter. Nonguerrillas say, "I don't have time for all that!" Meanwhile, guerrillas are building contacts and deepening client relationships through these media.

Here are a few opportunities missed by nonguerrillas with their "can't do" attitude:

- "Telemarketing doesn't work because people don't like to be called at home!"
- "Blogs are just a fad and could create more distractions than they are worth!"
- "News releases are a bad idea because the media never gets the story right and you can't control the message."
- "Twitter text messages are far too short to use for our purposes."

It seems for every new media that exists, there is a naysayer there to throw water on the possibilities it brings for nonprofit marketing. Imagine the day the first telephone was placed on the nonprofit marketer's desk way back in the 1900s. Surely one of them must have said, "You mean out of all the other things I have to do, I now have to pick up and talk into this contraption every time it rings?" While on the other hand, the guerrilla marketer back then picked up the phone and said, "Operator, get me Mr. Smith, please!"

If you are technophobic, it's time to set up an appointment with your technoshrink today. Get over your fears of the computer mouse! So much is changing in communication today—it would be a fatal mistake to ignore new technology in your organization's marketing. It's not just time to accept technology, you need to embrace it. Become proficient in all types of technology and master new media channels like Facebook, MySpace, Twitter, YouTube, and web resources like Google, Technorati, Flikr, LinkedIn, and Plaxo. Guerrillas are up-to-date on all these and they keep refreshing their knowledge of new tools and channels that come out continually. Most of these media are free or very inexpensive to use—that's magic to the ears of the guerrilla marketer. The internet is the guerrilla's best friend.

But it is not only the internet that is changing the way people connect. Even traditional mass mediums are in transition, too. Cable and satellite have fragmented TV audiences into very specific niche markets. You can find a TV channel that fits almost every lifestyle or interest people have. That's good news for you as a guerrilla marketer; now you can select media that get your message to the specific types of people you want to reach. Print media are deconstructing too. Newspapers are adding websites with multimedia and are engaging in interaction in ways never thought possible. On-demand printing and self-publication have created new opportunities for nonprofit guerrillas. All media are fragmenting and audiences are getting smaller and defined by smaller niches. Traditional marketers think about mass markets; guerrilla marketers think about marketing to individuals. Though people may assemble at times in large groups and may fit in nice neat demographic clusters, the fact is they never lose their sense of individuality and they prefer to be treated like you understand that.

Get Them Saying "Yes" with Permission Marketing

Perhaps you have heard salespeople say, "We need to get our customers saying yes!" This is one principle that is the secret to getting momentum going with the people you want to reach. Researcher Robert B. Cialdini says in his book *Influence: The Psychology of Persuasion* (Harper, 2006) that when people are asked to perform a small favor, such as wearing a ribbon, displaying a sign in their yard, or signing a petition, they are far more likely to agree to make a larger commitment afterward. Can you think of ways to get people saying yes to you? They can say yes by signing up for a free newsletter or e-book. They can say yes to a free DVD. When people come to your website, offer them a free gift in exchange for their e-mail address. When they sign up to get the free gift, report, etc., they will be much stronger candidates for a deeper relationship with your organization.

There are so many people who want to reach the same people you want to reach, it is increasingly important for you to get permission from them to market to them. Will people really ask you to market to them? When they sign up for your newsletter or free resource, they are saying yes to you. What is really special about that is they will actually come to anticipate your marketing. Blogs are a good example of permission marketing. Many people have said yes to nonprofit marketing when they have subscribed to the blog feed of their favorite organization. The helpful articles and service journalism found on these blogs keeps people coming back for more. Not only does this kind of marketing educate the public, it also establishes greater credibility for the organization. It gives their most active supporters a viral marketing tool to show to others who are not involved yet. The same goes for social media like Facebook.

Organizations start by establishing a permission relationship using the social networking tool, then the relationship grows through contact into a much deeper relationship. It works because new media give people what they want, which is dialogue, not monologues. While traditional marketers are busy pushing messages out to targets, guerrillas are having conversations with individuals. People are more likely to say yes to something helpful than they are to say yes to shelling out their hard-earned dollars to something they do not understand or know very well. But once the relationship is established and the value exchange of your organization is evident, they will become generous supporters.

> Guerrilla marketing is first and foremost about
> your mind-set. It helps you reframe the issues
> that you face in getting the word out
> about your organization in ways that
> make the most of your resources.

CHAPTER 3

The Guerrilla Marketer's Personality

THERE ARE 12 PERSONALITY QUALITIES found in those who make an impact and find success in nonprofit guerrilla marketing. Many of these traits may already be a part of your persona. Others are qualities you must cultivate in yourself to experience the best you can be in marketing your nonprofit. There's no guarantee that if you can practice all these you will have success. But if you don't have them, you will find success hard to achieve. Set a goal to sharpen

There are 12 traits found in successful guerrillas. If found in great measure, these traits will enhance the potential for success.

yourself into a guerrilla marketer by working these qualities into your daily life.

Trait 1: Guerrillas Have Imagination

One personality trait you need in great measure is imagination. Nonguerrilla marketers make the mistake of thinking imagination means being the most creative. Even the most expensive advertising agencies can miss this point. It is not how creative and slick you can be that gives your message the most impact. There are plenty of snazzy ads that don't work and numerous commercials that are entertaining or funny that can't sell anything. It's not the most artistic advertisement that makes the difference—it is the one that grabs the most attention. That takes imagination, not art.

- It is not the most beautiful envelope in the mailbox that gets opened—it could be the one with the most stamps on it.
- It is not the celebrity endorsement that wins the heart of listeners to your radio commercial—it's the way you make them feel famous when they hear it.
- It is not the most technologically innovative e-mail tools that makes them open your note instead of deleting it—it is the compelling subject line.
- It is not the artwork on your billboard that gets it noticed—it's where you put the billboard.
- It is not the compelling reasons for supporting your cause that tips the scales—but your timing in asking for support.
- It is not the urgency of your messages that gets a positive reaction—but that you have obtained permission for them and they were anticipated.

Take a lesson from Pulitzer Prize-winning photographers. They are not the ones who make the news. They don't engage in planning the events of history; they are simply present and put the frame around the moment. They zoom in on the right part of the picture to catch the eye and tell the story. They have timing that clicks their shutter at just the right second. They portray the real, raw, energetic, or joyful emotion that gets a gut reaction from the person looking at the image. The Pulitzer-winning photos are not always the most artistic images, but they are usually the most honest and relevant for the moment. You need to be in your moment and ready to position the eyes (and ears) of the people you want to reach in the right way. You can frame how people experience your marketing in ways that may not get the awards and accolades of the advertising industry, but that cut to the heart and get people responding to you.

Trait 2: Guerrillas Are Patient

Most people give up just before their marketing has a chance to work. Few marketers seem to have the perseverance to make enough impressions with the people they target. What if your organization quits just before the people you want to impact were about to adopt the new healthy behavior you have been advocating? How do you know that the work you have been doing isn't about to start taking hold in your community? A little patience goes a long way. Don't give up the fight before your battle plan has had a chance to work.

Guerrilla marketers know that to get someone's attention and evoke a response from them, you need to reach them up to nine times. The fact is people will rarely act on something they see only once. For most people, they need to see something, think about it, be reminded they saw it and were thinking about it, then be jolted again by seeing it a few more times before they act on what they have seen.

Here's the kicker, though: Before anyone sees something once, you have to show it to them three times before they realize they have seen it. That's because people are constantly bombarded with attempts to get their attention. Researchers say that people see between 1,500 to 3,500 appeals for their attention every day. People filter out much more than just advertising that tries to reach them; they block out hundreds of distractions all day long. There are a lot of sensory events in a single 24-hour period. It can easily become overwhelming. Stop reading for a moment and take inventory of the noises and sights all around you. Is there the hum of a climate control system running in the background? Are people walking by talking? Get a load of that wallpaper pattern on the wall. Look, a bird! Your brain blocks out these potential distractions so well that you have to make yourself pay attention to them to notice them usually. The human brain has a coping mechanism called the Reticular Activating System (RAS) that manages the daily function of consciousness and filters out unwanted stimuli. It's a good thing, too. Imagine if you actually heard every single noise around you. Imagine what it would be like to notice everything you actually see. It would drive you crazy. Some people have greater ability to block out unwanted distractions than others. But most people have a natural physiological ability to ignore your marketing.

One way to break through the natural attention filtering people do is through repetition. To break through the clutter of all the other things that are clamoring for the attention of the people you want to reach, you have to keep saying the same thing repeatedly. So it plays out like this: If they saw it once, you said it three times. If they saw it twice, you probably said it six times. As the computation goes on, you see that if they saw it nine times you probably said it 27 times. The power of patient repetition plays in your favor, and people who have been exposed to your message that many times will generally know about you and be responsive to you.

Some marketers will say they get much better response than that from their media outreach without all repetition. Congratulations to them! There could be a number of reasons for that. This is more art than science. But chances are great that more responsive people targeted by their media are being exposed to their message in 27 other ways they may not have considered. They may have a great location that people see every day on their way to work. Their supporters may be talking them up more than they know, or they are just plain blessed with good luck. For the rest of us hacks out here, we need a dose of good old-fashioned patience while our message is repeated enough to get response.

Trait 3: Guerrillas Are Active

Guerrilla marketing is not passive. With all the competition for the attention of the people she wants to reach, a guerrilla knows she can't expect success to fall in her lap. You have to make your own opportunities in nonprofit marketing. As movie producer Samuel Goldwyn once said, "The harder I work, the luckier I get." In guerrilla marketing the emphasis is on taking action. Too many marketers expect they can attend to their marketing for a season, lay it aside to work on other projects, and come back to do some more marketing when they feel they need to. But if you understand that your marketing really is a circle of activity that starts with your ideas and ends with the ongoing sustainable behaviors of the people you want to reach, you know you can't afford to take a stop-and-go approach.

Another way outreach can lack action in nonprofit marketing is when marketing is treated like an academic affair. There are many Ph.D.s involved in nonprofit work, and sometimes it seems social sector marketing can get bogged down in scholastics. Looking at many of the marketing books available on social sector marketing is like going to a college textbook bookstore—there's some real sticker shock on the prices of the books, and these tomes can be very complex to understand. Attend a few of the nonprofit marketing conventions and workshops and be prepared to meet some of the most educated people on earth. Not that there is anything wrong with education, or having an erudite understanding of the principles of marketing. Problems arise when marketing planning doesn't translate into action.

Good marketing is not defined by good didactic standards; it is defined by results. The people you want to get to adopt a new healthy behavior are not going to care what theoretical model of behavior change you are using. Those in the segments you target won't be inspired to take action by your anthropological insights into social stratification. Donors can't reach for their checkbooks if they fall asleep when you are presenting the case for your organization's needs.

In nonprofit marketing there are far too many ways to get sidetracked from taking action. Having a personality trait that is defaulted toward action will keep you from getting stalled in your marketing. While others are sitting in seminars, adding education credits to their resumes, and publishing articles in academic journals, you could be getting the results—that is, if you are geared toward implementing change with a take-action mind-set.

Trait 4: Guerrillas Are Sensitive

There is no substitute for understanding the moment you are living in. If you want to become a guerrilla, you will have to learn to focus on what is happening in the world. When you are objectively aware of current events, technology, public opinion, and even the emotions swirling around you, you can become more responsive to people and meet them at a time when they are most likely to respond to you. There is a little bit of a social forecaster in every guerrilla. They keep up-to-date on issues that could impact their mission and they try to position themselves to be in the best place for the most impact. Being able to respond in a time of crisis for relief organizations is expected, but what is less addressed is the impact of disasters on nonprofits that are not relief-oriented in mission. Over the years, natural disasters like tsunamis, hurricanes, and floods have affected all kinds of nonprofits, even those not directly connected to bringing relief. Some were caught unaware when lack of building materials jacked up the cost of expansion programs. For others, funding streams dried up as people redirected their charitable giving to fuel the relief. Every nonprofit organization needs to stay on top of everything that is going on. Who knows, you could discover a huge opportunity around the corner for you to enhance the effectiveness of your association before another group finds it.

But there are more events than acts of Mother Nature that can impact your mission. All around the world the population is changing. In the developed world the population is aging. Starting in 2010, Baby Boomers will be hitting retirement age at the clip of 10,000 per day every day until 2030. That means there may be a growing pool of volunteer workers headed your way. It could also mean you will need to adapt your fundraising approach as more of your best donors could be living on fixed incomes. Many of these Boomers have executive experience and could form a new wave of social entrepreneurs, thus multiplying the competition you face overnight. Is your organization ready for what comes next?

Sensitivity means you are aware that a new much more ethnically diverse generation, the Millennials, are coming to the front and center of the world stage. Demographers say this generation (born 1980–1996) is even more civic-minded that their Boomer parents were. They are a generation waiting for a cause to rally behind. Could there be a boon for your cause waiting in the wings? This generation is not only more advanced in technology out of preference—they demand it. If this generation communicates mostly to each other by texting, it would be insensitive (and dumb) for nonprofits to refuse to embrace strategies using text messaging.

Understanding others can pay big dividends if you pay attention. Guerrillas are sensitive to what their prospects are doing, what they want, what they read, and what they think as much as possible. They read the same books and newspapers, subscribe to the same blogs, listen to the same radio, and watch the same TV programs as the people they want to reach. That way they know what people are doing and are aware of things that could affect their opinions and actions.

Trait 5: Guerrillas Are Confident

It's a good thing to have the confidence to go out into the marketplace and compete for your cause and ideals. But, perhaps not surprisingly, your need for self-confidence will not be tested most from outside by opponents of your organization as much as it could be tested from within. Cartoonist Walt Kelly's character Pogo said it best, "We have met the enemy and he is us." You won't have as many problems standing against those who oppose you as you will have taking a stand against those who support you but have mistaken ideas about marketing. You know the drill; you plan a powerful marketing strategy and implement a branding and marketing campaign that is destined for the case study history books. All of a sudden, out of nowhere, a well-meaning fellow do-gooder confronts you with an urgent plea to change course. The moment has come for you to put into practice a little ego strength. You need the self-confidence to stick with the media campaign, to not change the strategy until it has time to work. It takes a lot of confidence to resist the urgings of your bored graphic designer to make something look cooler. Your promotion committee members may be tired of the message on the radio spots—but stand firm. Everyone in your organization will be even more sick of seeing your media long before people in your community will have even noticed it.

Resist the siren song of changing marketing strategies before you have given the plan a chance to work. Even your spouse and family might get into the act. Just smile lovingly at them and stay the course. That is because out in your market are people who are at various stages of responsiveness to you. Some haven't even noticed you for the first time. Many others could be on the verge of response. Your family, friends, and co-workers are tired of your marketing because they have seen it so much. They have become jaded to the message and they are ready for some variety. It will take all the inner strength you have to not listen to the people you care about and respect the most who are trying to talk you into turning your marketing into a colossal waste of time, energy, and money. Guerrillas don't give into the pressure to flit from one strategy to another because they know that marketing has a cumulative effect. They know it takes a while to make it up the hill, but they are confident there are sweet rewards on the other side of the mountain.

Trait 6: Guerrillas Are Aggressive

Guerrillas know a good deal when they see one. When they realize there are 200 marketing weapons (many of them free) available, they are ready to pounce. They know all that needs to happen is for them to leverage as many of them as possible with a little assertive action. Most nonprofits only dedicate a small fraction of their resources for marketing impact. Good stewardship of donor dollars is important, but if your organization cannot sustain momentum because of timidity, what good is it? The best programs for your community are of no value for social change if people don't know about them. How can word-of-mouth work if your volunteers don't know which direction to point people toward? How will they understand where to go to learn more about your organization?

You don't have to always spend money to make an impact, but you can't be reticent to engage in a fast-changing competitive market. Imagine you are in a room full of people and someone walks in and leaves thousands of dollars on the table and says, "Anyone who wants this money can have it. It's there for the taking for whoever wants it." In such a situation, the best course of action would be to be among the first to take advantage of the incredible offer. While some are waiting to see what others will do, you could be aggressive and take the giver up on his astonishing gift. But nobody really leaves money on the table in that way do they? Sure they do. There are resources beyond your imagination laying before you if you will only be aggressive enough to take advantage of them. Not using the marketing weapons available to you is like leaving money your organization needs to achieve its mission on the table. There is no good reason to not take advantage of the tools and technology in your arsenal.

There are two kinds of nonprofit marketers: frogs and lizards. Frog marketers sit comfortably on their marketing lily pads and wait for opportunities to come within their reach. At the right moment, when they see what they want, they plan to stick out their tongues and—zap! Sometimes they can go for a long time and see nothing and get nothing. Lizard marketers, however, are more aggressive. They don't wait for what they need to fly by them, they get up and go hunt down what they need. They do not rest until they find it. People who are not guerrilla marketers wonder why guerrillas seem to be ubiquitous in their marketing. The answer is not that guerrillas are everywhere; they are just everywhere the people they want to reach happen to be looking.

Trait 7: Guerrillas Are Innovative

Organizations in the nonprofit world are usually built around an inspirational idea that represents a new way of thinking or a means of making things better. The energy that comes from such idealism can be stimulating. But in nonprofit marketing romanticism can create problems. The worst thing you can do in marketing is fall in love with your product. As said before, you need to keep a people-oriented focus and be clearly aware of what is going on in your market if you are going to be competitive in rough economic times. Nonprofit marketers are always working to get people to embrace change. But the irony is nonprofits are usually the most resistant to accepting change within their own organizations. The phrase, "We never did it that way before" was coined in the social sector. As Shakespeare might say, "We'd rather bear those ills we have than fly to others that we know not of."

The opposite of people-focused thinking is a program-focused mind-set. This programmatic approach is what makes nonprofits want to remain in their comfort zones and keeps them from embracing change. It's easier to stay with what you know than head into the uncharted waters of innovation. You need to be able to adapt and change as the audiences you hope to reach are changing. The marketplace is not static; even the marketplace of ideas is changing. Being able to adapt and thrive in a shifting environment is a guerrilla personality trait worth refining in yourself.

Practically speaking, nonprofits are also often among the last to upgrade their use of technology and incorporate it into their regular work. Recently, great advancements in internet communication have made possible ways to enter new social networks of people using Web 2.0 sites like Facebook, MySpace, Twitter, and YouTube. Journalism has changed since the advent of blogging, and each day RSS feeds syndicate news content to millions.

There is a rapidly growing market of people using social media. Meanwhile, nonprofits are still blocking the use of new media on their servers and keeping their employees from using blogging and other web-based social interaction tools to reach people. These same organizations will think nothing of paying to fly a troop of faithful workers to a convention or seminars and workshops on the other side of the country. Why do they do this when the same possibilities for networking exist every day on the internet for free.

On the other side of this, be careful not to get hooked on change for change's sake. Studying the trendy is fun and rewarding, but it can also be distracting. If you only study the trendy newsworthy things, you can miss doing a lot of basic things that can help you in your work. Many nonprofit marketers frustrate themselves (and their organizations) trying out new tactics, when their real problem isn't that they don't have the right strategy—they just lack fundamental marketing practices. Even the largest organizations sometimes try to reorganize around some new idea to bring about more effective results, when the truth is if they would only live up to the plans they made before the reorganization, they would already be better reaching their stated objectives.

Trait 8: Guerrillas Are Generous

As a nonprofit marketer, you spend a good deal of time thinking about how you can get others to give. But one way to prime the pump of generosity is to become a little more giving yourself. People like to get things. "Free" is one of the sweetest sounding words in the guerrilla marketer's vocabulary. Can you develop a free specialty item to give the people you want to support you? A free calendar, a refrigerator magnet, even a nice ink pen can start the influence ball rolling. When you give people something of value, it puts them in the one down cycle of reciprocation and makes them psychologically more inclined to want to return the favor to you. You don't always have to give away something physical. Even digital gifts are appreciated. A free report or an e-book might do the trick.

Imagine you are working for an advocate group that seeks to improve marriage relationships and communication. A little generosity from you to couples could go a long way. You could give away some relationship-building help in the form of a free e-book. With a little local research you could identify "101 Amazingly Fun Yet Free Date Ideas" in your city. In your e-book write a couple of paragraphs per date idea describing ways people can reconnect with their spouse without having to spend a lot of money. One page of the e-book could promote the relationship communication seminars your group offers and drive people back to your website to sign up for your courses and your e-mail newsletter, and expose them to your blog for the first time. The free e-book would be available through your site and could easily be passed along virtually via e-mail by others. It will become like a satellite probe from your organization sent out into cyberspace to promote your work and position you as an expert on relationships. Distill the e-book into a news release to media outlets, and newspapers and local TV reporters may pick up your story. A subject like that could easily become a topic of conversation on the morning talk radio in your town. Soon you could become the designated relationship expert in your community and beyond.

It all starts when you give away something of value. It's easy to do; just figure out ways you can help people succeed. Are there any stinky problems people have you can help solve? Is there a way you can legitimately help people achieve their goals? If what you help people do is compatible with the values of your organization, there is no reason why you should not try it, especially considering the potential for building goodwill among the people you want to reach most.

Trait 9: Guerrillas Are Good Storytellers

Most people are not bookish. They don't like to read statistics. They seldom look at graphs and charts for entertainment purposes. Most people get most of their information from stories in electronic media such as radio and TV. They are attracted to the internet with all its interactive multimedia. All day long people hear stories. They pay attention to the stories about what politicians are doing in the Capital. They watch reality programs and TV shows and keep up with the stories of how characters interact with one another. The songs they listen to tell the stories about how relationships have gone good or bad. Listen in to the conversations going on around you in the coffee shop sometime, and you'll hear people telling each other stories about other people.

Some people are oral communicators, and their only method of communication is storytelling. Oral communication experts say oral communicators don't have the ability to follow literate communication methods. Oral communication is not merely a spoken version of written content. It includes communicating in ways that take into account how people who are not literate retain information. On the mission field the most illiterate of people have been the people reached through chronological storytelling of the Bible. Missionaries are astounded at how quickly oral people become biblically literate. Why? Think about it. A completely illiterate person has no way to store information on paper. They have to store everything they know in their mind. As such, an oral communicator can run circles around a literate person when it comes to Bible literacy. While the literate person is still looking for chapter and verse, the oral communicator just remembers the stories.

Social marketers can lecture people about sanitary water practices in some cultures until they are blue in the face, but the people they want to help won't understand what they are talking about until the marketers can couch the needed information into the form of a story.

Researchers say people with the lowest incomes and education levels are more likely to be functionally illiterate. The ease of using oral communication tools has led to the situation that even very educated and highly literate people are becoming de facto post-literates with oral communication preferences. That's why guerrillas don't merely bore people with pie charts, alarming stats, and long written treatises in the form of annual reports. They put a face to the figures and they know how to tell the stories that motivate people to get involved. People love to know what other people do. By spotlighting personal stories guerrillas provide the social proof people need to get involved. People who give don't give to programs, they give to people who have a plausible narrative about how they will make things better. They like to give to people who tell them about the story's happy ending.

One way to incorporate storytelling into your outreach is to use social media. Social media allows people to experience the heartbeat of your leaders and understand the perspective of the people your nonprofit serves. These days the people who follow you in social media could move to join you in your cause when you include them into the storyline of your work. They could be following your brief text message "tweets" on Twitter (more on Twitter in another chapter) and really begin to understand how you are implementing your program of change and want to join you, too. They may even start by promoting what you do in their own social networks. To get your message to the people you want to reach, you need to take the message to them in the way that is most appealing to them intellectually and emotionally, in the form of stories. To paraphrase a popular song, give them stories to talk about.

Trait 10: Guerrillas Are Focused

Nonprofit marketers face the same temptations for-profit companies face to expand their products, programs, and services to gain more share of the marketplace. For some companies the desire to develop line extensions draws them into ill-conceived products and wasteful expenditures. Companies that expand their product lines into marketing flops often don't realize their mistakes until they have lost millions of invested dollars. Highly successful companies can be the worst offenders in this losing game. Success builds confidence and enlarges their egos so that they believe they can have huge success in anything else they attempt. As a nonprofit leader, you can't afford to waste time, money, and energy on too much diversification. You have to stay on target to keep making progress toward your objectives. Guerrilla nonprofits don't lose focus by moving into areas that are beyond their core competencies. They are aware there is a potential to drift from their original mission and lose the chance to do greater good. Look at your organization's plans. Surely you are doing a lot of activities. Are any of them diluting your efforts? You may be wondering how you can expand what you are doing so you can reach a greater number of people and solve more problems. But instead you could be setting your organization up for failure if you get beyond your core values and corporate mission.

One way to guard your organization from *mission drift* is to ask yourself some tough questions when you are thinking about adding a new program. For example, what would your organization still be doing if you faced a 20 percent budget cut next year? Italian economist Vilfredo Pareto once postulated that 80 percent of the effects come from 20 percent of the causes in any given situation. The theory is that most of the progress of a typical nonprofit could be coming from just 20 percent of the organization's activities. Looking at what your organization is doing, can you see the same principle at work? What if you had to cut your budget by as much as 40 percent or even 80 percent, what would your organization still be doing? If you can identify what you would be doing regardless of what your circumstances are, you will find what your organization values most. More than likely, these will also be the things you do the best. They are your core competencies.

This exercise will help reveal what is really important to you. If you maintain a laser-focused loyalty to your core competencies and values, you will shape your organization into being the best it can be. Nonprofit leaders are often visionary people who can easily get off mission because they are highly attuned to the needs in their communities. For some people, staying focused will require a lot of self-control. Many nonprofits never met a need they didn't think they could solve. And the most successful organizations can let the acquired hubris from past successes lull them into sapping the strength out of their nonprofits if they are not vigilant.

The rewards for being focused far outweigh the perceived loss of not being involved in extending your services and products into new areas. Don't do more stuff; do what you do better. Improvements come from a variety of means. Perhaps you can leverage technology to do what you do more efficiently. You might be able to eliminate a cumbersome process. Trimming some of the fat in your organization could free some of your most creative people to do an even better job at what they are already doing well. Build on what you do best and make it better. Excellence is a far greater reward than diversification. As guerrillas innovate, they maintain focus to keep them from blurring their vision.

Trait 11: Guerrillas Are Constantly Learning

A guerrilla knows the local library like the back of his hand because he is always in research mode. He has read all the relevant books on the topics that impact his work and improve his nonprofit marketing. He is constantly scanning the books at the bookstore and is often online finding out what is new that can help him improve his effectiveness. The instinct to keep learning is insatiable in the guerrilla nonprofit marketer. In a changing marketplace, what used to work may not work in the present. What is working now will change in the future. Just ten short years ago the internet was a brand-new public communication channel. Social media had not been invented yet. Now these tools are the best friends of the guerrilla marketer. When these new tools arrived, guerrillas were among the first to leverage them for their work because they are always ready to learn something new.

Staying on top of your field and innovations in nonprofit marketing is only the beginning of what should be expected of any marketer. Guerrillas take it a step further. They know if you stay up-to-date on areas that are just a bit beyond your field, you will find ideas and concepts that will give you the edge over your competition. Knowing more about diverse topics will open your eyes to new ideas and ways to solve your organization's marketing problems.

Here are some ways to keep your zeal for learning alive.

- *Read entire books.* Many people fail to get beyond the first few chapters of books they read. If you actually finish the books you read, you will be far ahead of most people.
- *Attend a seminar or workshop that is completely unrelated to your work.* You will meet a new network of people and will gain insights into the common perspectives others have in their fields that may also apply to yours.
- *Write down new terms, book titles, and names of people you read about or hear mentioned.* Then look them up on Wikipedia. By digging deeper, you will find many useful nuggets of information.
- *When traveling, put audio books, seminars, or podcasts on your MP3 player and learn as you go.*

- *When you have conversations with people, ask them what they are reading.* You will be glad you did. Many of your colleagues and friends have great reading lists. Don't be the last to read the most important books.
- *Skim sections of the newspaper you don't normally read.* Try to find something that is new to you and explore what it is about. At the very least, learning in new areas will help improve your relationships with potential donors. Imagine how impressed (and inclined to support you) a bank VP would be when he discovers that you understand something about his work.

As you read books that are related to your field, be sure to post online reviews on all the relevant books in the topic along with your real name and organization's web address. Your insights could capture the attention of the person in the right position researching books in your topic and it could drive them to look at your reviewer profile with your URL on it. Guerrillas make the most of every opportunity.

Trait 12: Guerrillas Are Enthusiastic

In nonprofit work, the emotional stakes are often high. When you are aware of so many needs, the concern you have for others weighs on you. The urgency you feel for your cause to succeed can work into your spirit and can make you come across to others as unhappy and dour, when you really are passionate and concerned. Many nonprofit marketers work long hours and for little pay. It is understandable how you can get to a point where you feel drained when you are always giving. But for the sake of your cause, you need to get your energy level up and your enthusiasm needs to shine through to others. An enthusiastic disposition is a powerful guerrilla asset in nonprofit marketing.

Zig Ziglar said, "Your attitude, not your aptitude, will determine your altitude."

Learn a lesson from the for-profit world next time you go to one of the successful businesses in your town. When you enter a high-quality store, you are sure to get a smile from the employees there. People seem genuinely happy you are in their shop. Are they being phony? No, they know when customers come into their stores they expect enthusiastic and friendly service. Don't you? They know that customers are not interruptions to their work—they are the reason for their work. Happy customers mean more profits and greater job security. What if you went into a local retailer and found a bunch of grumps working there? Wouldn't you climb into your car after the experience and wonder what their problem was? A company with a bunch of sourpuss employees will not last long.

> Having clear vision about where you are taking your organization can inform the purpose of your marketing.

To really achieve success as a guerrilla you need contagious enthusiasm. Compassion is easier caught than taught. To get started improving your attitude, there's no need to be cheesy or seem pushy. Just start with a smile. Unknit those eyebrows, practice greeting people with enthusiasm in the mirror until you can do it naturally and comfortably. By practicing more enthusiasm in your work, you are likely to feel more energy and get more joy out of your work. It is very rewarding when you can revive the love for your work that originally brought you into the nonprofit sector. As you maintain the energy level you will see your productivity improve and people will be more attracted to you and your cause.

Chances are high you will see a guerrilla marketing opportunity today, if you train yourself to look for it.

CHAPTER 4

How To Turn Your Mission Statement Into a Marketing Tool

YOUR CAUSE CAN BE THE MOST IMPORTANT ONE in the world, but people won't be interested in what you are doing unless you can make a meaningful connection with them. You need to find a compelling and inspiring way to describe why you exist, what it is you do, and why it makes a difference in the world. Nonprofits are required by U.S. law to state the purpose of their work in the form of a purpose or mission statement. But just because you have satisfied the letter of the law and attained a 501c3 status doesn't mean you have done what you need to do to persuade the people you want to reach that your cause is relevant. As we mentioned before, people are not likely to assume what you offer is a commodity they immediately need. Most organizations have stated mission objectives, but they usually don't use these statements to inform how they do their marketing. Guerrillas know that what they are doing is more important than merely going by the letter of the law when communicating their mission. They take the time to turn their mission statement into a guerrilla marketing weapon. The stakeholders in your cause will judge your every move when you present your organization as a solution to needs in the community. So guerrillas pay very close attention to how they submit themselves for community consideration. Nothing is left to chance.

What a mission statement can do for your organization:

- Helps strategic planning and capacity building
- Helps your organization develop stronger brand messages
- Keeps everyone working toward the same objectives
- Affects how you approach and treat people
- Permeates all your messages and media

Your mission statement also determines how you will measure success. Progress is not determined by how much money you raise, how many volunteers you recruit, what kind of campaigns you stage, what your organizational chart looks like, how you keep records, or even how you relate to your board. These are very important things, but they are not the most important thing. The most important thing is how well your organization effects sustainable change that fulfills your mission. All the other important aspects of your nonprofit are necessary, but, if you are not careful, they can become a drain on your ability to accomplish your mission. You could work your way into failure without realizing it.

In traditional for-profit businesses, guerrillas stay on track by maintaining a focus on profits as the measuring stick of successful performance. They don't look at how many sales transactions they make. They are not over-focused on the traffic in their stores or their websites. They track three things: profits, profits, and profits. There are many businesses that have a lot of transactions staging continual sales promotions but are still going out of business. They are busy, busy losing money. To them it is about sales records, when it should be about profits.

How do you take the profit-producing principles of guerrilla marketing and apply them in the nonprofit context? Not everything in the for-profit world is a fit for the social sector—but guerrilla marketing is a perfect fit for nonprofits. So what do you do when profits are not the driver of your organization? We have never encountered a nonprofit that couldn't use a little more cash on hand. But in nonprofit guerrilla marketing, money is not the motive, impact is. The reason behind the guerrilla marketing principle of focusing on profits in business is to keep the main outcome clear to marketers. In business, the main challenge is to keep the company from losing focus on making profits. A nonprofit guerrilla keeps a sharp eye on his real bottom line, too; he is not waylaid by extraneous details that distract him from accomplishing the mission. Your organization profits most when your marketing makes the most impact toward your stated objectives. Do you have what guerrillas have, the ability to know what profits your

> In order to mark their progression towards success, guerrillas develop clear benchmarks by writing their goals and objectives down.

mission, or what lacks profitability for your organization's desired outcomes?

Clarifying Your Nonprofit's Vision

Your mission statement keeps you on track for accomplishing the bottom line of your organization, but it also helps you become more attractive to the people you want to reach. People will judge what you do against what you say you are supposed to be doing. If there is any difference between the two, you could come off looking like a phony or worse, a hypocrite. It is important to make sure what your organization does is the same as what it says it does. Is your marketing writing checks your organization's actions can't cash? A mission statement keeps your organization credible with your community if applied to your everyday work. Looking at your mission and your nonprofit with fresh eyes may help you identify ways you are sending unintended messages. Guerrillas don't send unintended messages. They are self-confident enough to ask the tough questions that help them know what people think about them.

Your job as a guerrilla may be to openly question the sacred cows (or even the Purple Cows) if they are keeping your organization from experiencing the outcomes your mission statement claims you are after. The tricky part of casting a vision is not finding good things to do. Most nonprofit leaders have a high sense of awareness about needs, and there is no shortage of things that need to be done. The challenge in vision casting is identifying the right things for your organization to do and to not get sidetracked doing other good things that distract you from your stated purpose. Surely you are doing a lot of good things, but is your organization doing the right things?

As you develop your mission statement, make sure you properly evaluate your nonprofit. Management expert Jim

COULD YOU BE CONVICTED FOR BEING A SUCCESS AT YOUR MISSION?

As an exercise, ask yourself if your organization were on trial for accomplishing your mission, what would be the evidence used to convict? What would the charges be? Who would the lawyers interview as witnesses? Could your strategies stand up under cross-examination? What are the exhibits that would be used in the case? If the media were covering the trial, what would be the headlines?

These are the metrics for your organization's success. Keep track of them.

Collins says in his monograph, *Good to Great and the Social Sectors*, (Jim Collins, 2005), "A great organization is one that delivers superior performance and makes a distinctive impact over a long period of time." Often good strategy is more about what you say no to than what you say yes to. It is a good thing to know what you are best at and stick with it. Collins uses the example of the hedgehog from Isaiah Berlin who divided the world into two types: hedgehogs and foxes. A fox is a cunning creature because he knows and does a lot of things, but he is often a victim of his own schemes. Meanwhile, the hedgehog knows and does only one big thing and he is practically invincible. Have you made your mind up about what goes on your "To don't list?" Collins suggests social sector leaders use the *Hedgehog Principle* to root out things that distract from what should be your true focus. He says you should learn to say "No thank you" to things that fail the Hedgehog test. "We examined the Hedgehog concepts of the good-to-great companies. We found they reflected deep understanding of three intersecting circles:

1. what you are deeply passionate about,
2. what you can be the best in the world at, and
3. what best drives your economic engine."

Making the right choices doesn't mean you will have fewer troubles or obstacles. Doing the right thing is sometimes hard. But as Michael Allison and Jude Kaye point out in their book, *Strategic Planning for Nonprofits* (Wiley, 2005), "Even roller coasters arrive at their destination if they stay on track."

Evaluating Your Situation

Why should you be the last to know what is happening in your organization? Nonguerrillas let things happen to them; guerrillas stay current by continually gathering information from inside and outside their organization. They don't merely gather enough information to confirm their biases; they want to know what is really going on. In the rapidly expanding nonprofit sector, you have to be proactive about getting and using information. Information is a powerful tool in the hands of a guerrilla.

One way to get a true picture of where you stand is to conduct a SWOT analysis. S'wot is that, you ask? SWOT is an acrostic used in marketing that represents the internal and external issues you need to study to find out what your current situation is. The letters stand for: strengths, weaknesses, opportunities, and threats. Every situation is unique. There is no single approach we can give you that will reveal all the issues and information you need to help you make the right choices. But it is safe to say that every organization has internal and external factors influencing their present situation, and having an awareness of what is going on helps you remain competitive in the marketplace.

Strengths

Find what you can do better than anyone else. Guerrillas don't try to do everything; they have an acute sense of focus. They don't expand what they do; they do what they do best, even better. Anything worth doing is worth doing well. But not everything that is done well is worth doing for what you are trying to achieve. The things you do well need to be the things that help your organization accomplish its goals. So, unless you change your mission, you may even have to stop doing some things even though you do them well.

Weaknesses

What is it you don't do well? Where does your organization need to improve to achieve your objectives? What relationship skills do you need to develop? What technology do you need to master? Guerrillas are not afraid to try new things if it will help them achieve their mission. But on the other hand, they don't get hung up in trying to be somebody else. Are you trying to be good at something you will never be good at? Don't get stalled in spending too much time fixing what is wrong if it takes away from time you could be spending doing the things you already can do right.

Opportunities

What is going on outside your organization that could become an opportunity for your nonprofit? Spending time with your clients and other stakeholders helps you identify the openings or opportunities for sustainable change. Guerrillas don't walk through life looking at their shoes; they have their heads up and are alert to see the possibilities all around them. Chances are high you will see a guerrilla marketing opportunity today, if you train yourself to look for it.

Threats

Missed opportunities abound when people don't really study their community, but also if you don't know what is really going on, it can come back to bite you. What external threats could hinder your organization from achieving the mission? Guerrillas watch for threats headed their way by keeping up with current social trends, tracking the political climate, and watching economic indicators. They know it is wise even to keep an eye on the weather.

Guerrillas don't just gather information, they share it with others in their organization in writing so the entire operation can benefit. Putting your findings on paper also helps you focus your ideas and makes it easier to communicate with and mobilize others. Your SWOT analysis can be used to create a priority list of tasks you will accomplish in your marketing. When organizations prioritize their marketing and communications through the positive input and involvement of their team, board members, and volunteers, they are more ready to embark on a strategic mission to change the world.

Finding the Purpose of Your Marketing

What good is all this information if you can't put it to good use in your marketing? Doing your homework about your situation and keeping your focus on the bottom line won't make a difference until you can leverage all you know strategically for advancing your organization's cause. The strategic plan that is written and placed in a three-ring-binder notebook that sits unused on nonprofit leader's bookshelf is almost a proverb in the social sector. Guerrilla marketing is not an academic affair; it's a matter of taking action.

Every organization has its own DNA, and, despite people trying, there is no single marketing template that works in all situations. All this background and analysis you are doing is meant to be put to good use in planning a marketing attack that is perfectly suited for your organization in your present situation. When planning a guerrilla marketing attack, the objective of the marketing has to be clear. Advertising and marketing that does not have clearly stated goals is ineffective. It is hard to evaluate if your marketing investment is worth your time, money, and energy if the purpose is unclear to you. Guerrillas put their goals on paper (or on their computers) in the form of result statements that are based on their intended outcomes. We are not ready to write a marketing plan yet, but we are ready to write your guerrilla marketing mission statement.

The Three-Sentence Guerrilla Mission Statement

If you already have a written mission statement for your organization, we are not trying to minimize the important planning or vision casting your organization may have already undertaken. We consider that an integral part of your mission focusing and situation analysis. Rather, we want to help you enhance the work you have done and fortify it with power for guerrilla marketing. Be honest. If you are like many organizations, you have a mission statement that sounds academic or institutional. Is reading your organization's mission statement also a good cure for insomnia? To mobilize people you have to capture their imaginations. You have to stir their hearts. You have to make them believe you can deliver on your promises. Most mission statements don't do that well. Maybe what you need could be called a "mission restatement." Whatever the case, a guerrilla mission statement helps you turn your mission statement into a marketing tool. It can help you clearly focus your current purpose statement in ways that also serve to get the attention of the people you want to reach.

Guerrillas know that every point of contact your organization has with people is marketing. Your mission statement touches everything you do and is seen by everyone you connect with. With something that important, it makes sense to look at it with an eye for marketing. Why is it that mission statements are often written academically or by committees? Shouldn't they be written with the intent of using them as persuasive communication? Even the Declaration of Independence, though drafted by a committee, was written by a single person with a knack for words, Thomas Jefferson. Your mission statement should be written with no less thought than the most expensive advertising campaign receives. There is no need to change the legal purpose statement used to register your nonprofit with the government. But you wouldn't expect a Super Bowl advertisement to be written by lawyers, would you? Restating your purpose with a marketing mind-set can help you connect better with people. Of course you will have other sorts of marketing messages that support your organization in your outreach work, but what if all people could see was your mission statement? Would it pique interest in them for your cause? Ask yourself, if your mission statement came up in an internet search engine (a very likely scenario), would you want to click it? What would be the key words people used to find you anyway?

Here's how you write your guerrilla marketing mission statement. Remember, the three things that will make your organization the most successful are:

1. your passion,
2. what you are best at, and

3. a clear sense of what is the bottom-line impact you are trying to make.

Sit down and analyze all the data you have and cull everything you know about what your organization does and is down into just three sentences:

1. *Why do you exist?* (Make sure you are talking about your passions.)
2. *What does your organization do?* (This is where you talk about what you are best at.)
3. *What difference does it make?* (Describe the impact your organization is making.)

Keep them short. Putting too much information in your phrases will make your audience's attention spans start to

MARCH OF DIMES

Why do you exist? *Our mission is to improve the health of babies by preventing birth defects, premature birth, and infant mortality.*

What do you do? *We carry out this mission through research, community services, education, and advocacy to save babies' lives.*

What difference does it make? *March of Dimes researchers, volunteers, educators, outreach workers and advocates work together to give all babies a fighting chance against the threats to their health: prematurity, birth defects, low birth weight.*

wander. Imagine you are going to use this as your "elevator speech." Suppose you have just gotten on an elevator, and as soon as the doors close, another person in the elevator asks you to tell them about your organization. The time it takes to go from the first floor to the second floor, you must tell them what they need to know about your nonprofit. If you can't say who you are, what you do, and why it is important in 30 seconds, your organization is too complicated to become the subject of people's conversations. You may have bigger problems than marketing.

After you have written your sentences, you can enlist help in wordsmithing and polishing them. But getting the statements first from your heart will change you forever. These statements become the tools you can use in your progression toward unimagined success for your nonprofit.

CHAPTER 5

Guerrillas Focus on People

To be a guerrilla you have to love people. If you want your non-profit to grow and impact the world, you need to become a student of human nature, even if your primary objective is protecting animals or the environment. You have to understand people; the planet is crawling with them! We feel sorry for those folks who say they would love their work if it weren't for the people. People are all we have. Every day you are marketing yourself to people, so you should take it upon yourself to become an expert on them. Guerrilla marketers know they need to understand their target audiences better. Knowing who you are trying to reach is the starting place for good marketing. It not only dictates how you will present your message, it also shows you the best channels for reaching them. For example, you cannot effectively buy advertising if you don't have a clear idea of your target audience.

Presently, there are four major generations of people that are not only the targets of your marketing efforts but are also actively involved with nonprofits as donors, volunteers, and clients:

1. Silent Generation (born: 1925–1945)
2. Baby Boomers (born: 1946–1964)
3. Generation-X (born: 1965–1979)
4. Millennial Generation (born: 1980–1996)

Each of these generations have perspectives and needs that differ from the others. This chapter profiles these generations and suggests what you need to know about them to be successful in reaching them. By learning what their outlook, needs, and wants are, you can anticipate how they will interact with your organization and use this information to organize your marketing strategy.

As you read the profiles, keep in mind that not every point will apply to every individual. We are not trying to create stereotype caricatures. Instead, we are looking at macro level trends that are generally true about each generation. People in each generation share similar experiences that create a common background among their age-group peers. As always in guerrilla marketing, individuals matter most, so use this information as a starting point to making your organization more attractive to people, not as the ending.

The Silent Generation

KEY CHARACTERISTICS: Achievers, leaders, established, influential, hard working, corporate, gatekeepers, and sometimes revolutionary

BASIC DEMOGRAPHICS:

Median age: 71

Years they were born: 1925–1945

Number in the segment: 52 million

Background

Nicknamed the Silent Generation by a 1951 *Time* magazine article that mistakenly portrayed them as less enthusiastic and significant than their parents and grandparents' generations, the people that make up this group are far from silent. They were born in a very difficult time in the United States. On their birthdays (from 1925 through 1945), the country was either in desperate economic hard times or engaged in world war. Because times were tough, most families chose not to have children or perhaps could not because of war. Therefore the Silent Generation is the smallest of the major generational cohorts now living in the United States.

Despite the hard times into which they were born, the Silent Generation is also known as the "Lucky Generation" because the timing of their birth gave them unique opportunities throughout their lifetime. The United States experienced nonstop upward growth in per capita Gross Domestic Product (GDP) from 1945–2000. The Silent Generation is considered "lucky" because they were born just in time to get in on the ground floor of unmatched historic economic prosperity in America.

The Silent Generation is lucky also because they experienced the most intact family life in the history of the United States. Their childhood was most like the *Ozzie and Harriet* show than any other generation now living. As teenagers they were given more autonomy and disposable income than their parents enjoyed. The members of the Lucky Generation were the teenagers of the 1950s, many of whom were also influenced by the Beat Movement (a precursor to the more socially liberal Baby Boomer Hippie). Many of these became leaders who went on to shape radical changes in society and culture up to today.

As young adults they experienced rapid upward mobility and opportunity more than previous generations. Maturing into established adults, achievement-oriented Lucky Generation members built corporate empires and became legendary cultural names like Marlin Brando, Elvis, Bob Dylan, Woody Allen, Eric Clapton, and Rev. Martin Luther King, Jr. Beatnik author Jack Kerouac wrote the generation's defining book *On the Road*. The Beat Generation was swilling cappuccinos long before anyone else thought it was fashionable.

In the 1950s when the Russians launched the Sputnik satellite, many young Silent Generation members took it as a personal challenge to them. That event charged them with the energy that built the new economy of America—and inspired them to work toward a future without limits or rivals. Most of the corporations and organizations that form the foundation for the U.S. economy and infrastructure were formed doing their lifetime.

Many members of the Silent Generation remain as the active founders or CEOs of these organizations. Famous Lucky Generation leaders include Astronaut Neil Armstrong (and 10 more out of the 12 men who have walked on the moon), Warren Buffet, Ted Turner, Calvin Klein, John McCain, John Kerry, and General Colin Powell.

Outlook

■ *Personal responsibility in context to others.* Those of the Silent Generation strongly believe in such things as duty, honor, and country. They tend to believe each person should make the appropriate sacrifices to see to it that the whole group experiences success. Their combined ethics of hard work and commitment to one another have made them successful in many ways. This generation is still one of the most influential groups of people now living.

- *Group-oriented relationships.* This generation has always been group-focused. As teens, group dating was popular with them. They had their "gang" of friends they spent time with in their younger adult years. Many of them served in the Korean War together. As they grew older, the Lucky Generation remained loyal to their friends, helping them get established where they could. To be friends with one Silent Generation member brings the potential to be included in a very large group of other influential networks. Their influence and position often makes them the gatekeepers to implementing new directions in the country.

- *Take charge leadership.* Lucky Generation people know how to follow leaders. Since they are used to living and working in a group, they appreciate it when someone takes the reins of leadership, provided they do so with humility and respect toward others. A kind and polite (yet strong) leader with a clear vision is preferred to a leader with an egalitarian collaborative decision-making approach.

- *Revolutionary problem solving.* Silent Generation problem solving can sometimes become revolutionary. They like to take apart the problem, find the solution, and work on the long-range strategy that will reverse the negative direction. They will leverage all their relationships toward the goal and put their agenda ahead of everything else until they accomplish the desired change.

- *Manage the money.* The Silent Generation tends to be frugal with money, which may come from hard economic times into which they were born. They'd prefer to review expenditures as a group and hear the justification for each one from their leaders. They also want to see that money is spent to mobilize the most people toward the collective goal.

■ *Analog technology*. They remember when you could fix things with your own two hands (and not have to use a call center in India) and they knew how to do it themselves. This generation may not be the handiest with digital technology, but they know how to do a lot of other technical things that have been forgotten by younger generations. This is the generation with the know-how that put a man on the moon using slide rules and a computer that had less memory and computing power than the average cell phone.

■ *Corporate institutions*. The Silent Generation is a good fit for the corporate world. The most successful corporations now existing were built by them. They do not distrust corporations as much as they distrust individuals with hidden personal agendas (who might corrupt it). They will fight to preserve the purity of the organization at almost any cost.

Messages that Attract

■ "Look how far we have come together!"
■ "Here's what your part in this task includes . . ."
■ Stories of how older adults are energizing a larger movement of people
■ Get endorsements from leaders they respect
■ Don't make the mistake of overlooking or underestimating them
■ Respect and ask for their contribution
■ Recount the historic foundations they laid
■ Lay out the long-range vision
■ Make sure they understand the continuity with the past

The Baby Boomers

KEY CHARACTERISTICS: Optimistic, moralistic, educated, passionate, team-oriented, and self-developing

BASIC DEMOGRAPHICS:
Median age: 53
Years they were born: 1946–1964
Number in the segment: 78 million

Background

American Baby Boomers came of age in a time of unprecedented prosperity in the United States. Their optimistic attitude comes because they tend to take material things for granted. Their generation has always been the focus of interest in general society as they have had the starring role during every phase of their development. Rather than aspiring to the American Dream, Boomers have been born into it. They are the most educated generation in American history, and they value and respect education. Baby Boomers are insatiable learners who are constantly on a quest of personal development.

Boomers have brought sweeping social and cultural change to the United States throughout their lifetimes. They have a more informal approach to life that changed the business world from formal suits and ties to "business casual." Their tastes in music, movies, and design have shaped the present American culture. In addition, they have changed the social values in the United States with regard to women's rights, racial equality, changes in sexual mores, and the rearing of children. Baby Boomers have a strong need to define what they do in terms of morality and right and wrong. They are the force behind movements from the Hippies and Free Love to the Jesus People and contemporary Christian music.

As the first generation that was raised on TV, they have shaped the world with technology innovations in just about every area of learning, especially in physical science, sociology, psychology, and technology with inventions such as the personal computer, the internet, satellite networks, etc. Most of America's technical engineers are Baby Boomers.

Outlook

- *Youthfulness.* Boomers don't want to be kids forever, but they do want to keep younger by intensely questioning established ways and bringing the youthful sentiment of looking at things with fresh eyes.
- *Moralistic.* Boomers tend to see everything through the prism of right and wrong and good vs. evil. A good way to get a Boomer's attention is to spotlight an injustice.
- *Purpose driven.* Boomers are driven and hard working, and tend to think a person needs to pay his dues and work his way to the top. Position is the outcome of creative action, hard work, and dedication.
- *Personal gratification.* Many Boomers value relationships for what they get out of them emotionally or in how they help them develop themselves. When relating to people, the loyalty of friends is highly valued. Boomers also want respect from others for their achievements.
- *Give a little face time.* The generation that gave us Woodstock loves conferences and large gatherings. These are places where Boomers thrive; they like to mingle with others and form relationships. These relationships are not too deep, however, because Boomers are slow to commit.
- *Consensus building is important to Boomers.* They value egalitarian leadership. They prefer to work on problems in teams and task force groups. Give them a place to meet regularly and a team of competent people, and they feel they can change the world.

■ *Taking personal responsibility.* Boomers want to lead people movements that solve problems. They believe that if people would take personal responsibility seriously enough, most of the world's problems could be resolved.

■ *Spend the money.* Boomers are focused on the present more than the future. For this reason, they have always had the tendency to spend more than save. They want to spend in ways that have measurable impact in the present.

■ *Digital immigrants.* Baby Boomers are playing catch-up in using new technology in daily life. The primary technology that shaped Boomers was the telephone. Many prefer to talk on the phone to e-mail and other forms of communication. However, when Boomers master the use of a new technological tool, they are very proud and let everyone know about it.

■ *Civic minded.* Boomers care deeply about human rights, fairness, humane practices, and building trust. They will join organizations that agree with their values and they love working to right the world's wrongs.

■ *Attitude toward institutions.* Boomers do not believe that large organizations can be trusted to always do the right thing. They will not sign up for something just because it has the official stamp of approval from a large organization.

Messages that Attract

■ Taking responsibility
■ Life adventures
■ Demonstrations of passion
■ Self-defining moments
■ Morality tales
■ Clearly stated objectives and goals
■ Novel approaches
■ Overcoming social threats

- Pushing traditional boundaries
- Learning from younger generations
- Institutions transcending themselves
- Youthful energy
- Best practices
- Proven methodologies
- Challenging established ways
- Second half of life impact

Generation X

KEY CHARACTERISTICS: Balanced, self-reliant, skeptical, entrepreneurial, savvy, and efficient

BASIC DEMOGRAPHICS:
Median age: 36
Years they were born: 1965–1979
Number in the segment: 66 million

Background

Generation X came of age in the shadow of the Baby Boomers.
Also called the Baby Busters, this generation is the next smallest
generational cohort in the United States. The smallness of their
numbers is due in part because in the late 1960s and 1970s there
was a widely held belief that overpopulation was a planetary
crisis (much on the same scale as global warming is the planetary concern of today), also the expanding use of the birth control pill (made available since 1960) contributed to the fact that
fewer babies were being born during these years. Throughout
the '70s and early '80s divorce became more common in the
United States, with nearly half of all marriages ending in
divorce. This generation is the children of these divorcées. They
became a generation of latch-key kids who learned to become
self-reliant taking care of themselves after school until their

working parents came home. Growing up in divorced or blended homes where both parents had full-time jobs also caused the generation to seek to prioritize the balance of work and family when they reached adulthood. Busters seek the right balance in life, being careful to not neglect their families while working for organizations or causes that employ them.

For the Generation X, the perspective on life is not as optimistic as the generations before or after them. They tend to feel that the economy has never given them a break because they have had to struggle and delay their opportunities to be leaders or attain prominence in the working world. Further exacerbating the perception is the unwillingness of the Baby Boomers to yield room for their generation inside the organizations where they have established predominance. Growing up seeing the high-profile failings of leaders in positions of authority in everything from politics (Watergate) and business (Enron) to religion (PTL) has made this generation cynical when thinking about leaders. Busters are not impressed with credentials and position. It has been said this is a generation that doesn't believe in heroes. To gain credibility with the Buster, one has to demonstrate competence, show results, and lead a balanced personal life.

Because opportunities have not been forthcoming for them, Generation X has become entrepreneurial in their outlook, seeking to build their own opportunities. As pragmatists, they want to see results at the bottom line. But they envision a working world where people matter more than organizations and they will not commit themselves without reserve to any organization.

The Gen X contribution to present-day society includes family-friendly concepts such as popularizing home schooling, paid maternity leave, and stay-at-home fathers. Busters are known for their creative workspace environments with space to play games, change scenery, and have private conversations. Generation X brought the world Google, Yahoo, Wikipedia, and eBay.

Outlook

- *Savvy self-reliance.* Busters value their ability to make their own way. Busters tend to trust their intuition more than they trust others. There's a little entrepreneur in just about every Xer.
- *Balance in life and work.* Generation X wants to leave time for fun and recreation. They also want sincere relationships at work; no schmoozers or fast talkers allowed.
- *Reluctant to commit.* Because many Busters come from divorced backgrounds, many have abandonment issues that make it hard for them to make relationship commitments. If you push too hard for commitment and loyalty, he'll likely walk away or find a work around.
- *Networking by working together.* The Gen X way to network is to develop relationships through work. They make the organizations they work with more efficient by cultivating deeper connections with co-workers.
- *Respecting competence in leadership.* This generation respects people who show they know what they are talking about by what they are able to accomplish. They are unlikely to be impressed with people due to their rank or educational background.
- *Alternative approaches to problem solving.* They are practical realists who will look for new solutions that work rather than trying to adapt a failing system.
- *Money.* The Buster approach to money is to hedge against losing it. They want to squeeze every ounce of value out of it. They want to know what every cent is doing. They want to know how the money is protected against economic failure and individual corruption.
- *Digital adaptives.* Generation X wasn't born with the internet or with wireless connectivity. But they have made up for lost time! Since technology can make them more efficient, they are attracted to it.

■ *Glocal (Global + Local) Concerns.* Xers are concerned about the state of the economy, the national debt, and health care because they feel their indulgent forbearers, the Baby Boomers, have left them with a litany of problems to solve. Global warming, social injustice, poverty, education, and other issues also concern them. These are seen pessimistically as just a few of the problems they feel they have been saddled with from prior generations.

■ *Distrust institutions, avoid them where possible.* Generation X are not fans of traditional institutions because they doubt their leaders are there because they are competent. They are more likely to see them as there as a result of some political maneuvering they have done.

Messages that Attract

■ People who are effective
■ New and alternative approaches
■ "You are respected!"
■ "You can be in the driver's seat!"
■ Show the benefits of cooperation
■ Show them how money is being used effectively
■ Show the family life of leaders
■ Balanced work and recreation

Millennial Generation

KEY CHARACTERISTICS: Ambitious, authentic, relational, collaborating, civic-minded, high energy, self-confident, and sometimes, a little vain

BASIC DEMOGRAPHICS:
Median age: 20
Years they were born: 1980–1996
Number in the segment: 86 million

Background

Generation Y is still coming of age in the United States. The youngest of them is 14 years old. This ambitious group of young people is also called "Echo Boomers" because their size (86 million) is even larger than the Boomer population. Their numbers are only partly due to the size of their Baby Boomer parents' generation; they are also the product of the rapid increase in immigration in the United States. This generation is more culturally and racially diverse than other generational cohorts in America.

The fact that Gen Y is also known by another name, "Millennial Generation," is a reminder that one thing that marks them is their ability to choose among a range of options for just about everything they want or need. Millennials have had a mind-numbing range of options for their consideration because they have grown up in a consumer-driven era where the various products and services around them were always striving for market share by differentiating themselves with endless value-added benefits. Echo Boomers are used to a lot of options and tend to be very choosey customers!

A typical Gen Y childhood experience of going to the dentist is an illustration. Besides what dentist they go to, they have their choice of several mouthwash flavors, color of disposable sanitary bibs, headphone music styles (if they forget their iPods when they come), what kind of sunglasses they want to wear as the dentist shines the light in their mouth, the color of rubber bands in their braces, etc. The list could go on!

Besides having multiple choices for every situation, the Millennial Generation has also been constantly encouraged and uplifted by their parents and general society. They have been protected by the school system from any feeling that they may in any way be inferior to others. Everyone seems to have been telling them from their earliest years that they are of special intelligence, gifted with talents no others have, and they can be or do anything they set their mind to. As a result, Millennials are the most self-confident generation in history. This confidence lends itself to powerful feelings of ambition. Yers truly think they can achieve anything. Sometimes their self-confident tendencies express themselves in outright vanity.

Their approach to life is not with trepidation and caution; instead, they boldly seek to drain every bit of benefit out of every experience and every activity they attempt. They are not afraid to try new things and are at times too extreme in how close they get to the edge. This is exemplified in the many Yers who choose to get extensive tattoos and body piercings. They adopt radically dangerous pastimes such as skateboarding down stairway handrails, doing extreme bicycle stunts, and even "surfing" on the hoods of cars. The world is their oyster!

Not all Echo Boomers live on the wild side, but most of them have a galvanized sense of community that is in many ways similar to the values held by the WWII "Greatest Generation" when it comes to having a civic mind-set. The aftermath of the attacks of 9/11 seared in this generation that the real heroes are civil servants like policemen, firemen, and soldiers who have been celebrated in the public forum as long as they can remember. This generation truly wants to give back like the civil servants of our country. Even the musicians and celebrities they admire are giving back.

They are polite, hard working, and ambitious, so whatever organization they work with gets their best efforts as long as their bosses constantly tell them how great they are doing. In fact, Boomer managers have fallen in love with the Y Generation. They admire their youthful outlook and their sense of civics so much that in many places these Millennials are getting promoted past the Generation X. Because they are in demand, Echo Boomers tend to skip from place to place when opportunities for advancement come up. And why shouldn't they take the opportunities? After all, despite their lack of skills and experience, they honestly feel they deserve it. What's not to love about them? The last thing an Echo Boomer wants to hear is that in some way they don't measure up. For this reason, the thing that bothers them most is to be told they are not experienced enough or skilled enough to do something.

Gen Y is hardly out of the gate, and already they have contributed technology advancements that are multimillion-dollar international blockbusters. Two examples, Facebook and MySpace, are leading the pack (not ironically, two web-based media tools that help launch one's ego into cyberspace) with a seemingly endless stream of new social media applications being developed. The Echo Boomer generation is a generation of tinkerers who have known no period when technology wasn't readily available to them. As such, technology is not as daunting or impressive to them as it is to other generations.

Outlook

- *Big ambitions*. Echo Boomers are very ambitious. They want to try it all and do it all and expect to be rewarded for their efforts. They don't believe they necessarily need to "pay their dues" to get where they are going. They are working now for their big break. To them leaders are achievers.
- *Hardwired relationship networks*. Gen Yers don't have to remember to keep in touch with people because they tend to be in almost constant contact with the people they are closest to through instant messaging on the social web and text messaging via their cell phones.
- *Constant social networking*. Social media like Facebook and MySpace are important tools for cultivating relationships to Gen Y. Many in their generation have abandoned e-mail and telephones. With tools like Twitter, they can even stay in their social network through text messaging.

- *Relaxed view of leadership.* Millennials are relaxed around authority figures because they have been raised to think they are inferior to none. They come across as poised and relaxed around leaders. If a leader is seen to be a competent achiever, they want to get to know them personally.

- *Collaborative problem solvers.* Echo Boomers have a cadre of friends in their network that can help them solve problems. Their ease of communicating in social networks makes them natural collaborators in problem-solving situations.

- *Money needs to be controlled.* Gen Y are not as cynical about money and the economy as Generation X but they tend to see money as something that needs to be controlled tightly.

- *Technological natives.* Millennials are comfortable with technology. They are easily bored with new technology and because many have the ability, they often want to tweak technology to their specifications. They are a generation of customizers, not just customers.

- *Giving back to make a difference.* Like Boomers and Xers, Generation Y has adopted many causes to their generation such as ending global warming, poverty, human trafficking, and educational deprivation. The big difference is this generation truly believes they can solve these problems.

- *Customize institutions.* Echo Boomers don't have quite the amount of mistrust of institutions that Boomers and Xers have. They are not "brand loyal" to any institution. Instead they want to blend them ("mash-up") together into new outcomes.

Messages that Attract

- "Give back, make a difference!"
- "Come together, work with others!"
- "Go to the edge!"

- "We can do this!" (positive outlook)
- Spotlight others in their cohort who are achievers
- Reality-show style stories
- Transcending cultures
- Explore, discover something new
- Tales of extreme risk or radical methods
- People having fun together
- Show variety of options
- Tell stories using social media

Developing a Profile of Your Most Active Segments

Hopefully these profiles will get you started identifying who to target with your marketing. These sketches can be used along with demographic and primary research data you gather to form a profile of your preferred target audience. A good practice for your organization is to create a composite "persona" profile of your most active segments and use it for planning outreach. A profile of your typical donors and volunteers helps your organization anticipate the needs of your supporters. Give your persona profile a name to personalize your audience like "Bobby Boomer" or "Jenny GenX." You can use a picture of an actual person from the target audience, or purchase one from a stock image website that represents the entire segment, and hang their image in your office or where your team plans your work. This will help keep you and your team from thinking about people like they are numbers and from treating individuals like they are projects.

> Marketing without research is like
> building a house without establishing
> a solid foundation for it.

CHAPTER 6

Guerrillas Understand Their Marketplace

NONPROFIT LEADERS HAVE A MIXTURE OF attitudes when it comes to doing research in their marketplace. A few look at research as the panacea for their problems. They are addicted to doing research, but usually are not equally hooked on applying what they learn with active marketing. Others see all the numbers and charts in research reports and have nightmarish flashbacks to high school math. They think research is as irrelevant to their mission as algebra is in their daily lives. Some avoid research because they fear the results might prove to them that they need to do things differently. They are usually right.

But research doesn't have to be an intimidating experience to be effective. It is not wasted energy when done correctly. And it doesn't have to be complicated. For example, if you look at a for-profit company's website to find out who in the company is the best person to call about becoming partners with your nonprofit before you dial their number, you are doing research. You are also making yourself more credible with the people whom you call. Research can make your organization far more competitive when seeking grants also. There are a lot of good reasons to do research.

We don't intend to try to talk you into doing research in this chapter. The fact is you are already doing research, even if you are unaware it is research. All nonprofits in creating programs for their target audiences find out in the process of doing so if people like what they offer or not. You may think you are doing programming, but when you roll out a product or service to the public, you are testing if your ideas work and are getting feedback about them. When you send out something in the mail or launch a new website, you are going to find out if they are effective or not by using them. Wouldn't you rather find out ahead of time if your new ideas are going to appeal to the people you want to reach? Isn't it better to test your marketing promotions with a smaller group and see what the response rate is before you sink a lot of money into a huge advertising flop? Marketing without research is like building a house without establishing a solid foundation for it. It doesn't matter how good the architectural designs are or whether the design gets accolades from other architects. If you build your house on sand, you have only yourself to blame when the foundation of your house can't weather the storms of the real world. The same applies to marketing. It seems obvious to guerrillas that "marketers" should want to know everything there is to know about their "market." How can you do effective marketing without having a deep grasp of your marketplace?

Leveraging Information for Your Nonprofit

A part of your due diligence in promoting your nonprofit is to understand your marketplace as well as you can. In warfare, guerrillas are always in research mode; they thrive on good intelligence. They gain their competitive advantage by doing reconnaissance. The key differences between a guerrilla marketer and a non-guerrilla are how they use their time, energy, imagination—and information. Guerrillas don't just get what little information they can use to get by on, they find out what information they have to have to help them draw a straight line between where they are now and where they are going to be. They have a relentless attitude of getting and leveraging information as an advantage in their cause. They are continuously learning. Research is an indispensable tool in the arsenal of the guerrilla marketer for marketing planning.

> By learning more about the people the nonprofit wants to reach, guerrillas are better able to link their message to solutions that appeal to them.

You can be a guerrilla researcher too. Start by understanding your customers, partners, and stakeholders. Next, master an awareness of what makes your prospects tick. After that, become an expert on your marketplace and industry. Then, know your competition better than they know themselves. Finally, always be spying on yourself.

Guerrillas know that research doesn't have to be expensive to be effective. They are

Guerrilla Marketing Planning	Guerrilla Use of Research
Situation analysis	Helps you understand your market. Identify target audiences. Spy on your competition and yourself. Identify opportunities for your competitive advantage. Design intelligent positioning.
Goal setting	Find the purpose of your marketing. Looking at the goals you have achieved in the past can help you in setting new objectives. Leverage data from your tracking system.
Communication strategy	Design your call to action. Identify media channels for your message. Apply demographic data in media buying. Pre-test messages. Pilot programs and products.
Marketing attack	Keep momentum in your attack by watching response and conversion rates. Manage your resources, networks, and marketing weapons.
Tracking	Collect and use information from responses, sales, and donations. Watch response metrics and maintain follow-up. Track sales and donations.
Assessing impact	Calculate retention and comprehension of messages. Measure if your goals are helping you achieve your stated mission.
Evaluation	Compare results to objectives and goals. Listen to feedback. Assess skills and educational needs. Start your marketing circle again.

willing to invest in unconventional means to get the research results they need to make the right decisions. You can put more of your time and energy into the research and save money. That is not to say you don't need proper methodology. Too many organizations think that because the intention of their cause is pure, they can get by without doing research correctly. Don't kid yourself into believing that the good karma your organization may have with the universe somehow excuses you from research excellence. You have the same communication problems that the product marketers are spending millions of dollars trying to overcome. What you are doing is far more important that figuring out if a new snack food tastes cheesy enough to customers. In addition, you are likely to have more barriers to adoption of your product than the snack food market researchers have to theirs. If anyone has room for communication error, it is the manufacturer of products that are nonessential to living. You, however, have a cause greater than theirs, so you should take research more seriously than they do in keeping with the importance of your task.

Steps in Nonprofit Guerrilla Marketing Research

1. *Define the research problem.* Start by identifying the questions you need answered. Why are you doing research? Define what the problem is you want to solve. Social marketers call this stage doing epidemiology. That's a great way to think about your marketing research problem. Imagine yourself as the guerrilla doctor giving your organization's marketing a checkup. Ask questions that help you identify the symptoms, make a prognosis, and prescribe the remedy for what is ailing your nonprofit.

2. *Determine the kind of research you need.* There are two kinds of research, primary and secondary. As backward as it may sound, always start with secondary research first. Secondary research includes reading existing research found in the form of reports, books, and interviews of experts. A good place to start is with the data your organization already has on hand in the form of sales, responses, feedback, evaluations, and records. Primary research is

research conducted firsthand by the marketer. Once you know what is available, you will know what information you need that you don't have yet.

3. *Identify the method of research.* Two types of research methods exist, qualitative and quantitative. Quantitative is scientific research using probability samples and statistical data (surveys, observation, experiments, etc.). With the right sampling methods you can ask just a few hundred people questions and get an accurate picture about what millions of people think, feel, and do. Qualitative research (focus groups, interviews, ethnography, etc.) helps you get the answers about why things happen. This form of research gives you the closeup view of individuals, but is not reliable for extrapolating assumptions about large groups of people. Both forms of research are useful.

4. *Design the research.* This is the part where you create your research strategy and develop research instruments like survey questionnaires and focus group discussion guides. The biggest part of this phase is knowing how to ask the right questions. The second biggest part is keeping your biases in check and yourself open to listening to the answers. Third is staying focused on your objective of finding information you will actually use. Are you measuring attitudes or behaviors? Do you want to evaluate awareness or satisfaction? Your budget also has an impact on the kind of research you design.

5. *Collect your research data.* Now, this is the fun part. You get to peek inside the minds of the people you want to reach. Don't stop until you have the right amount of information. Have you found enough secondary data to know what you don't know? Do you have enough completed surveys of the right kinds of people to constitute an accurate sample? Are you listening and watching closely enough?

6. *Tabulate and analyze the data*. Another fun part of research is looking at the data you have gathered and making sense of it all. You will be editing, coding, and categorizing your information. This is a very important time to remind yourself to remain objective. Also, the more thorough you are at this stage, the better your results will be when you apply your data in your marketing strategy.

7. *Report and apply the research in marketing*. Your report may only serve to confirm what you already "knew" or you may find yourself in the uncharted waters of a new discovery. As you write your report, recruit the help of others who have the expertise to help you understand the implications of your data. The main reason half of all research is not used is because researchers fail to make recommendations and application of their data. Guerrilla marketing researchers draw conclusions and make recommendations for taking action in their research reports.

Digging for Secondary Information

Before you conduct primary research, make sure you are aware of what data already exists that can help you in the form of secondary information. Following are some of the best sources.

The Library

Librarians may not look like dangerous people, but they are because they are dangerously savvy about where to look for the information that could burst the bubble of your bright, but mistaken, ideas, or debunk the pet theory you have been nursing. On the other hand, they might lead you right to the information that opens up your mind to a new idea that becomes a tremendous advantage for your organization. Market research can help you test your ideas before you sink your time, energy, and money into taking a new direction. A librarian is a good person to have on your marketing team.

There is a gold mine of information available to help your nonprofit if you are prepared to do a little digging at the library. Government census data and reports, economic data, productivity statistics, information from news and trade associations are sitting on the stacks waiting for you right now at the branch library. University libraries often have sociological studies, scientific journals, and host forums that could inform you about topics of interest to your nonprofit's cause. Your librarian can help you devise a strategy for harvesting the kind of data you need. Start with your local library. You don't have to head downtown to get what you need. Even the smallest library has access to enough information to keep your nonprofit in the know with reference materials, books, periodicals, and databases.

Chamber of Commerce and Economic Development Authority Office

After the library, head over to your local chamber and EDA. These offices are often found in the same building. They have gathered information about your community you can use in practical ways. They can help you navigate the regulatory and zoning issues of your community, and they can put you in touch with key business and community leaders who can help you with your nonprofit. The chamber also hosts great networking events.

The Internet

The web has a lot of the information you need available with only a click of the mouse. Know the difference between internet *directories* and *search engines*. *Directories* are edited by humans (and machines) and organized by subjects instead of compiled by keyword results. You will find information in directories you can't find in the massive lists of data displayed in search engine results. Directories like AboutUs.org, dir.yahoo.com, and directory.google.com are good places to look. Also Wikipedia, the free encyclopedia, is an excellent resource. *Search engines* organize information based on a variety of algorithms and formulas, mostly by keywords and page ranking data gleaned from automated search spiders and robots on the web that crawl all the pages on the internet looking for keywords, links, and tags. Google.com and Yahoo.com are excellent search engines to use in your research, but also consider other sources like Dogpile.com and AltaVista.com.

Internal Information

If only you knew everything you know. Many nonprofits spend time and money looking outside their organization for information, when the information they need is right under their noses in the form of data and reports already available. You can get a lot of insight from studying your organization's sales and other response information. Also, getting to the front lines with your volunteers and paying attention to what people in your organization are talking about at the water cooler can reveal helpful insights.

Why Guerrillas Do Primary Research

The book you need most for your nonprofit isn't available at your public library or local bookstore; it is one you need to write yourself. You can write the book on the people you want to reach by doing original, or primary, research. Doing primary research isn't just a nice idea, it is vitally important to the success of your organization. Primary research doesn't have to cost an arm and a leg, but it is not free. To be effective, your organization will have to make an investment in it. Here are a few benefits gained from doing primary research:

- Defines the purpose of your marketing
- Keeps you from making stupid mistakes (ask your spouse)
- Gives you a realistic picture of your present situation
- Identifies and creates competitive advantage
- Fuels creativity
- Helps identify and segment your target audiences
- Clarifies your market niche
- Provides insights into how to differentiate your products, programs, and services
- Keeps you in touch with trends in the changing marketplace
- Useful in developing your nonprofit's identity
- Gives you the outsider perspective
- Gauges perceptions, satisfaction, and awareness
- Clarifies which marketing mix and media channels are best
- Changes mistaken assumptions in your organization
- Beneficial for prioritizing budget planning
- Makes practical use of response data, sales metrics, membership, and donor records.

Managing Survey Error Like a Professional

Designing and conducting surveys is not as difficult as you might think, but it is more than we can describe in detail here. There are two excellent guerrilla resources on this subject. They are: *Guerrilla Marketing Research* by Robert J. Kaden (Kogan Page, 2006) and *More Guerrilla Marketing Research* by Robert J. Kaden, Gerald Linda, and Jay Conrad Levinson (Kogan Page, 2009). In the meantime, here are a few items to get you started.

The first thing you need to know about survey research is that all surveys are wrong. All surveys, no matter who conducts them, have a margin of error in them. You have no doubt seen the disclaimers in survey reports where the researchers state their survey has a specific degree of error. For example, they state their research has a confidence ratio of 95 percent and a margin of error of plus or minus 5 percent, and so forth. What they are stating is the degree to which they are wrong. That's not being pessimistic about surveys; we want to make a point. Good researchers have a plan for managing survey error. If you don't have a conscious plan for managing survey error, you are setting your survey up for failure before you even start. Managing research inaccuracy requires diligent attention no matter who conducts the survey.

Many nonprofits do surveys very poorly; they don't have an effective strategy for scientifically sampling the opinions and preferences of people. They design their questions poorly and jump to wrong conclusions when analyzing their data. And they often give advice and believe conclusions that are based on their own faulty research. Bad research is just wasting time, energy, and money. If your organization is going to conduct a survey, make sure you have a plan for managing the amount of error in your research. The four kinds of survey error are: sample error, question design error, response error, and reporting error. Apply the same error management principles used by the research professionals and get a handle on the accuracy of your surveys.

1. Sample Error

Solution: A proper random sample

Many nonprofit surveys are conducted with little thought for statistical sampling. Nonprofits usually pass out a few surveys and expect that the results will give them answers to their questions. To get good research you have to ask the right people, in the right number, selected in the right manner to get a predictable level of accuracy in research.

- *You need the right people.* For example, you can't ask one group of people what another group thinks—how do they know? You need to make sure the people you ask in your survey fit the description of the people you want to learn about.

- *You need to ask the right number of people.* You can't hand out 35 surveys, tabulate the results from 13 responses, and call it scientific research. If the group you want to study is very small, you need to conduct a census of everyone in the group. If the number of people in your study is very large, you will need to select a cross section of people that represents the whole group.

- *You need to select people in the right manner.* You need to get a random selection of people in the study group using scientific sampling techniques. Don't be intimidated by the talk of science; it's easy to randomize. Done correctly, your survey could ask questions of just 400 people and get an accurate representation for millions more people. Learn how to conduct proper research sampling, and your organization could become the only expert on your entire target audience.

2. Question Design Error

Solution: *Properly designed questions*

Anyone can write a survey question, right? Well, yes and no. Anyone who knows how to write them can, but you have to learn how to design questions properly or you will bias your survey results. To write good questions, you need to think about your research objectives and the people you want to query. People can't tell you everything you want to know. Also, you need to avoid asking leading questions, watch out for questions with unclear meaning, and have balanced scales for respondents to use when answering.

Designing questions also means managing your expectations. Often nonprofits think they can ask the collective wisdom out there and get answers to the deepest secrets of the universe—paper or plastic? Humans are also very poor at predicting how they will behave in the future, so they can't really tell you if they will use your new product even if they say they will. People can best tell you who they are; what they do, what they have done and know; and what they think and feel. Beyond that, it gets more difficult.

3. Response Error

Solution: *A proper number of respondents*

Even some of the most highly touted research is based on so few respondents that the findings are misleading. Dare we say wrong? For example, a popular approach is to conduct polls and surveys through websites to find out what people think or feel about a particular subject. These polls don't tell anything about what the general population of people thinks, they only tell what the people who took the poll think. The results are not scientific because they do not employ sampling methodology. Even if questions are correctly designed and the people you survey are the right people, you still have to contend with the statistical monster margin of error. If your survey sample says you need 400 people, then 299 are not enough. You need to keep working until you get the right number of randomly selected people answering all your properly designed questions.

Some surveys are too long. When nonprofits decides they are going to conduct a survey (unfortunately a once-in-a-lifetime experience for many), they often think they might as well ask their target audience *everything they always wanted to know, but were afraid to ask before*. But if you make your survey too long, fewer people will be willing to complete your survey and you really ought to throw out incomplete surveys. You will need to keep the survey short enough so people will fill it out completely. Does all this sound too hard? Nobody said science was child's play. Good research can be hard work. But if you hold on and keep up until you get the proper number of responses, you will be rewarded with the sweet nectar of scientific accuracy!

4. Reporting Error

Solution: *Guard against research bias*

Many nonprofit leaders fool themselves (without knowing it) by looking at data in ways that confirm their biases. If you want to see something, you will see it. Science calls for objectivity! You need to be objective when you analyze data. Sometimes that isn't possible. You may be too close to the situation to be objective. That's when it is time to call in a professional researcher who can help you make a dispassionate assessment. If you get professional help, make sure you include them in all aspects of your research design. A good researcher can't take a survey conducted with bad methodology and magically make it scientifically accurate with his analysis.

Other problems arise when researchers are not equipped to analyze the data from the survey they have conducted. The results are accurate, but the reporter doesn't know enough about the nonprofit's cause, advertising, or marketing principles to make a proper analysis. Sometimes the culprit of faulty research reporting is the researcher's lack of skills in handling information in a database or calculating percentages and weighting cross-tabulated data. If you want to become a skilled researcher, you can. But like anything worth doing, it will take work and dedication.

Focusing on Focus Groups

A focus group is a group of six to ten people who meet together for an hour (or two, but no more than that, please) to discuss a focused topic. There is an objective moderator who guides the conversation along the topic without taking the lead or lecturing on the subject. The conversation is recorded (audio or video) for summarizing, reporting, and showing the sponsors of the research what participants said. You can use focus groups to test programming, try new products, and get an insider's perspective from the people you want to reach with your product, program, or message. Focus groups are a quick and fun way to get useful research.

A few tips for designing a focus group:

- Get an objective person to lead the discussion, someone who doesn't have an agenda to get people to say what you want to hear.

- Only invite people into the group who fit the exact description of the people you want to reach. Use a screening interview questionnaire to identify them.

- Pay the participants for their time (usually $50 each). Don't worry; this won't influence their opinions. They will be more committed to speak up if they are getting paid.

- Assure participants you will only use their comments in your research and not their names. Help them know they will not be contacted about their comments.

- Limit the people who see or hear the recordings. Don't distribute the participants' personal information.

- Alert people they are being recorded and allow people to leave if they don't want to be recorded. Get people to sign a release giving permission to record and use their comments.

- Develop 10 to 15 questions to guide the moderator in leading the conversation along the areas where you want to focus discussion. Only the moderator needs to see the questionnaire. Avoid being too rigid with keeping them on the exact path of the questions. Try to get a free-flowing discussion going. You just don't want a focus group that lacks focus!

■ On major projects, use a professional focus group facility. They are designed with a one-way mirror on one wall with an observation area for people sponsoring the research. If the leading stakeholders in your project are present in the observation room, they will learn a lot more than if they just read a report.

In-Depth Interviews and Ethnographic Research

You can learn a lot by going out and talking to people directly where they are. Ethnographic researchers are participant observers who use this form of research frequently. You can do interviews too, find people who fit the profile you want to study, and ask them questions similar in nature to those you would ask in a focus group. You won't need to pay the people you interview, but you could provide a meal or refreshments. Don't let what you provide become too much of a distraction, though (like a noisy restaurant, etc.). Use the same approach you used in the focus group. Screen people to find out if they fit the group you want to study. Have 10 to 15 questions in mind that you want to ask. Let the conversation unfold naturally; don't try to drive the conversation too much, unless the people you are talking to get too far off topic.

Case Studies

Some really good ideas come from studying a particular instance of a behavior you want to learn about in detail. How did your most active people become that way? What drives them to get so involved? Who were the key players in helping them grow? Conversely, who has recently dropped out of your program? What happened? What were the events leading up to them leaving? Also, new people have started coming to your program.

How did they find out about you? What did they like most? Study a situation in detail and glean as much insight from it as you can.

Secret Shoppers

Send in your own spies who can help you evaluate your nonprofit. Recruit and train people to visit your organization's locations for you. Train them how to record their impressions and get them into a report you can use for planning. When selecting your secret shoppers, make sure they are objective people. Pay them as you would a focus group participant to assure their diligence in recording and reporting back to you.

Guerilla Marketing Research Advantage

Research is a weapon in your arsenal that helps you fight against mediocrity and ineffectiveness. If you are not doing research, start right now. But don't stop there. Fifty percent of research in the business world is currently collecting dust on a bookshelf somewhere. Don't let that happen to your research—act on what you learn.

Guerrilla marketers have a plan to make use of the research they do. By learning more about the people their nonprofit wants to reach, guerrillas are better able to link messages to solutions that appeal to their target audiences. Guerrillas take what they learn in research and use it to build a competitive advantage.

> Without take-action guerrillas,
> nonprofit marketing would digress into academ-
> ics and would only exist in plans stuffed into
> three-ring binders gathering dust on the book-
> shelves of executive directors.

CHAPTER 7

Mini-, Maxi-, and E-Media Weapons

ASK THE AVERAGE NONPROFIT EXECUTIVE DIRECTOR what marketing is, and you'll be told that it is advertising. Guerrillas know this is nonsense. Advertising is only one weapon of marketing. How many weapons are most organizations aware of? Maybe five or ten. How many do they use? Three at most. Guerrillas are aware of a full 200 guerrilla marketing weapons and make use of about 40 of them. More than half the weapons are free and yours for the taking!

This chapter along with Chapters 8 and 9 contain all the weapons divided into eight categories. They are presented in no particular rank or order because there's a 200-way tie for first place. Still, you will come across a few weapons that deserve red neon asterisks inside your head. Your job now is to select as many of these weapons from your arsenal as possible and then put them to use.

Mini-Media

As a small nonprofit, you will have little competition in the mini-media. Larger companies will not use these types of weapons because they are not as fast on their feet as you. Mini-media costs are low, and you will be the star of the show when using these weapons. Here is where your small size is an advantage.

1. *A marketing plan.* Be prepared to hear your executive director and board members rave about your excellent work as they see your marketing plans in easy-to-understand writing. Many nonprofit communication leaders don't get the funding they want because they can't show their leaders that they have a plan for using their budgets effectively. A marketing plan is your road map to a successful marketing campaign. You don't have to write a wordy document either; you can write your marketing plan in just seven sentences. (More about the Seven-Sentence Marketing plan in Chapter 20.)

2. *A marketing calendar.* Make a 12-month summary of all your guerrilla marketing activities by creating a list with 52 lines, one for every week in the year. In five columns across the list write 1) number of the week; 2) thrust or emphasis for that week; 3) marketing weapons used; 4) budget for the week; and 5) results at the end of the week (i.e., responses, dollars, rating scale, etc.). By the end of

the year, your annual marketing report will be easy to prepare and will reveal your stunning results.

3. *Identity.* The real reflection of your organization's personality. Build your reputation on truth, not a slick media facade. Your brand should be your authentic promise.

4. *Business cards.* Guerrilla business cards do double duty as marketing weapons, having more than just their name, address, and phone number. They also include the story of the benefits the nonprofit is bringing to the world and inviting the participation of others.

5. *Stationery.* The look of your stationery can reflect the feeling of credibility and stability for your nonprofit. If you use it in direct mail, a lot of people will see it. Get it right.

6. *Personal letters.* Not name-merged letters, but real letters written from one person to another. In a personal letter you can speak from the heart as a friend talking to another, including references to the other person's life. Talk about the other person and not yourself, and you will have their rapt attention. In this day of computers and desktop publishing, make sure your personal letters look, sound, and feel like a personal communication.

> By using many combinations of the 200 guerrilla marketing weapons, your company will greatly enhance the likelihood of nonprofit marketing success.

7. *Telephone marketing.* Not for the fainthearted, telephone marketing comes with a lot of rejection. But research shows that up to 51 percent of people will listen to telemarketers. If you build genuine rapport with the people you call, your nonprofit can reap the rewards of positive responses.

8. *A toll-free number.* If your organization has (or wants to have) a national scope, make it easy for people to contact you by phone with a toll-free number. People are accustomed to using toll-free numbers when contacting national organizations. If you are a smaller nonprofit, a toll-free number gives your organization the feel of a larger one.

9. *A vanity phone number.* If your phone number also spells out a word using the letters on the telephone keypad, it can make your number easier to remember and dial. If you use a word as a mnemonic device for making your phone number memorable, make sure the word you use supports your brand message. When promoting your phone number, don't forget to also include the actual numbers for people using cell phones with QWERTY keyboards. Most people who have these type devices don't know how to dial these kinds of numbers on their phones.

10. *The Yellow Pages.* If your nonprofit offers a service, program, or product that other organizations or companies also offer and are listed in the Yellow Pages, you need to be there too. Use the space to give more than just the basic information. Include as much information as you can, and speak in the language of benefits.

11. *Postcards.* Direct-mail postcards are a cost-effective way to send a targeted message to your community. Rather than constantly change your message, try sending the same message more than once. Test your copy by sending different messages to separate smaller lists, then send the card with the copy that gets the most response to your entire list.

12. *Postcard decks.* Companies that prepare coupon and postcard decks give nonprofits affordable access to larger audiences. The low cost of promoting in card decks allows organizations to enjoy regular visibility to

customers who anticipate receiving them in the mail. If you offer a service, product, or program that has a fee, include a discount coupon and watch for people lining up at your doors.

13. *Classified ads.* These small advertisements are useful for reaching people with services and programs. Classified advertisements are easy to test. They give access to local preferred targets and provide an affordable means to reach national audiences also.

14. *Yard signs.* Depending on city zoning laws and home-owner association rules, placing your message in the front yards of your supporters is a low-cost way to connect with a targeted community. Even prospects can get into the act. Once someone has agreed to place a sign in their yard, chances are high they will say yes to helping your cause in other ways.

15. *Free ads in shoppers.* These free local papers give your organization a money-stretching way to get your message to the community for the price of a little time filling out a form with your message. Some periodicals also look for articles to increase readership and add pass-along value; providing such content increases your visibility.

16. *Circulars and fliers.* They contain less information than brochures, are easy to make, and very flexible. Distribute them on the street, stick them under windshield wipers, leave them on the counters of local stores and offices. They even can break the ice to start an advocacy conversation.

17. *Community bulletin boards.* Look around, they are every-where: in stores, laundromats, on the college campus, at the local cafe, etc. Place your messages in front of the people you want to reach at no cost to you.

18. *Movie ads.* Put your message in front of a captive audience of potential clients and supporters using the advertisements that appear in theaters before movies start. You

can target people by tying your message into films that fit the theme of your cause. People exposed to theater advertising consistently show greater recall of ad messages. This may be because while they wait, there is nothing else they can do but view your message.

19. *Outside signs.* Down through history people have used signs to convey all kinds of meanings—everything from road directions to political statements have been rendered on signage. Signs can become advocates in your cause too. Tie your signs into your brand message, and include your meme and value messages. Signs can simply direct people to your location, or subtly reinforce the decision-making process. Brainstorm how you might use signs in your organization's cause. Who says your signs have to be stationary? Guerrillas love mobile signage.

20. *Street banners.* If you find the right locations for your banners, you can get your message to thousands of people at a very low cost. Some towns report their street traffic statistics on their municipal or chamber of commerce websites. If they do so in your town, you can use the information to find the best locations for your banners. Check local regulations, then place your banner near the path of cars, alongside the tracks of trains, or on the shores of waterways. You can even make your banners visible to landing airplanes.

21. *A window display.* If you have a location with high visibility, you can use your windows as a stage to get attention and make your point. Make your windows serve as tools to create interest and invite people inside. With window displays, find creative ways to change them regularly.

22. *Inside signage.* These signs act as silent advocates for your cause. They inspire confidence, reinforce your message, and teach. They can be placed in locations where people

might be tempted toward negative behavior, suggesting positive alternatives.

23. *Posters.* They could be as simple as a blow-up of your flier, display ads, or brochures. Colorful posters are the best kind. Try not to crowd them with too much clutter. Sometimes a picture can say more than copy ever could. Posters capture attention and create an environment favorable to your brand. They can support your educational messages and add emotion to your appeal for response. Don't neglect to provide accurate contact information so people can respond to you.

24. *Canvassing.* Take your message door to door, car to car, store to store, or even trade show booth to trade show booth. To make your outreach the most effective, make eye contact with people, smile, and get the name of the person to whom you are talking. Bring a visual aid or do a demonstration for the most impact when you tell your story. People respond 68 percent better to what they see than what they only hear.

25. *Door hangers.* A brochure that is designed to hang on doorknobs can give you massive targeted exposure in a brief amount of time and for very little money. Include a tear-away business reply response card, and you have a powerful guerrilla marketing weapon. Door-hanger bags can contain free samples, a DVD, a newsletter, anything you can fit into the bag.

26. *An elevator speech.* This is a 15-second presentation that summarizes your organization's work and why it should matter to people. Your three-sentence guerrilla marketing mission statement makes a great elevator speech. Learn to use it without sounding canned. Use it as a conversation starter—big things happen as a result of small conversations.

27. *A value story.* Tell a success story about how your organization poured value into another person's existence or made the world a better place. Don't bore with extraneous details; talk about the values that appeal to the people to whom you are addressing. When people perceive something is of value, they willingly pay (or donate) a premium for it.

28. *Repeat clients.* It took your organization a lot of time, energy, creativity, and money to get the clients and supporters you have now. Don't ignore them to death like most organizations do. Expand your share of your customers' attention and increase response from them with repeated contacts.

29. *Letters of recommendation.* When noted people give recommendations showing their support for your work in an open letter, it lends credibility to your nonprofit. It works like the blurbs you see on the back of books where other people recommend the author or his work. Social affirmation is a powerful guerrilla marketing weapon.

30. *Attendance at trade shows, events, and conferences.* Guerrillas can be found wherever people are gathered because they know that community events and conferences are fraught with networking opportunities. Pick the events that are most likely to attract the people you want to reach.

Maxi-Media

Another option for you are the maxi-media, the category of larger, costlier, splashier, and more traditional media. These are 19th- and 20th-century weapons, still effective although lots of the luster has gone.

31. *Advertising.* Paid advertising is a very important weapon in your arsenal, but it should be only a fraction of what

you do in your guerrilla marketing attack. Too often, organizations start and stop with advertising because they have a narrow view of marketing.

32. *Direct mail.* Focus your mail campaigns on a single, clear, and powerful idea. Test your copy by sending three versions of your mailing to a smaller sample of your mailing list. Then, send the one that gets the most response to the entire list. Don't be afraid to repeat sending the same message if it works. Repetition increases response and recall.

33. *Newspaper ads.* Newspaper display ads allow you to target nationally, regionally, locally, ethnically, professionally, economically, by activity, monthly, weekly, daily, and many more ways. Hang on to display ads that work for you and use them again and again.

34. *Radio spots.* Everywhere you go there is usually a radio playing. Listen and you will hear radio music in the background or a news or talk show being listened to in the foreground. You can leverage the intimate power of radio with commercials by being a guest on a talk show or sponsoring a remote broadcast. Radio is very targeted; find out what your target audience listens to before you start your radio outreach.

35. *Magazine ads.* Even with the advent of digital media, the number of print magazines is still growing, with nearly 20,000 periodicals actively being published. There are two types of magazines, consumer and trade. When you think of magazines, think of a huge target with your audience right in the bull's-eye. There is magazine for just about every activity or idea, so there is a good chance there is one the people you want to reach are reading.

36. *Billboards.* Use no more than six words to remind people of your message. The best copy you can put on a billboard is "Next Exit" because outdoor advertising is an

excellent tool for raising awareness about your non-profit's location.

37. *Television commercials.* Despite the numbers of obituaries written, TV is not dead. The proliferation of new viewing options with cable, satellite, and internet has created more TV, not less. It's a very affordable and powerful medium you can use to deliver your message with sight, sound, and emotion.

E-Media

The newest category in the 200 weapons is e-media. Most of these were not even a gleam in a software engineer's eye at the time *Guerrilla Marketing* first turned up on shelves in bookstores and libraries. They nonetheless merit a category all their own, and a hefty one it is.

38. *A computer.* If that one-eyed monster on the edge of your desk frightens you, it's time to stare your fears in the face. A guerrilla makes the most of the latest technology. The computer has put powerful marketing tools in the hands of anyone who can handle a mouse. Now anyone with an internet connection can become a marketing force.

39. *A printer or fax machine.* Using the latest user-friendly desktop publishing tools, you can use your printer and fax machine to create and send powerful print collateral that is useful for your organization's cause.

40. *Social media.* Recently invented and already indispensable, social networking sites have shown they can do more than merely communicate about trivial things. In a very short time they have made people celebrities, built fortunes, and even fueled revolutions. Your advocacy message can also be propelled forward virally through these

FROM THE FRONT LINES

NAME: Kivi Leroux Miller

WEBSITE: NonprofitMarketingGuide.com

BOOK: *The Nonprofit Marketing Guide* (Jossey-Bass, 2010)

"Nonprofits need to start thinking of themselves as media-moguls or at least mini-moguls. You can be the publisher and the broadcaster, using very affordable and easy-to-learn tools, and take your message directly to the people who matter most to the success of your organization and to your good cause."

networks with the investment of only a little time and imagination.

41. *Forums and chat rooms.* Besides the forums and chat rooms on major websites and search engines, there are countless discussions taking place on local and targeted websites. A brief search on the web will take you right to the people you need to speak with. Before you chime in, lurk behind the scenes and get to know the key players in these groups.

42. *Internet bulletin boards.* You can post information on targeted websites for free with only the cost of spending the time to register a profile. Use these spaces as you would use classified advertising, except remember to include a hyperlink back to your website or landing page.

43. *List building.* When someone comes to your site, you have no doubt done a lot of work to get them there; don't lose contact with the people who have shown the most interest in you on the internet. Ask for their e-mail information, and it doesn't hurt to ask for their address, too. Also, keep track of names and addresses you gather in other ways. Don't let people fall through the cracks.

44. *Personalized e-mail.* Office software and e-mail marketing services allow you to name-merge your messages to the people on your e-mail lists. People love the sound and sight of their own name. Make sure when you send your e-mail messages, they see their name along with your organization's name.

45. *An e-mail signature.* The footer of your e-mail is a powerful viral marketing tool. You may not realize how much your message gets forwarded all over the internet by the people you communicate with. Make your e-mails work harder at marketing by including your organization's message and contact information at the bottom of all your e-mails.

46. *Canned e-mail.* When people complete an action on your website, such as subscribing to your e-mail newsletter, registering for an event, or making a donation, your site needs to respond to them with automated confirmation e-mails. These automated messages also provide you a place to do a little guerrilla marketing. Beef up the marketing value of the copy on your responders. Add automatic suggested-selling to your shopping carts, offering products with messages like "People who ordered [product] also liked [product]." Or, "If you like [program], you may also like [program]."

47. *Bulk e-mail.* Guerrillas don't spam! The internet is full of people who are trying to take advantage of the ease and

affordability of using e-mail for marketing. Don't risk having your organization's web server blacklisted by breaking antispam protocols. You can, however, find companies who have affordable opt-in bulk e-mail lists to use in your marketing. Also, a fusion guerrilla marketing partner often has a great opt-in bulk list you can share.

48. *Audio and video postcards.* Your advocacy message or donor appreciation message can have a personalized flair with audio or video postcards sent by e-mail. The video is hosted on the sending server and plays directly in the reader's e-mail. This tactic can add value to and increase readership of your annual report as well.

49. *A domain name.* Carve out some real real estate for your organization in cyberspace with an original domain name. A URL (Uniform Resource Locator) that is the same as your organization's name (or meme, if it's short enough) is not just a convenience, it is vital for your marketing. If your website or blog is hosted on the URL of a free server like blogger.com or wordpress.com, you don't look like you mean business as much as having your own domain does. As handy as these free services are, it is best to not use their domains as the main URL for your organization. You want your web address working to brand your nonprofit on the internet. Having your own unique URL also makes you more credible to search engines.

50. *A website.* Should your organization have a website? Depends. Do you want to be visible or invisible to the world? If your organization doesn't have a page on the internet, you are missing a vital channel of communication. Today simple-to-use and affordable website tools exist so that organizations of any size can have an effective

and useful website. For many, the first place to look for information about anything is the internet; make sure your nonprofit is represented well there.

51. *A landing page.* When you advertise on the web with banner ads or links, you need to drive people to a page on your site that is designed with the decision-making process in mind. If people click a banner advertisement or link of yours on another site, they are in a thinking mode that follows the offer made in the ad message in the banner or link they clicked. Make sure when customers click through to your site that the page they land on has a logical flow from where they came from.

52. *A merchant account.* Don't leave money on the table because your organization doesn't accept credit card payments or donations online. Guerrillas make it easy and convenient to pay. Get a merchant account for your organization. If you don't have one yet, in the meantime, use a service like PayPal to hold you over.

53. *A shopping cart.* It is one thing to promote an event, product, or program; it is quite another to have an online means whereby people can register and pay. The internet is a direct response medium. Make sure when you stir people to act, you make it possible to do so immediately online with a shopping cart.

54. *Auto-responders.* Clone yourself with automated tools that advocate for your cause on the internet 24 hours per day. Think through the decision-making process and program your auto-responders to communicate with individuals in ways that close transactions through repeated contact. You can create a daily, weekly, or monthly (any time frame is possible) educational program that is delivered right to the e-mail inboxes of your target audience on a schedule that starts from when they sign up.

55. *Search engine ranking.* When you write on the internet, you have two audiences reading your work, humans and machines. Humans are emotional and creative and can read between the lines and catch the artistic nuances of your messages. But on the internet people use machines to find you. Machines can't read between the lines, they can't intuit what you mean unless you come right out and say it with the exact words their human searchers are looking for using search engines. When you write, make your copy friendly to web robots and internet spiders by using links, keywords, and tags to communicate your meaning.

56. *Electronic brochures.* These do the almost same duty as printed brochures, except they cost a lot less to distribute. Add them to your e-mails; include them in your canned e-mail and auto-responders also.

57. *RSS feeds.* Shorthand for Really Simple Syndication, RSS feeds are just that, a simple way to syndicate your content all over the internet almost as soon as you publish it. RSS feeds work for blogs and other social media, and can also be formatted for use to feed subscribers information about pressing needs or urgent news.

58. *Blogs.* Blogging can increase traffic to your organization's website and help increase ranking with search engines. Your blog's content can prompt discussion with readers who will respond to your message online.

59. *Podcasting.* In less time than it takes to have a telephone conversation, you could be syndicating your message to the MP3 players of thousands. Podcasting is a great tool for interviewing, talking about case studies, and giving vital updates.

60. *A personal e-zine.* Publish your own digital magazine. Include stories, articles, pictures, and promote your events,

programs, and products. If you do a quality job, you could even sell advertisements in your e-zine as a fundraiser.

61. *Ads in other e-zines.* Discover what digital brochures are popular with the people you want to reach and place an ad in them.

62. *E-books.* A series of blog posts could easily be turned into an e-book. An e-book can be an essay paper, story, or report in PDF format. The best e-books are typeset to look great if printed. Sometimes e-books have the same valuable impact of a published print book.

63. *Content provision.* Find ways to repurpose the content you write in reports, blog posts, and e-mails as articles for other websites and publications. Don't ask for a fee, instead, request a credit or link back to your website.

64. *Webinars.* Any workshop, seminar, training session, or meeting can also be conducted online using free or paid online meeting sites. By offering online webinars, you can open doors to the world.

65. *Joint ventures.* In the for-profit world trillions of dollars are generated in joint ventures. Could there be an organization that makes a good partner for yours? Keep your eyes peeled for the right partner and the right timing, and in the meantime, develop the plan for rolling out your collaboration. Always plan the exit strategy before you start. Nothing lasts forever.

66. *Word-of-mouse.* Make it easy for people to forward your content by sending links and embedding your message in the social network profiles. Free plug-ins are available for your website or blog that format and send your content to other networks with the click of a "Share This" button.

67. *Viral marketing.* Viral marketing on the web can take your organization to the top of people's minds in a hurry. The

creative combination of sights, sounds, information, and imagination can spread around the globe very quickly with great volume and velocity. To learn what is viral, pay attention to the things people forward to you. They are probably the best object lessons.

68. *Commercial sites.* For-profit websites allow you to create profiles and communicate your values to other customers. You can also develop a for-profit partnership with a company looking for cause marketing collaboration.

69. *Click analyzers.* Software and internet-based services exist that can help you analyze how people use your site. Before you redesign your organization's website, make sure you know what works and doesn't work. You'd hate to remove a button on your website that makes you thousands of dollars per year.

70. *Pay-per-click ads.* Just as the name implies, you pay only when people click on your advertisement. In pay-per-click the customers come pre-qualified as prospects. Nonprofits like pay-per-click because they have more control over their advertising budget. You can set how much you invest in ads and never go over. If you set a budget of $100 per day, the websites increase the rotation of ads until they get their quota of clicks for that day. Each exposure has advertising impact even when people don't click your ad.

71. *Search engine keywords.* Keyword analysis tools can help you investigate the words people are searching for on Google. Use the words that communicate your message that are also searched for more often on the web.

72. *Google Adwords.* You can purchase placement with your keywords on Google and get your information at the top of search engine results very affordably.

73. *Sponsored links.* Some websites place your links in prominent positions for a nominal fee. As a nonprofit, you may be able to strike an arrangement with these sites on a pro bono basis. Placement in highly ranked sites will also reap search engine ranking benefits.

74. *Reciprocal link exchanges.* Trade links in a quid pro quo arrangement. You post a link to their website on yours if they do the same for you.

75. *Banner exchanges.* Some companies create banner networks where the cost of a banner display ad is simply putting a line of code in your website that allows other banner ads in the network to appear on your site.

76. *Web conversion rates.* Do you know what percentage of people who come to your website, shopping cart, or landing page actually close a deal with you by signing up, making a purchase, giving a donation, or subscribing? When you know this metric you can experiment until you can increase the percentage of closed transactions on your site. Once your web conversion rate is optimized, you are ready to drive more traffic to your site through viral and paid advertising.

New media has changed the face of communication forever.

CHAPTER 8

Info-, Human-, and Non-Media Weapons

THIS CHAPTER CONTINUES TO LIST THE 200 guerrilla marketing weapons of advertising opportunities awaiting you. Many are free and available to anyone. Take advantage for your nonprofit.

Info-Media

Most media imparts information, but some media are all about information rather than have it be merely a peripheral reason for their existence. Some of these media are old. Some are new. All are capable of turning your organization around to meet your goals. And some can do that for free.

77. *Knowledge of your market.* A good place to start your guerrilla marketing strategy is by researching as much as you can about your target market. Nobody should know more about your market than you. And if there is someone who does, make friends with them and learn. Knowledge increases creativity and is a powerful competitive advantage.

78. *Research studies.* Locate existing research about your target audience in libraries, on the web, and in organizations like your chamber of commerce. Then, design original research objectives to find out what you don't already know with surveys, interviews, and focus groups.

79. *Specific customer data.* Many organizations keep records of clients and maintain lists of supporters, but too few study their lists and analyze their records looking for ways to add more value to their primary targets lives' and get deeper support from their donors.

80. *Case studies.* Write brief documents that tell the story of how your organization has saved the day in the past. Your proven track record is also a great marketing tool for attracting donors and other supporters. Resist the urge to make it overly academic, unless that is the audience you intend to reach with your message.

81. *Sharing.* Guerrillas apply the saying, "the hand that gives, gathers" by being generous people who share what they have in ways that help others succeed. You can share information, content, good ideas, your facilities, etc. Helping people succeed can open up a lot of important doors for your organization. Guerrillas also share

marketing tactics with each other. They know if they share something that worked for them, other guerrillas will likely share their successful ideas, too.

82. *Brochures.* Use them to start a relationship with your prospects by providing attractive and useful information—not just organizational jargon. Brochures with titles that contain phrases like "How to.." and "Five Ways to . . ." attract readers. Don't just pass your brochures out, offer them in ads and on your website for free in exchange for e-mail and address information. Between 25 to 33 percent of people requesting a brochure will make a purchase, so be sure to include an order form and a phone number.

> When nonprofits comprehend the likes and dislikes of reporters they stand a greater chance of getting good stories put into the media.

83. *Catalogs.* List all your resources and programs in a catalog along with a form to request more details, order products, or enroll in programs.

84. *Business directories.* Put information about your organization in places where people are looking. Getting listed in professional directories usually is free; all that is required is a little time filling out a form.

85. *Public service announcements (PSA).* Broadcasters air PSAs about events, programs, and products as a community service for free.

86. *A newsletter.* Each time you send out a newsletter, you reconnect with the people who have raised their hands to know you and be involved with you. Reward them with updates about your organization, but don't just include

insider information, also provide useful content for people who are not yet involved. Your newsletter will become a pass-along promotional tool in the hands of your supporters.

87. *Speeches*. Public speaking gives you visibility and credibility with the people you want to reach. The goal is not for people to give you applause, it is to get response from people and gain support. Guerrillas don't get distracted from their purpose seeking accolades; they want supporters and customers.

88. *Free consultations*. If your nonprofit offers services based on fees as a means of generating operations revenue, you can offer a free one-hour consultation. Free consultations help you demonstrate your skills and establish credibility with your intended audience. Free is the most powerful word in the guerrilla marketer's vocabulary.

89. *Free demonstrations*. Offer a demonstration of your service or product to the people you want to reach. Take your product on location or stage a large-scale demonstration at a place of your choosing. Do whatever helps people get the message.

90. *Free seminars*. Host a seminar in your community and put your expertise on display. Besides being great for community education, these events provide a venue for your potential supporters to see you in action. Don't put the pinch or hard-sell on the people in attendance; instead, use the time to establish credible contact and identify those who are the most interested.

91. *Articles*. If you enjoy writing, you can market your nonprofit by producing helpful articles. Write articles that give people information or produce benefits in their lives. Think like a service journalist writing articles with "Five Healthy Choices for . . ." and "Ten Ways to . . ."

These kinds of articles have wide appeal. One guerrilla thinks of herself as a refrigerator reporter because her tips and ideas end up being posted on people's refrigerators.

92. *Columns.* If your articles are consistently good, you may end up published or even syndicated in print and on the web. There is a ton of credibility that comes from being published. Offer your columns for free in exchange for credit with your organization's name, website, e-mail, and phone number.

93. *Writing a book.* Speaking of credibility, nothing gives you a faster track to guru status than writing and publishing a book. Save up all your research, articles, and blog posts and organize your original concepts into a book. You don't have to have the book already written to find a publisher. Learn how to put together a query letter and winning book proposal.

94. *Publishing on demand.* Great strides have been made in self-publishing with the advent of print on demand. Now you can produce a book and sell it through top online booksellers without having to print large quantities; the books are printed as they are sold. This gives your nonprofit a faster track to putting your expertise on display. Books also make excellent gifts to potential donors.

95. *Workshops.* Lead workshops that get people interacting and building skills. Workshops are more than part of your educational programs; they are also great channels for marketing your nonprofit. You can also use these events to sign people up for other programs or services.

96. *Teleseminars.* Your seminars and workshop sessions can be televised on cable access channels, local broadcast TV, and now with new internet technology, streamed live on the web or stored online on video sites like YouTube.

97. *Telethons and infomercials.* Informative or entertaining programs that also ask for action from the audience can increase response, raise awareness, and boost support. No other medium is better for showing your product or programs in action. TV is also great place to ask people to call your phone number or visit your website.

98. *Constant learning.* Guerrillas have a lifelong love for learning. They don't try to learn all about everything, but they want to learn one thing after another. They have a competitive advantage in their nonprofit marketing because they learn about more than marketing or advertising; they also are students of psychology, technology, social trends, politics, and economics.

The Human-Media

Many media are things. Others are people. There are so many that as people we decided to create a category of human-media. When we say they are about people, we're really saying that they're about you and also that they *are* you. These overlooked marketing weapons are far too powerful to be missed—and they alone can have more of an impact than all the others combined in raising awareness for your cause.

99. *Marketing insight.* Many organizations have no idea what marketing is. Some even perceive marketing as contradicting their values. You can speed past these organizations by availing yourself of an education in marketing with seminars, workshops, the internet, and the numerous volumes of marketing books published each year. Insights may come slowly, but rest assured, your real world experience and insatiable interest in marketing will yield practical applications that benefit your organization.

100. *Yourself.* As you increase in your understanding of marketing and adopt the personality traits of a guerrilla, you will become a major asset to your organization. Keep honing your skills, improving your attitude, developing your attributes, and staying humble. The world needs your input.

101. *Your employees and volunteers.* Be sure your people are on the same page with your guerrilla marketing plans. Especially keep them up to speed when you start something new. Nothing can sidetrack a strategy faster than a receptionist or staff member who doesn't know what is going on or isn't on board with the plans.

102. *A designated guerrilla.* You are learning about guerrilla marketing, but you may find you are too busy or not in the right place to lead the marketing attack for your organization. Your nonprofit can still benefit from guerrilla marketing principles by designating someone in your own ranks who can get excited about the thought of aggressive, proactive marketing. You will need someone with the staying power and courage to make it their responsibility.

103. *Employee attire.* Your appearance can have an impact on your effectiveness for positive or negative. Your employees (and volunteers) need to understand that the way they dress conveys meaning to the people you want to reach and also influences those who are considering supporting you. Depending on your type of work, an affluent look could be as much a detriment as an unkempt look in other situations. Know the appropriate clothing medium.

104. *Your social demeanor.* Pay attention to how you conduct yourself around people. Etiquette is important not only in face-to-face social situations, but also online and on the phone.

105. *Your target audience.* Knowing your target audience is a marketing weapon because having a clear understanding of them helps you develop the right messages and find the right media channels to reach them. While nonguerrillas try to reach markets, guerrillas market to individuals.

106. *Your circle of influence.* Your world is full of relationship networks. If you pay attention to the people in your life that are (or could be) influenced by your message, you can have a large impact. Some relationships are closer than others, but all your relationships are part of your network. Cultivate positive influence in your network.

107. *Your contact time with donors/volunteers.* Some nonprofit leaders miss opportunities for greatness because they are too busy to listen to their customers. Others listen but are too busy dismissing their complaints or observations. You need your customers, Value every contact with them.

108. *How you say "Hello" and "Goodbye."* The way you greet people says a lot to them about how much you care. When you treat people well they remember it and tell others about you. Warm greetings, smiles, eye contact, and using the name of the people you communicate with have more than social value; they add credibility to your marketing.

109. *Your teaching ability.* Anyone can give a one-sided boring lecture. Guerrillas learn to teach people. In 1956 Dr. Benjamin Bloom identified a taxonomy of three educational domains: 1) cognitive: thinking skills; 2) affective: feelings or emotions; and 3) psychomotor: behavioral or physical skills. Becoming proficient as an educator has value in many ways. Knowing how to teach trains you to understand what inspires and motivates people (affective domain), grasp how people think (cognitive domain),

and give people skills they can apply in their lives (behavioral domain).

110. *Stories*. Storytelling is more than just the latest nonprofit buzzword; it is a way of connecting with a majority of the people on the planet. People of all walks of life are living as oral communicators, depending less on literate forms of communication. Stories connect with people because they include characters, plots, and settings, not program descriptions, slogans, and pie charts. A good story will hold people's attention for an hour and win hearts forever. A dry organizational message will have them looking at the clock and thinking about how to excuse themselves.

111. *Advocacy training*. Guerrillas conduct regular training sessions. In your organization's training you can spot and troubleshoot problems, share insights for effective outreach, teach skills, and inform. Regularly scheduled training also provides a means to update your staff and volunteers with the very latest information about the progress of your marketing attack.

112. *Use of downtime*. When you are between projects, the temptation to use that time in unproductive ways is great. Nonguerrillas use the lull between projects to relax. They are unproductive during downtimes. Guerrillas use downtime to do research, develop new strategies, network with contacts, and anything else that helps keep the competitive advantage going.

113. *Networking*. Guerrillas make time in their schedules for regularly attending networking events, and they keep their eyes open for networking opportunities at other times. Stay in touch with your contacts. Help them succeed, and they will help you.

114. *Professional titles*. Your job title doesn't have to be a generic term like "director," "founder," "president," or

"manager." Think of an inspiring way to communicate what you do that also builds interest in your cause. You can change your title to something that grabs attention like "Planetary Health Technician" for a nonprofit environmental advocate. The title isn't just amusing; it makes a nice bridge for a conversation about ecology with a new contact.

115. *Affiliate marketing.* Vendors of the various products you use often have referral programs that can earn a commission for your organization. A nonprofit with a large e-mail mailing list can recommend a book on Amazon in their newsletter and receive a commission on the sales to use for their cause by signing up for the associates program.

116. *Media contacts.* Publicity professionals charge a lot of money for their services because they have collected an extensive list of media contacts and cultivated relationships with media professionals. You can do the same thing they do and become your own publicity specialist. Develop a professional relationship with media contacts, understand the nature of the reporter's business, and look for ways to become a trusted source of information. You may become the default spokesperson for your cause.

117. *A-list customers.* Make sure you treat your best supporters with the utmost value and respect. You can distinguish your A-list customers from your B-list customers. Treat your B-list customers like royalty and your A-list customers like family.

118. *Your core story.* Think about the ways your organization has impacted the lives of real people or real situations and develop a core story you tell when you talk about your work. Make sure the story describes a problem involving the people to whom you're telling the story and how your solution to that problem can make their life better.

119. *A sense of urgency.* If you want people to catch the same vision you have, your marketing needs to exude a sense of the urgency of your mission. People are far more likely to take action when they believe the cause is pressing than when they think there is plenty of time to act.

120. *Limited time or quantity offers.* While your organization will always have needs, you can create an urgency to respond by extending limited offers. Some nonprofits create special groups of donors who are limited in number of memberships. To be a part of the group, the donors have to act quickly. This is not just a tactic to get response; it also helps you identify people who have a natural propensity for taking action.

121. *A call to action.* Guerrillas work backward, starting by developing the call to action in their marketing materials before they start developing their attention-getting messages. The fact is, it is not the advertisement that gets the attention that matters most. It is the one that gets the most response.

122. *Satisfied customers.* Success stories help build the confidence of your prospects. Most people would rather not be the first person to try something new; they would rather hear from someone just like them who went before them and had a good experience. Show your results by putting your winning track record on display.

The Non-Media

This category is definitely not about the media. The non-media can make a substantial increase to your contributions, but they won't do so in standard ways. Because they are not officially "media," we don't want them to escape your notice. In fact, we're shining a bright light upon them by including them.

123. *A benefits list.* This may take some time and might make you blush, but do it anyway. Make a long, unabashed bragging list of all the ways your organization benefits people and the world. This is no time to demure. You need a comprehensive list of all the good things your nonprofit brings to the table. Your marketing messages and meme will not be wordy, but your benefits list needs to be extensive. The list you create will become the tool you use to craft winning marketing messages. You may only focus on one or two of the items on your list in your marketing, but your list will become a valuable guerrilla marketing weapon and be used in many ways.

124. *Competitive advantage.* Don't ask yourself what do they have that you haven't got? Ask yourself what can you have that they haven't got? Could it be the way you deliver or perform your services on-site? Maybe you can be more personal, faster, cheaper, or cleaner. Expertise and information can give you an advantage. Exercise your imagination, invent your competitive advantage, and live up to it.

125. *Gifts.* A small gift from your nonprofit warms prospects to respond to you and reinforces the relationship you have with existing customers. There are countless types of specialty advertising items available. You can put your logo, name, and meme on calendars, ink pens, key chains, etc. These are good ideas, but it's best to find something that reinforces your message and is useful to recipients.

126. *Service.* Nonprofits tend to avoid thinking of their clients as customers, so when they see the plethora of resources and books available for improving customer service, they glance right past them. Despite what you feel about the term, customer service is a major part of

your organization's marketing. When people call your organization, do they hear phrases like "I am sorry, that's not my department?" Listen to what your customers want—anything they want—and develop a reputation as a problem-solving organization.

127. *Public relations.* When you think about public relations, think more about the relationship your organization wants to have with the public than you think about how to get your news into the media's bloodstream. Some say there is no such thing as bad publicity, but if you think of PR as your nonprofit's relationship with the public, who in their right mind would want a bad relationship with the public? (More about publicity in the next chapter.)

128. *Fusion marketing.* Nonprofits have a long history of working with partners from the for-profit world. But fusion works nonprofit to nonprofit too. A school can partner with an animal shelter for volunteer workers and education purposes. A church can provide coaches and counselors to the local YMCA chapter as a community project. A legal services nonprofit can work with a civil rights group sharing publicity. Your job as a guerrilla is to find the partners with the best tie-in to your message and needs.

129. *Barter.* With all the manpower and networking connections you have as a guerrilla nonprofit, there are scores of companies and individuals who would be willing to offer products and services for you if you also shared your resources with them. Your museum facilities might make a great annual meeting place for a sign company who could install an outdoor sign for you and dress up your location. A pet rescue organization could board the pets of a painter during his vacation and get a nice coat of paint on the kennels in return. With bartering, everyone is happy.

130. *Word of mouth.* Equip your clients and supporters to speed up the spread of your good news, by preparing a brief document summarizing the benefits your organization offers. Putting the words in their mouths makes it easier for people to talk you up to others.

131. *Buzz.* Look for opinion leaders and work to get their phone lines (and LAN lines) crackling with conversation about your products, programs, and information. Find what is unique about your nonprofit that makes it a conversation piece. Give a sneak peak of a new program to an elite few media mavens, or leak a shocking research report and soon the buzz about your organization will start. Find out how your target audience gets information and get your concisely designed message there.

132. *Community involvement.* Nonprofits usually are trying to get the community involved with them, but when you become involved with the community outside your own particular cause, you make new contacts and find many incidental marketing opportunities without really having to try. A sports league nonprofit that adopts a mile of highway also sometimes gets a sign that displays their name on the side the road for all to see. A speakers club or professional organization that tutors at-risk students becomes the leading story on the evening news. Whatever you do, do it from a sincere concern for your community and you will become a genuine neighbor and not just another nameless stranger.

133. *Club and association memberships.* Just as community involvement makes you a familiar face in the crowd, membership and participation in social clubs, country clubs, civic clubs, service associations, professional groups, and trade associations adds social capital to your marketing and makes you a known quantity around

your town. Membership also has the advantage of putting you on a first-name basis with other leaders in your community.

134. *Free directory listings.* Find the directories that connect with your target audience and list your nonprofit there. Include more than your contact information, also include your meme and other messages.

135. *A tradeshow booth.* Take your nonprofit's message to three or four trade shows per year. People at trade shows are there for a purpose, and you should be too. You are there to close sales, sign people up, and take names for immediate follow-up. Stick with that plan; don't let your goals get sidetracked by peripheral attractions. Make sure you are at the shows that attract the kind of prospects you want to reach. Universities go where future students can be found. Health-care nonprofits are where the focus is on medicine and health. Pick the right event, and you may make all the sales and discover all the leads you need.

136. *Special events.* Put together an event designed to get your organization on the front page of the news and on the social calendars of your target audience. Events can be celebrations, community fairs, conferences, or anything that gives you a reason to gather both existing customers and prospects under the same roof (or big-top tent). A special event can also be a reward for your best customers or largest supporters and makes a great time to ask for an annual pledge.

137. *A name tag at events.* When you attend a conference or event and are given a name tag, don't just put your name on it; everyone does that. Put your message on your name tag too! Instead of saying "Hello, My Name is John Doe," write something that makes you stand out in the crowd. Say "My Name is John Doe, I am turning children

at risk into world leaders!" Why blend into the crowd with a *me-too* name tag?

138. *Luxury boxes at events.* You don't have to be the sponsor at an event to capitalize on the energy of a large gathering. Set up a reception area sponsored by your organization. If you can, find a sponsor who can help you get a skybox at the game and invite potential donors and supporters.

139. *Gift certificates.* People are always looking for ways to give gifts to their friends and family. Why not let them give a gift to you in their friend's name or the gift of your services or programs? Mention the gift certificates in your organization's newsletter, and on signs in your location, and teach your advocates to talk about them, too.

140. *Audio-visual aids.* This is a sight-and-sound generation; include visuals and audio in your presentations. Left-brained people will tune in to the facts and figures you may talk about in your presentation, but don't leave out the right-brained people who will pay closer attention when you have images and sounds associated with your message.

141. *Flip charts.* Add flip charts to your arsenal of communication tools. You can't always pull up a PowerPoint slide show or multimedia presentation on your computer. Flip charts are very flexible tools that allow you to keep the conversation flowing in the right direction in advocacy situations. These charts give you another useful way to use your display advertising, posters, and testimonials as face-to-face marketing tools.

142. *Reprints and blow-ups.* Make enlargements of magazines and newspaper articles that have been written about your organization. Include copies of these articles in your media kit, mail them along with letters you send, and hand them out at events.

143. *Coupons.* Get your target audience clipping out your advertising and have them bring it to you to help you measure the most effective print media in your guerrilla campaign. Include a different tracking number for each publication where you place your coupons. Coupons reward people with a discount for taking action, the action of responding to your marketing.

144. *A free trial offer.* Like free consultations, free trials remove the risk of doing business with your organization. A non-profit magazine or newspaper can offer one month for free for new subscribers to get them signed up. Once you have made the connection, a good number of the new subscribers will keep subscribing.

145. *Guarantees.* You can remove the feeling of risk from the list of concerns your clients have about your products and services by offering a guarantee to prospects. A guarantee will set you apart from your competitors in a hurry. A clinic with a ten-minute guarantee or the visit is free sounds better than one where a prospect has no clue how long they will have to wait. Don't guarantee vague things like "satisfaction" or "friendliness"—make it something specific. Describe how they will be satisfied and tell what your friendly service will entail.

146. *Contests and sweepstakes.* There is no faster way to build a mailing list than by holding a contest. Find a prize that people want that also supports your message and let people register to win it on your website; also put entry forms on the counters in businesses around your community. Don't just have one winner, have ten winners. And when you announce the winners, don't do it in a corner—alert the media. Contests are fun, list-building, publicity events that put your nonprofit on the top of the mind of the people you want to reach. Don't have any

money for prizes? Barter them with other organizations. You are a guerrilla after all.

147. *Baking or crafts ability.* Your talents and hobbies can help you market your nonprofit. Make a batch of cookies and take them to the local radio station to cultivate closer relations with your media contacts. Make an inspiring plaque in your garage workshop and give it to your A-list supporters as an act of appreciation for their involvement.

148. *Lead buying.* Besides asking for referrals from your supporters, you can also purchase or rent existing lists of names of people who could become leads for your organization. Purchase the list of attendees at the conferences you attend, or get a copy of the membership of the associations to which you belong. Opt-in e-mail and direct mail marketing lists are available through direct marketing companies.

149. *Follow-up.* The biggest problem most nonprofits don't know they have is a follow-up problem. Like the majority of businesses, 68 percent of the contacts organizations have are ignored to death. A guerrilla doesn't close a sale, he begins a long-term relationship. After the sale, guerrilla nonprofit marketers have a plan for sending a thank-you follow-up note to new contacts within 48 hours. They also have plans for staying in touch with their contacts that stretch out into the future at 90 days, six months, nine months, a year later, and so on. With so much competition in the nonprofit sector, following up is great hedge against failure.

150. *A tracking plan.* Advertising forefather John Wanamaker is famous for saying, "Half the money I spend on advertising is wasted; the trouble is I don't know which half." If you want to know where your organization's marketing is working or not working, you will need to develop

a tracking system. Every client, each campaign, all your marketing materials need consistent observation. Where do patrons of your theater company come from? How did your donors first hear about you? You are investing your time, energy, imagination, and money into marketing. You might as well know what is paying off and what is not.

151. *Marketing on hold.* Try to keep the time your customers and supporters spend on telephone hold to a minimum. But while people are on hold, instead of listening to music, they could be listening to information about your organization's great programs. Encourage listeners to on-hold messages to ask your advocates about your products or events and train your staff to be ready with the information.

152. *Branded entertainment.* Soap operas are the original form of branded entertainment; these daytime dramas were originally sponsored by detergent companies. In the '70s social marketing behavior change messages were featured in "very special" episodes of popular TV programs. Your message, product, or service could become part of the storyline in a movie, or other entertainment as well. You don't have to be in the movies or TV; remember "We Are the World" way back in 1985? Consider how you can get your nonprofit's name up in lights in TV, radio, podcasts, videocasts, and event sponsorships.

153. *Product placement.* Your products could also become part of the storyline in entertainment just by being part of the scenery. If your product is a behavior, the characters could be modeling the healthy activities your organization promotes. Who says secret agents can't also have compost heaps in their backyards?

154. *Being a radio talk show host.* Your credibility as a community advocate increases with your exposure as a radio

talk show host. Investigate in your community what radio stations offer open slots for shows on AM and FM radio. Often these stations handle all the production details; all you do is plan the programming.

155. *Being a TV talk show guest.* Local TV and cable access shows are a good place to start as a TV guest. Nonprofits use their small TV beginnings to stair-step their way up to larger and larger markets for advocating their regional and national causes.

156. *Subliminal marketing.* Most decisions people make are made unconsciously based on factors that are not obvious to them. For example, a person may not realize he is buying a new briefcase to appear wealthier to others, thinking only the faux leather finish looks like a good deal to him. Most marketing psychology is Skinnerian, appealing to the conscious mind. Guerrillas also understand human psychology has Freudian implications for marketing to the subconscious mind.

> Good marketing doesn't happen instantly. It takes repetition and time before your message has a chance to sink in with your prospects.

CHAPTER 9

Attributes and Attitudes of Your Organization

GUERRILLA MARKETING WEAPONS CAN ALSO reflect the personality of your organization. Take a look and see what might work for you.

Organization Attributes

Donors and volunteers are naturally attracted to companies that demonstrate specific attributes. The truth is that the more of these attributes you have, the more poised you are to reach your goals. It's obvious right from the start.

157. *A proper view of marketing.* As good as guerrilla marketing is, it is not the cure-all for everything that is ailing your nonprofit. It won't work instantly. It seldom gives you the exact results you hoped for. A lot of people—most people—will ignore even the best of your marketing outreach. However, your organization needs marketing to survive in today's competitive marketplace. If you understand the limitations of marketing, you will have realistic expectations and be more willing to give it time to work.

158. *Brand name awareness.* Name recognition is a powerful form of subconscious marketing. Many people make purchase decisions merely because they are familiar with the name of the products they choose. Guerrillas get name recognition and credibility with customers through repetition.

159. *Intelligent positioning.* Determine what you want to stand for in the minds of people. What is your niche in the marketplace? Your marketing battle plan should serve to establish your position with your prospects and clients. Does your nonprofit do something nobody else can? Can you do what you do in a way that nobody else does? Brilliant positioning strategy comes from knowing who you are and understanding your market better than other organizations do.

160. *A name.* Nonprofits are notorious for having names that only make sense to a few insiders. It's better if your name reflects who you are and what it is you are doing. If you are just starting out, you are in a good position to select a good name. Make sure it is easy to pronounce and spell and, above all, isn't nonsense to outsiders. Your name

will be seen in a lot of places—on lists, in the phone book, on the web. Let your name help you in your marketing instead of becoming a hinderance to outreach.

161. *A meme.* It is the lowest common denominator of your idea, an elementary unit of communication that can change the behavior of people. It only takes a second to grasp its meaning. Memes can be symbols, such as the Red Cross, or words like "Only you can prevent forest fires." Make sure your organization has a meme to propel your cause forward to success.

162. *A theme line.* A theme line is a set of words that express the spirit of your organization. Your theme line isn't a throw-away program theme used for a year and then set aside; it should be created to last a long time, maybe a hundred years or so. You should use your theme line (and your meme) in all your advertising, on your website, in e-mail and other media like your business card— carve it on your hand if you want. You want people to think of you whenever they see or hear it.

163. *Writing ability.* The old adage is true, "Readers are leaders." But if this is true, what does that make writers? If you know how to write, you have the potential for a tremendous competitive advantage. Your organization can churn out influential blog posts, articles, and editorials that inject your viral marketing messages into the public bloodstream.

164. *Copywriting ability.* The same applies to those organizations blessed with someone with the creative ability to write advertising copy. Many organizations spend large amounts of money paying for creative talent. If you have the chops to write good copy, you can give your nonprofit a head start in the race toward finishing your task.

165. *Headline copy talent.* In direct marketing headlines can make or break a campaign. If you have someone on board with the skills to write the kind of headlines that get people clicking on links and opening envelopes, you can turn almost any kind of media into a powerful marketing weapon. The headline is often the name of the game in guerrilla marketing. Don't underthink it.

166. *Location.* No longer is the physical location of your non-profit the determining factor in your success. Instead of moving into the high-rent district of your town, you can move to the no-rent district of a spare bedroom and establish a world-changing nonprofit using the power of the internet. To move in to this kind of location, all you need is an excellent work ethic and an intimately understood computer.

167. *Hours of operation.* We no longer live in a 9-to-5 world. You know from experience, no doubt, that the needs you are serving can't always be attended to in an eight-hour day. Your organization needs hours that fit with the 24/7 age we are living in. Your website, e-mail auto-responders, telephone answering machine marketing, etc., are all allies in your nonprofit's cause. Could you open earlier or stay open later to serve clients better? What about the people who are missed because they work the all-night shift?

168. *Days of operation.* Some churches are beginning to realize many people will never be able to attend church if services happen only on Sunday morning. They are now starting to offer services on other days as well. How could your organization's weekly schedule be altered to help you accomplish your mission?

169. *Credit cards acceptance.* Your organization may have values that are opposed to the abuse of consumer credit, but

your organization should accept credit cards anyway. Many people never carry cash, and when they respond to your appeals on the internet, credit cards are a must-have for transactions. You can encourage the responsible use of consumer credit with the way you handle transactions.

170. *Financing available.* Nonprofits like schools and hospitals are familiar with offering payment on credit. But multi-payment options can also serve donors, program participants, and people who purchase your products. Making financing available brings down the barriers to response and is appreciated by your customers.

171. *Credibility.* You can't buy credibility; you earn it with consistent service, quality, and effort. It comes from great service to your clients. It is seen in your attention to details and in how you treat others, in presenting your nonprofit's message or yourself. People talking about your organization to their friends lends credibility. When you relate to the public, give talks, write articles, you gain credibility. Don't only focus on gaining credibility, though; pay attention to actions and activities that might cause you to lose it.

172. *Reputation.* Over a long period of having consistent credibility, you gain reputation. It takes a long time to acquire a good reputation; it can be only a matter of minutes to lose it. Guerrillas know that having and maintaining credibility and a top-rate reputation are vital for getting good marketing response. Make sure all the people who are associated with your organization are aware of their fragile stewardship of your nonprofit's most important asset, your reputation.

173. *Efficiency.* Doing things efficiently within your organization is important, but we are not talking here about mere internal effectiveness. Efficiency is also a guerrilla

marketing weapon. Customers don't like to wait on slow, inefficient service. If you do what you do proficiently, your nonprofit will be attractive to people. McDonald's is a for-profit example of a company that turned efficiency into a competitive advantage. How could your organization become more efficient?

174. *Quality.* The two most important lessons your organization can learn about quality are: 1) quality is the number two reason people will support your organization; and 2) quality is not what your organization does, or what products or programs you produce, it is what your customers get out of your organization.

175. *Service.* The best marketing in the world won't motivate a customer to purchase a poor product or service more than once. Put a premium on giving the best service to your community your organization can give.

176. *Selection.* What your organization offers is as much a part of your marketing as any other tactic you could use. Make sure what you are offering isn't just what your organization happens to be producing. Offer the products, programs, and services that resonate with your target audience. Never offer a program merely because your organization always has. Link your message to the life solutions people want.

177. *Price.* What does your target audience have to give up to benefit from your organization? Sometimes it is money; sometimes it is giving up a behavior. Pay close attention and make sure your prices are not a barrier to participation.

178. *Upgrade opportunities.* Offer your customers the opportunity to enlarge the size of their transactions with you. Offer subscribers to your magazine a recommended book. Suggest to people signing up for a year's membership to your

museum to sign up for two. Bundle your fundraiser products in sets of three or four and increase the size of your orders exponentially.

179. *Referral program.* What if your organization could know the people your people know? Of the donors who support you, how many of their friends would also support you? Do your best volunteers also have friends who are their hard-working twins? The way to find out is by establishing a referral program. This kind of program makes it easy for your clients and supporters to help you meet their contacts. Conduct a referral emphasis regularly, try twice a year, and ask your members to list three people who might also be interested in your work. Send out an e-mail asking for the names you need. Give your people prewritten letters and e-mails to send to their contacts. Then get ready—you are about to grow.

180. *Spying.* You don't have to go incognito to do a little reconnaissance on your competition. Just order their products, or attend one of their programs and see what they are doing. You need a reality check on your competition, but also don't fail to spy on yourself. Send in the secret shoppers, order one of your products, or call your phone support center and see how your nonprofit is performing. The purpose of all the spying is to give you a clear picture of the reality of how your organization is doing.

181. *Testimonials.* More believable than any marketing copy you could write are the sincere words of a satisfied person touched by your organization. Think of the people you have helped the most or experts who could certify you have impacted the world in a positive way. If you have truly earned the praise of another human being with your work, ask them to put in a word for you in a written testimony. The best testimonies talk about problems that have

been solved, not how sweet people think you are. Anonymous testimonials may be needed in some cases, but if at all possible get the real name and address of the people who give their testimonial. Use these testimonies in print, on the web, post it on a sign, and use them in presentations.

182. *Extra value.* Guerrillas give a little extra in everything they do because they know in their hearts that those that give also receive. The guerrilla focus on customer needs leads them to fulfill these needs while giving more than expected.

183. *Noble cause.* Nonprofit guerrillas already have a cause they believe in and they are careful to cultivate for-profit businesses sponsors who are looking for noble causes like theirs. However, there are other causes served by other nonprofits that are compatible with your organization that might become a worthy, though perhaps secondary, cause for your nonprofit to support.

Company Attitudes

The company attributes we explored earlier in this chapter were about your company. The company attitudes we list now are about your mind. All these attitudes ought to be descriptive of your company, but in reality, they are descriptive of you. They begin with you. They flourish because of you. They win over donors and volunteers because of you. Maybe 10,000 people help you do these things, but we know these attitudes come from your heart and rest on your shoulders. We know how much they can mean to your company.

184. *Easy to do business with.* Build bridges with your target audience by being easy to work with. Nonprofits that place hurdles in front of their customers through

bureaucratic policies and complicated processes not only limit their effectiveness, they send people walking the other direction when they enter the room.

185. *Honest interest in people.* We feel sorry for those people who say they would love their work more if weren't for the people. When you care about people with a genuine passion, it shows in everything you do and makes you attractive. Also, a genuine interest in people leads to insights that give your marketing more impact.

186. *Good telephone demeanor.* The people who call your organization deserve your very best. Phone calls are not interruptions to your work, they are your work. Of course there are a few callers who waste your time, but for the most part the people who contact you by phone are the people you are serving or who want to help you in your work. Make time to get some telephone training and learn how to get the most out of this important medium. Learn how to make people feel valued and important when they talk to you on the phone. And by all means, smile. Your smile will shine right through the phone lines—people can hear it.

187. *Passion and enthusiasm.* If you are not interested in every working moment of every day and focused on achieving your organization's mission, maybe it is time to consider another vocation or mission. If you don't have passion, which is the supreme expression of enthusiasm, it will show in your results. You owe it to your cause to cultivate a passion for your work.

> Nonprofits can succeed or fail on the basis of their ability to initiate and maintain great intentional relationships.

188. *Sensitivity*. A guerrilla marketer cannot plod through life focused on himself. The lack of ability to empathize with others is not only immature; it is a death knell for your marketing. Learn to see things from the perspective of others. Be sensitive to your marketplace, the economy, the present moment in history, your prospects, their families, the time of year, the competition, your track record with customers, and more. You are fighting an uphill battle if your understanding of your environment is not evolving constantly.

189. *Patience*. Good marketing doesn't happen instantly. It takes repetition and time before your message has a chance to sink in with your prospects. When other marketers don't see the results in a short amount of time, they revamp their websites, develop new media, and many quit altogether. A guerrilla is patient because she doesn't expect marketing to work in a hurry. Marketing can't work miracles, patience does. If you don't have patience, or can't develop it, hand the marketing over to someone who has what it takes.

190. *Flexibility*. Inflexible things can break. What is flexible can adapt to a changing environment. Flexibility has more to do with service and less to do with products, programs, and prices. Word-of-mouth marketing flows from the stream of flexibility. The more you can offer, the better you meet needs, the more people will talk about you to their friends. Don't be surprised when your organization is called on to be flexible—be ready.

191. *Generosity*. Guerrillas view marketing as a chance to help their prospects and customers succeed at their goals. They are extremely imaginative about what they give, shifting their generosity into high gear and seeing the world through the eyes of their customers and

prospects. Guerrillas share insights, information, gifts, and their precious time. Their websites are fountains of information, with articles, tips, free e-books, podcasts, videos, and sign-up forms for newsletters and free consultations.

192. *Self-confidence.* Replacing fear and doubt with self-confidence, guerrillas are confident because they do their homework. They know the messages that resonate with their target audience and they know what media is best matched to reach them. They are not swayed to change tactics midstream by well-meaning colleagues, friends, and family who would talk them into making the huge marketing mistake of quitting or changing before their marketing has a chance to work.

193. *Neatness.* For-profit companies like Disney and Nordstrom have build mega-million-dollar enterprises with their emphasis on neatness. Your organization can use cleanliness as a marketing tool, too. Look around your facilities, does the place look welcoming and clean, or cluttered and chaotic? What about your office, your car, your clothing? How about the bathrooms? You might not think of neatness as a marketing weapon, but ask yourself, when you travel by car would you rather stop and eat in a place with clean bathrooms? If people see your place of operations or person as sloppy, they are likely to think the same thing about your cause.

194. *Aggressiveness.* As in warfare, guerrilla marketers are always prepared for the attack. To be aggressive as a guerrilla marketer, you don't have to have a pushy personality; you need a take-action mind-set. Already you are taking action reading this book. Be aggressive in your use of the 200 weapons in the guerrilla marketing arsenal. Always be working to outsmart your competition

and aggressively keep marketing on the front of your agenda.

195. *Competitiveness.* Many nonprofit leaders might not warm up to talk of competition, but remember, some of the most competitive athletes compete with only themselves. You have to smell victory and want it to get it. You can't overcome feelings of failure until you have defined what victory looks like for you. Constantly work to improve your understanding of your market, of your customers, of how to use technology—stay on top of your game. Top competitors are not reactive, they are proactive.

196. *High energy.* Learning about marketing is meant to be more about doing marketing than about doing mental gymnastics. People who talk a good show about marketing are not guerrillas. Guerrillas are active and energetic. Implementing marketing plans takes energy. Talking about marketing, on the other hand, can be a relaxing pastime for some. If you never break a sweat while doing your marketing, you are not trying hard enough.

197. *Speed.* Time is a most precious commodity. Everyone, rich or poor, has the same amount each day. Time is fleeting for us all, all the time. Show people you value their limited resource of time with speedy service and they will stick with your organization. Try wasting the time of your supporters and volunteers and watch them trickle away one by one. They won't waste any time leaving. Today people are trained through their experiences with the internet and computer-assisted services to expect almost instant response. If they sign up for your program, they need instant confirmation. Return calls and e-mails promptly within 24 hours—make that 2 hours—scratch that. Try to do it in 30 minutes. Time isn't money, it's

more important than that. You can always get more money, but you can't get more time.

198. *Focus.* It is far better to get better at something you are already doing than to become mediocre at something new you are not yet doing. Keep your nonprofit from chasing after new programs and products if it means sacrificing doing what you already do well. Only 2 percent of people set goals, and of those who do, only the ones that keep their focus on the goals achieve them.

199. *Attention to details.* When you have contact with your customers, supporters, and prospects, keep in mind that what you might be tempted to think are tiny details are not of little importance to your clients. When you remember their name, it matters. When you know details about their lives and families, it matters. When you have to be reminded how you have met them before, it matters too. Listen to people. Pay attention to what they say. Ask questions and remember their answers. Attention to details is the difference between winning and losing.

200. *Ability to take action.* Guerrillas are active and engaged in their marketing. They don't automate their messages and customer relations. They are ready to steer their marketing and provide the power behind their strategies. Without take-action guerrillas, nonprofit marketing would digress into academics and would only exist in plans stuffed into three-ring binders and gathering dust on the bookshelves of executive directors.

Choose from these 200 weapons to build your guerrilla arsenal. Once you've selected them, put them into priority order, set a date for launching the weapon, and appoint a person to mastermind your use of those you've selected. Whatever you do, launch your guerrilla marketing attack in slow motion, only firing off weapons when you can utilize them properly at a pace that is comfortable emotionally and financially. After launching, keep track of which weapons hit a bull's-eye and which miss the target completely. Guerrillas always know which is which.

CHAPTER 10

Guerrilla Publicity

ONE OF YOUR GUERRILLA MARKETING GOALS will be to attract more coverage of your nonprofit's programs, products, and activities in the media. Nonguerrillas overlook the great marketing opportunities that exist in public relations. They needlessly spend money advertising events, products, and programs that could easily become news reports, articles, and online content on high-traffic websites. Before plunking down a lot of money on ads to publicize your events, consider the advantages of guerrilla publicity.

Nonprofits are a natural fit for public relations because often they are engaged in making their community a better place. You are news because you are doing something. Your job as a guerrilla is to get the word out about what you are doing to the public. Nonguerrilla organizations often treat getting publicity as something that happens miraculously; they are amazed and impressed when their organization gets a mention in the news. But guerrillas know that every day there are thousands of influential reporters out there who wake up each morning with a very hungry media monster to feed with news, information, and storytelling. When you realize that the media is always actively looking for good stories to tell, you have taken the first step toward becoming a guerrilla publicity guru.

Getting Media Play

Reporters are always in the lookout for news for their readers and viewers. If you have a story that fits their editorial needs, they will be interested in telling it. You will hardly be able to stop them. Nobody likes old news, so the reporter has a constant need for new information. The odds are in your favor with a little guerrilla patience that you will get the attention of key people in the media. Keep sending your interesting, newsworthy information and eventually you will get media play.

In addition to the traditional media, the web is filled with information-hungry media mavens. Bloggers and social media networkers are continually combing though available information, looking for new tidbits to share in their communication hubs. These people are often experts in their topics and pride themselves in being the one with the best and latest information. Make friends with these influencers by sending them the data

FROM THE FRONT LINES

NAME: Sandra Beckwith

WEBSITE: NonprofitPublicity.com

BOOK: *Publicity for Nonprofits* (Kaplan, 2006)

"Publicity can be a real asset to your organization. But it won't happen overnight. Publicity that gets the results you want and need takes time, planning, effort, and follow-up. You might generate positive media exposure in a few days, or you might need weeks or months. Realizing that success doesn't come overnight will help you manage your expectations and those of your administration and board of directors."

they need and they will become a conduit for your nonprofit's message. Like traditional reporters, bloggers have readers who are hungry for new information. Good bloggers know they need regular updates of relevant information to keep the interest of their readers, which may number in the thousands. Keeping a blog relevant takes a lot of work and a lot of information. If your news fits what these active writers want, they will feed it to their readers through their blog RSS feeds. Active users of social media also keep a vigilant lookout for information that is interesting for their MySpace and Facebook pages. Twitter users have scores, even thousands, of followers who like to receive 140-character "tweet" updates via web and cell phones. Guerrillas know they can often get more response from social media publicity than they get from advertisements.

Besides all the new Web 2.0 social media now available, websites are also looking for content for their regular updates. Your organization can help them fill their need for articles, calendar items, videos, podcasts, and reports.

You hear people talk about getting free publicity, but PR is not free, it is earned. You have to earn it by being interesting, relevant, and newsworthy. You earn it by networking. As with anything guerrilla, results start with a change in mind-set. The reason nonguerrillas don't get much media play and are amazed when they do is because they treat it as something that happens by chance. Their thinking is all wrong. They send out news releases occasionally and post a few items on their website, but they don't take the initiative to earn the attention of reporters and other media representatives. Guerrillas are far too active to sit passively by and leave one of the best tools for marketing their organization up to chance.

Benefits of Public Relations

Publicity yields so many benefits for nonprofits, it is amazing that more don't try to earn it. Don't be mistaken, reporters may not always be the nicest people when you contact them. They may not show any interest in your news and information. But with persistent effort, the cumulative effect of all your contacts with the media will yield fruit. Keep trying, keep smiling, keep the stories coming, and your nonprofit will harvest a bumper crop of publicity in due time.

Credibility comes with publicity, not from advertising. Advertising is a great tool for reminding people of the publicity they have seen about your organization. When people read about your organization in the body of a news article, or see your spokesperson as the expert on a newscast, they don't perceive your message as promotional. They see it as news. The more the people you want to reach see your organization in the media, the more propensity they will have toward supporting you. This always increases your chances that they will trust your nonprofit.

Your organization may want to be in the news not just for promotional reasons. Your presence is part of your advocacy. It's a helpless feeling as you watch or listen to people talk on the microphone with misleading, unhealthy information that are the very things your organization is designed to counteract. Let's use the example of an organization dedicated to hearing health that has no marketing budget. This can put them at the mercy of a hearing aid business with no doctors on staff. Let's say that this business advertises hearing aids to patients who really need audiology screening to check for the other health issues that cause hearing loss. Unless the organization learns to leverage the power of publicity and advocate for their cause, people who have deadly tumors will be walking out of the hearing aid store thinking all their hearing problems are solved. How tragic when what they really need is to check into the hospital for major surgery. The mission of your nonprofit benefits greatly from your understanding of how to manage public relations. By not actively engaging in marketing and public outreach, nonprofits needlessly complicate their work. In the example above, the hearing health organization could proactively advocate for their cause by developing a simple marketing plan and by having a strategy for regularly using news releases. It doesn't cost any money to create a plan and actively implement good community relationship practices.

Publicity brings valuable top-of-mind awareness to your potential customers too. People decide unconsciously what brands they buy based on the recognizability of the name of the products and services. An important part of your branding is getting your name on the minds of your target audience.

Another group who notice your media exposure is other media people. Suddenly you move to the top of their minds as the source for a story they are working on because they now know about you. Your name in print in a smaller market media can get the attention of a larger newspaper or magazine editor. A few articles and a magazine story later, and you could be asked to be on the national news.

Of course, PR has advertising value for your organization as well. Your nonprofit's events and programs can be announced to the public free of charge in the form of community calendars, public service announcements, and news reports. Advertising salespeople talk to their customers about media reach, impressions, and frequency to sell expensive space or time in their media. Your organization could have the same reach free of charge through publicity.

Community connections and networking are also improved by public relations. When your organization is mentioned in the media, often your phone starts ringing. People from other organizations across town that could become fusion partners with your nonprofit call you. A new volunteer is found in a woman who was just wondering what she could do to help the community. She sends you an e-mail because she saw your e-mail address in an article. Long-lost classmates come out of the woodwork to contact you when they see your face in the news. They could become valuable partners in your cause. All this could happen because of a little PR.

Now that we have convinced you to use PR, two keys that will help you in your public relations are to think about your relationship with the media and your relationship with the public. The latter is the most important. Some say there is no such thing as bad publicity, but if you think of PR as your organization's public relationship, who in their right mind would want a bad relationship with the public? Set a goal to always cultivate a good relationship with the public. Try not to overfocus on getting reporters to think about you. When you are perceived as trying to get them to do something for you, reporters become uncomfortable. Your news will naturally interest reporters when you are thinking about what their audience wants and not what you want.

The single biggest mistake nonguerrillas make is caring more about building and promoting their organization than engaging people and touching their needs from their perspective. Improperly relating to the media that way is just another dimension of what keeps nonprofits from experiencing community impact. PR is more understanding the public than just about understanding reporters. Relationships are important with media representatives, but if your story has real news value it will get reported even if reporters don't know you at all. If you know the public and understand how to create interest in your news, your PR plans will come together.

Create a Media Contact List

You can't do public relations without media people. It is very important to get to know them so a first step in your publicity strategy is to get the contact information you need about reporters and other media representatives. Think first about the audiences you want to reach and select the media they use. Imagine media as like taking a subway ride: It is important to be on the right train to get to your destination. If you are on the B train when you really need to be on the A train to get to where you are going, you'd better switch trains. The same applies to the media you use in publicity. If your target audience doesn't pay attention to them, you are wasting your time with them.

Make a list of all the relevant media contacts you need to reach your target audience. You can make your own forms on paper or in a spreadsheet, or use your computer's contact management software. Whatever you use, also include information and notes that will help you in publicity planning. Don't forget to include important contacts in nontraditional internet media like bloggers and social media mavens. Often the reporters who write for print media are the same ones who develop content for news websites. Get to know them.

Information to include in your media contact list:

- Name and position of contact
- Beat/type of reporter/preferred topics
- Contact information (address, e-mail, telephone, IM name)
- Media/publication name
- Media type
- Deadline information
- Best times to contact
- Preferences about news releases
- Editors and other staff information
- Notes about previous communications and stories

Develop Your Key Messages

Next, it is time to think through your media strategy. Draw up a plan for where you want to go and how you plan to get there. What media do you want to target with your outreach? Track your issue in the news using Google alerts and be aware of anything that could impact your mission or help tell your nonprofit's story. Brainstorm with your team, thinking of ideas and angles for your message. Your theme line ought to become a part of the storyline of the messages you send and you need to work in your meme when you can. Don't go in too many directions with your publicity planning, however. With PR it is impossible to control the reporting, but it is possible to think ahead about what kind of messages you should send to the public. The fewer themes you have, the easier it will be to manage output. Once your news is released, you won't have much control of the story, so it is best to think out beforehand what you want to say. Pick—and memorize—key messages that accomplish your advocacy goals. Think of themes that brand your nonprofit.

What Is Newsworthy?

What makes a story merit the attention of the public? Ask yourself, does the public want to know? Do they need to know?

Here are a few more angles for determining what makes the news.

- *Timing.* Is it really new or novel? Is it happening right now?
- *Significance.* How many people are affected by it? Does it have impact? Does it relate to a larger trend? Ask yourself, "Will people really care about this?"
- *Proximity.* Newspapers and media are looking for the local angle. Can you illustrate a national trend or news item locally by your release of information?
- *Prominence.* Is someone or someplace people have heard of involved?
- *Human interest.* Human interest stories need to evoke emotion like sympathy, laughter, love, etc. The most read stories are of personal triumph over adversity.
- *Unusual.* "Man Bites Dog!" Is something that is not the run of the mill going to happen?
- *Visual.* Is there something about your event that is really eye-catching?

- *New research results.* Do you have new findings from a survey or investigation that would interest people? Reporters love to report research findings.
- *Conflict.* Things that are controversial usually make the news or get attention. We are not suggesting you stir up trouble. But if there is a foe to overcome, like neighborhood crime, it has a better chance of making the news.

How to Write a News Release

Your organization's news won't be published if the media doesn't know about it. One way to inform them is by sending news releases. About 70 percent of what is published in newspapers is the result of someone sending a news release. Other media also use news release information for programming content ideas. You could even use news releases from other organizations and companies for content ideas for your media.

There is some controversy among marketers about how useful press releases are. Some say that since the media prefer to find their own stories, they don't pay much attention to news releases. That may be true for some, but not all reporters ignore news releases. Critics say reporters inundated with information have become so annoyed with news releases that they just toss them aside. Maybe some do, but think of all the junk mail you receive in your mailbox. You may throw a lot of it aside, but some of it you look at, don't you? Though you may be annoyed by the volume, it doesn't keep you from responding when you spot a good deal, does it? Guerrillas don't give up on a medium just because it is not currently in vogue. Many people don't like telemarketing and will never talk to telemarketers on the phone. However, guerrillas know that about half of people will talk to them, so they don't quit telemarketing. In the same way, guerrillas don't give up on sending news releases just because some people think they are passé. Keep sending your news releases because some will reap a response.

Writing a news release is also good discipline for your communication strategy. Procter and Gamble is famous for the practice of writing concise memos for internal company communication. They require their staff to write one-page memos that follow a strict five-part outline:

1. Idea
2. Background
3. How it works
4. Key benefits
5. Next steps

This discipline has helped P&G hold a major share of the market for the products they sell around the world. A news release isn't the same as a P&G memo, but the discipline of writing them can help your organization become better at telling your nonprofit's story to the public because it forces you to put your story into a brief sharable form. Writing and sending news releases to your supporters can also help keep your advocates on the same page with your marketing message by keeping them up-to-date with what is happening in your organization.

We can't cover everything about news releases in this chapter. You may want to read *Guerrilla Publicity* by Jay Conrad Levinson, Rick Frishman, and Jill Lublin (Adams Media, 2002). To get you started here are important details about news releases for your nonprofit.

1. *To whom will you send the news release?* Use your media contact list to find the right targets for your news. When necessary, customize your release to fit the audience.
2. *What is the angle?* What will make the story newsworthy? Can you connect to another national or international

story with a local angle? Remember to think from the audience's point of view and not only yours.

3. *Keep it to one page.* If a reporter is interested in your story and needs more information, she will contact you. Make your news release easy to scan and get the basic points. This helps reporters work faster, something they appreciate because they work on tight deadlines.

4. *What are the five W's?* Remember to include all the information about who, what, where, when, why, and how. As you write, include this information, and when editing, double-check that you are not leaving out an important element.

5. *Write in third person.* Even when your news release is talking about you or quoting you, it is important to keep the feel of objective reporting in your writing. In many cases news releases will be printed as written. By writing in third person you make it easier for your words to become the actual content of these reports.

6. *Who are you quoting?* Print stories need quotes, and radio and TV reporters need to know what kind of sound bites they can get from the story. Quote someone.

7. *The inverted pyramid.* Journalism 101 expects the important information to be at the top. Your lead sentence needs to summarize and tease the whole story while hooking the reader's interest. The rest of the news release fleshes out the details.

8. *Contact information.* Include all the data that helps the reporter know how to contact you to ask for more details. Proofread contact information to assure you have only accurate data.

9. *Describe any visuals.* TV needs visuals, and newspapers will send a photographer if there is an interesting picture. Unless you tell reporters what they might see, they

may not know what to expect. Include a brief blurb about visuals in your news release.

10. *Send your news release.* Know the preferences of the reporters you contact. Usually e-mail works best. However, some TV and radio editors like a hard copy of a news release to hand to a reporter when making an assignment and may prefer faxes and surface mail.

11. *Follow up.* Reporters are like anyone else; they sometimes need reminders. With all the information that is coming their way, you stand a better chance of making the news if you place a follow-up call to ensure they received your news release. When you talk, remind them with a ten-second version of your news.

12. *Repurpose news releases for other content.* You can use the information for other purposes. Stories can be placed in your newsletter, or developed into a series of blog posts. Don't waste all the good effort you put into writing your news releases.

Media Kits, Guerrilla Style

News releases do most of the heavy lifting for publicity, but it also advisable to assemble a media kit. These kits contain information about your organization with your mission, board members, staff information, and other data. It is not necessary to send media kits to reporters; you can post them on a page of your website. At the foot of your news release, provide a link to the page with the press information. Make sure your media page is easy to find through search engines and web directories. When you post your media kit information online, use both Word and PDF formats. This allows reporters to choose which format they prefer. Post larger size versions of photos. Print and high definition digital media demand it.

Hard copies of your media kit can be created and made available if you hold press conferences or meet face-to-face with reporters. Put your media kit in a folder with your logo, name, and theme line on the cover. There is no need to clutter your media kit with every brochure from your organization. Make your media kit a simple presentation that puts your organization's best foot forward.

What to include in your media kit:

- News release
- Tip sheet
- Fact sheet
- Policy briefs
- List and description of programs
- Published articles (about and/or by you)
- Case studies
- Staff bios
- Annual report
- Bio sketch
- Photos

Giving Reporters What They Want

You can set your organization apart from the crowd of news releases they receive by giving reporters the kind of information they want. The best way to know what they want is to actually read, listen to, and watch the media they produce. Imagine how frustrating it is for reporters to receive content from organizations that clearly don't know anything about their work. Watching and reading also helps you understand the audiences who use their media. When your news is relevant to their audience, reporters are most interested in you.

Be sure you communicate with reporters before your deadline and theirs. Nonguerrilla organizations wait until the last minute to send their news releases because they treat publicity as an afterthought. Your media contact list needs to include a record of the deadlines of your media contacts. Deadlines are not a mystery to the reporters, so don't be clueless about them. Ask. Other items to send reporters:

- *News release.* This is a one-page brief about a news item from your organization. Use news releases to communicate news only. Put other kinds of information in one of the formats from the list below.
- *Public service announcement (PSA).* Promotional information from your organization that benefits the public welfare are made-to-order media for nonprofits. Some may be timely, like news; others that are not time sensitive may be usable at any time. You can make a commercial about your cause, and many media will run it for free. Imagine that!
- *Event announcements.* Information about the time and place of an event that is open to the public is usually sent to editors of community calendars.
- *Media alerts.* These are short descriptive memos about activities with news value; for example, details about a rally or protest conducted by your organization. Include details that reporters need to answer the 5 W's and who will be available for interviews.
- *Editorial.* Write a first-person letter to the editor about issues that impact your organization's mission for good or ill.
- *Pitches.* In one page or less, propose an idea for a story or feature to an editor.
- *Tip sheets.* Brief bullet-point lists of helpful information can be included in sidebars and snippets in publications, such as "Five Keys to a Happy Marriage" or "Ten Ways to Spot Depression in Your Teenager." Tips often become larger articles.

■ *Fact sheets.* Write a summary of important data about your cause or organization. Some examples: a list of the number of meals served by your nonprofit in crisis relief or total pounds lost by members of your fitness program. Information about the dimension of needs your organization is addressing gives a snapshot of your important data.

■ *Backgrounders.* These are detailed briefs that give more depth of information about an aspect of your organization, leaders, cause, or programs.

■ *Reports.* Data gathered by your organization can also be useful to the general public. Create fact sheets from these reports and offer the full report to those who request more details.

■ *Academic papers.* Research conducted by universities or laboratories may support the case for your organization's mission. These reports can be announced in a news release and made available to reporters who want more detail. These papers can also be submitted to academic journals for publication.

■ *Survey results.* Results from your own surveys, polls, focus groups, ethnographic, or in-depth interview research can be summarized as a fact sheet or backgrounder. Make the report available upon request.

■ *Articles.* These are byline articles written by you or commissioned by your organization. Larger media may not be interested in these articles, but smaller trade and association publications will print or post them to their web media. Also, these articles are useful content to bloggers.

■ *Columns.* Continued public exposure and consistent quality could lead to a column in the general media. Perhaps more likely, consider syndicating your writings to smaller publications.

■ *Media kits.* Information about your organization with your mission, board members, and staff information as discussed above. Many of the formats discussed in this list can become part of your media kit.

65 Ways to Add Entertainment Value to Your News

Reporters know news is not merely about regurgitating facts; it has to get the attention of readers and viewers. News is also entertainment. Different media have different ways to be interesting. For example, still cameras need visuals, video cameras need action. Storytellers need settings, plots, conflicts, and characters. Below are ways to make your organization's news more interesting to read, listen to, and watch—and far more appealing to reporters.

1. Get expert opinions.
2. Recruit celebrity endorsements.
3. Make historical analogies.
4. Add some nostalgia.
5. Find the international connection and bring news back from abroad.
6. Find a local spokesperson.
7. Release a survey or case study report.
8. Employ a catchy phrase.
9. Sprinkle sound bites into your speech.
10. Use a clever chant.
11. Wear costumes.
12. Bring props.
13. Include pets and animals.
14. Do actions like crawling, walking, running, sitting in.
15. Put up a backdrop.

16. Meet in or in front of an interesting location.
17. Bring stacks of signed petitions.
18. Display interesting charts.
19. Make cut-out figures to stand beside you.
20. Present or hold a giant check.
21. Give away awards, prizes.
22. Hang banners.
23. Create or display sculptures.
24. Chalk art on sidewalks or walls.
25. Show scale with items that represent your statistics.
26. Create replicas.
27. Report massive numbers, people, items, or responses.
28. Make or give away food.
29. Hold a rally.
30. Sponsor a fair.
31. Get arrested.
32. Spend time in jail.
33. Host an autograph party.
34. Make unusual use of technology.
35. Report rejection or being denied access.
36. Use shock value.
37. Carry picket signs.
38. Put up posters.
39. Place yard signs.
40. Take a road trip.
41. Guide a tour.
42. Drive in a convoy.
43. Wrap your car.
44. Use mobile signs.
45. Throw, drop, jump over, climb up, or fly something.
46. Demolish or break something.
47. Burn an item or symbol.
48. Build a bonfire.

49. Light an eternal flame.
50. Find superlatives—biggest, fastest, oldest, etc.
51. Build a set or stage.
52. Build, decorate, or restore a house or vehicle.
53. Attempt a world record.
54. Paint a mural.
55. Create window displays.
56. Use puppets or stuffed animals.
57. Draw cartoons or caricatures.
58. Release an academic paper.
59. Host a symposium.
60. Sponsor expert panels.
61. Leverage making the national as local news.
62. Rank something, as the most likely, worst, or best.
63. Display extraordinary pictures.
64. Unofficially leak information.
65. Do skits or reenactments.

How to Relate with Media Representatives

Keeping up with reporters and having a good relationship with them is important for your organization. It is a good idea, when possible, to network with reporters and get to know them before you need something from them. Drop them an e-mail when you read or see something they produce that you appreciated. Add them as friends on Facebook and follow them on Twitter. Many media companies are requiring their staff to use social media, and you can quickly move to the top of their source contact list by connecting with them through these mediums.

Always be polite. The cliché "Never pick a fight with someone who buys ink by the barrel" is true. However, it is very rare when a reporter has a personal agenda against a nonprofit organization. Up to 60 percent of some publications can be advertisements. Hard news like crime and politics will always get the most coverage. After the other news is reported (and all the ads sold), often there isn't much room (or time) to cover stories from nonprofits. Don't get upset if your news release doesn't make the news. Reporters may be covering more important stories at the time. Keep sending your news and emoting your most positive vibes to reporters. You will make the news eventually.

A few more tips for good media relations

- Return calls and e-mails promptly.
- Tell them upfront if you have limited time to talk.
- Have a clear grasp of your message.
- Don't get off topic in interviews.
- Stay on the record.
- Be quotable; speak in good sound bites.
- Provide concise and accurate information.
- Define words and help with spelling.
- Don't tell the reporter how to write their story.
- Follow up promptly with additional details by e-mail if needed.
- Refer reporters to other helpful sources and provide the contact information for them.
- Don't ask them to contact you when the story runs.
- Let them know you read (and appreciated) the story when it runs.

Leading a News Conference

If your organization has a major announcement or an important crisis to address, one way to make to the public aware is through a news conference. When you hold a conference (also called press conference), make sure you have really big news. You would hate to have a party that nobody attends. News conferences are not for announcing a new program or staff member—unless the new program is funded by Bill Gates or the new staff member is Bill Gates. But when you have a major breakthrough or face a significant challenge that has impacted your cause or threatened your organization, a news conference is a good way to brief several media representatives at the same time and keep your message focused.

One way to make sure your news conference isn't devoid of people is to invite other guests or host the news conference during another event to assure people are there.

Ideas for a successful news conference:

- Send out announcements about the news conference to your media contact list.
- Schedule in midmorning so reporters still have time to file their reports.
- Watch for conflicting community events on the same day.
- Meet in a reasonably comfortable location.
- Provide refreshments.
- Have a designated spokesperson(s).
- Introduce speakers and use name tags.
- Provide press kits and other handouts.
- Put up a backdrop or meet in front of a location with an interesting visual appeal.
- Use props or other visual aids.
- Keep it under an hour.
- Allow time for questions and responses.
- Set the emotional tone according to the news you are announcing.
- Follow up and send media kits to reporters who couldn't make it.

When Communicating in a Crisis

Any organization can experience a crisis. Bad things happen to good people. Sometimes otherwise good people do bad things. When your organization faces a crisis or a scandal, you won't always have much time to organize a response and you won't be able to control everything the media says about you. Knowing that a crisis can happen at anytime, you should be prepared with a plan. Develop your strategy and even stage a few drills to improve your readiness. The reputation of your organization is too important to leave crisis communications up to chance.

Keys to handling communication in a crisis:

- Gather the facts of the situation as soon as possible.
- Contact your people and alert them early.
- Decide how your organization will respond or correct the situation.
- Set a goal for your communication.
- Prepare a statement.
- Tell the truth always.
- Communicate your next steps (or say you are waiting for more information).
- Designate a single communication leader.
- Be a source of information, take the initiative.
- Work with reporters (tell them you will respond in an hour).
- Decide if a news conference is needed.

> Guerrillas don't look at their organizational website as the single online tool they need for marketing their nonprofit on the internet; they think in terms of combinations of internet marketing weapons in their online marketing attack.

CHAPTER 11

Guerrilla Marketing on the Web

MOST NONPROFIT ORGANIZATIONS UNDERSTAND the importance of having a site on the internet with information about their nonprofit, but too few seem to understand how to get the most benefit from the internet. The internet is the guerrilla's best friend because the web is the greatest guerrilla marketing tool ever made. Guerrillas know they don't have to know everything there is to know about internet technology to get the most out of it. They know what they need most is to have the right mind-set for using the web. Instead of handing off their internet strategy to someone who doesn't understand nonprofit marketing, they stay proactively involved in making sure the internet is working hard for them. They don't look at their organizational website as the single online tool they need for marketing their nonprofit on the internet; they think in terms of combinations of internet marketing weapons in their online marketing attack.

A range of options now exists on the internet that have transformed the way nonprofits market themselves. Not only have websites changed communications, but newer forms of online networking have become possible in recent years with social media like blogs, Facebook, MySpace, Twitter, Flickr, YouTube, LinkedIn, Digg, Squidoo, Technorati—the list is seemingly endless, with new possibilities cropping up every day.

No one could have imagined back in 1984, when guerrilla marketing was first created, how the web today would make it so much easier to market effectively. Back in the early days of the internet, guerrillas were among the first to use the new medium to reach their customers. They were pleasantly surprised by the power of the web as a direct marketing tool, but that was when the internet was just in its infancy. Now, the web has matured, making the internet even better for guerrilla marketing.

Don't worry, we're not going to open up a fire hydrant of information about all the new potential now available on the web for marketing. You don't have to use all the tools we talk about, but consider which ones best fit your organization's mission and marketing strategies. The purpose of this chapter is to give you a review of the basics of internet nonprofit marketing and show you how your organization can effectively use the newer media for achieving your nonprofit's vision.

What You Can Do on the Web

There are so many possible ways to use the web, an entire book could not cover every angle of benefit for your organization. Here is a short list of 20 approaches you can take when using the web in your nonprofit work.

1. Research your target audiences, customers, and supporters.
2. Find and relate with fusion partners.
3. Take donations online.
4. Open a virtual location on the web.
5. Cross borders, expanding your nonprofit's reach globally.
6. Provide instant advocacy updates.
7. Penetrate new networks of people.
8. Stream live video telethon fundraisers.
9. Provide instant response and content delivery to website visitors.
10. Be accessible 24/7 to your customers and clients.
11. Educate people about your cause with online training.
12. Manage volunteers.
13. Send video and audio postcards.
14. Track response to your outreach.
15. Facilitate board of directors relations.
16. Relate to reporters and media representatives.
17. Save money on print materials and printed annual reports.
18. Give virtual tours of your facilities.
19. Get instant feedback from your target audience.
20. Save time by answering common questions with a FAQ page

The list of possibilities could continue much further. But considering just the list of above, could you say your organization has exhausted the benefits available. To nonguerrillas, the web is built for one kind of use. They see the internet in simplistic terms. For many, their website is a digital version of their print marketing materials and not much more. What a waste of potential! While there are some similarities between what you can do with print marketing and what you can achieve on the web, the internet is a different medium that requires a different mind-set from other forms of marketing.

Evaluate Your Nonprofit Website

Spend a few minutes looking at your organization's website. Ask yourself, are you making the most out of the potential available to you, or is your nonprofit's thinking limiting your results?

- *Planning.* Do you know exactly what you want to accomplish with your website?
- *Content.* What information will best attract visitors to your site and keep them coming back regularly?
- *Design.* There's a "hang or click" moment when people see your site. Do you understand what influences their choices?
- *Involvement.* How effectively do you use interactive tools like auto-responders, forms, and widgets?
- *Production.* How efficiently do you use software or content management systems to get your message online as quickly as possible?
- *Follow-up.* How much time typically elapses between the time visitors e-mail or request contact before your organization responds?
- *Promotion.* How visible is your website to search engines? Is it linked to and by other websites? Do you promote your site in offline media, mailings, and wherever else your name appears?

■ *Maintenance.* Do you constantly change, update, freshen, and renew your website?

Optimizing Your Nonprofit Website

If you found areas of weakness in your web marketing strategy, don't worry. We have a checklist of ideas for optimizing your site for maximum marketing impact. The list below will help you analyze what your next steps should be for improving your organization's website.

■ *Audience.* Start by understanding your target audience. Begin working with a clear idea of the needs and attitudes of your audience and the action you want them to take.

■ *Marketing strategy.* Integrate your website with the rest of your organization's marketing. Don't treat your web page as an afterthought. Your website needs to support your marketing and branding, having a similar look and feel.

■ *Theme.* The recurring theme of your site should support the actions you want your readers or website visitors to take. The same themes used on the cover of your brochures, newsletters, and advertising should be echoed on your homepage and on every page that follows.

■ *Control.* Beware of yielding all control of your website to technical support (IT) people; these people rarely understand marketing. Numerous nonprofits are hamstrung with pointless websites run by people who know all about the latest software and programming tricks but have no clue about marketing.

■ *Navigation.* Think through the navigation of your website, making it easy for users to find what they are looking for, logically, based on their point of view. Don't force your site users to interpret your navigational structure. Use standard navigational conventions when organizing your web page. Use "breadcrumb" navigation links on each page.

■ *Nonlinear thinking.* Understand that site visitors will not read your website in a linear fashion, going from page to page in order, but instead will jump around within your site in random ways. Provide navigation and information that keeps them oriented to the structure and message of your site.

■ *Speed.* Make your site fast loading by reducing the size of image files. Don't assume everyone on your site has a fast internet connection, and even if they do, they won't want to wait around for slow-loading files.

■ *White space.* Avoid cluttering your site with too much information or too many columns. Ample white space makes it easier to read content and spotlight the most important information.

■ *Color.* Your use of color should not make it difficult to read your site. Dark color backgrounds with dark color text are difficult to read. Just because you can read your website on your computer doesn't mean others can. All monitors do not display colors exactly the same.

■ *Readability.* Make the content on your site interesting and easy to read. Get the attention of readers with compelling headlines. Tease and link to stories on other pages from the homepage. Break up large sections of copy with sub-headlines. Use bulleted and numbered lists.

■ *Copy.* Chunk copy into smaller segments, allowing for more white space. Use links to provide the option of drilling deeper for information. Use as many subpages for depth as is needed by the reader. Don't put everything on one page to reduce the amount of scrolling necessary.

■ *Response.* Make it easy to respond by employing a clear call to action and by using forms, shopping carts, sign-ups, donation buttons, and subscription tools. Many people never respond because they weren't aware they were expected to respond.

- *Social networking*. Put social media links or buttons on your site that promote your organization's presence on websites like Twitter, Facebook, MySpace, YouTube, Flickr, etc.
- *Bookmarking*. Add social bookmarking tools that allow content to be easily shared by word-of-mouse on Technorati, Digg, Facebook, MySpace, blogs, etc. Easy-to-use plug-ins and widgets are available to make it simple to add this feature to your site.
- *Visuals*. Use images and videos that tell the story of the results of your work and give a sense of positive progress in your cause.
- *Capture e-mail addresses*. Make it easy and beneficial for users to give you their e-mail addresses so you can stay in contact with them. Offer an incentive that can be delivered digitally to people in exchange for their e-mail address. An e-book, MP3 audio presentation, or video are a fair trade for getting people to give you their contact information. Try not to let people leave your site without receiving an enticing offer of an incentive to leave their e-mail address with you.
- *Automation*. Using sequential auto-responders, you can create automated educational courses, tips, newsletters, prayer guides, quotes of the day, etc. in an e-mail that keeps you on the minds of the people who come to your nonprofit's website. The messages deliver automatically without any extra work for you after you set them up. They make your site work for you, even when you are sleeping.
- *Take payments and donations*. Start with PayPal or get your own e-commerce solution. Encourage people to take

action now to give a donation, make a pledge, purchase products, or sign up for your programs.

- *Tracking*. Use your website metrics to measure how many visitors who come to your website also sign up for your newsletter or online education courses. Work to optimize your site so you increase the percentage of visitors who sign up by tweaking what you offer and how you lay out your site.
- *E-mail newsletters*. Offer an e-mail newsletter to your site's visitors. Each time you send out your newsletter, it will bring subscribers back to your page if you link items in your newsletter to pages on your site. Pay as close attention to the copy in your e-mail newsletters as you would to any direct mail campaign piece or advertisement.
- *Privacy policy*. Post a policy on your site and link to it next to anywhere on your page that requests visitors give you their e-mail addresses. This assures subscribers you won't give (or sell) their information to third parties or spammers.
- *Opt-out option*. All your bulk e-mail communications need to provide an automated way for subscribers to opt out. This lets people manage the e-mails they get from you and helps keep your communication from being mistaken for spam.

Blogging with a Cause

If you are a nonprofit leader, you are often too overloaded with the work of accomplishing the mission of your organization to add new tasks to your to-do list. Who wants to add more work to their already overloaded week? Blogging sounds like another energy-draining marketing chore. You may be surprised to know that you already are doing everything you need to do to make an interesting and effective blog. By starting a blog, you can even use the everyday tasks of running your nonprofit to create tools that will help you find and keep new clients and supporters in a way that also reinforces to your existing clients and supporters that they made the right choice in working with you.

All that is needed is for you to repurpose your existing work in ways that make useful content for your blog. Blogging can help you sharpen your skills as an advocate, position you as a thought leader in your field, and is a free way to promote your organization. Blogging is well worth the effort you put into it.

Things you are already doing that could make you an interesting blogger:

- Talking to interesting people of all kinds
- Making presentations about your cause
- Reading books, articles, and blogs about your area of interest
- Keeping abreast of news, research, and the latest data on your topic
- Answering questions and handling objections about your cause
- Writing letters, e-mails, editorials, and articles on your subject
- Leading outreach and promotional efforts for your organization

A blog post doesn't have to be very long to be effective. The length of your average e-mail is probably longer than your blog posts have to be. The ideal blog post is between 100 to 300 words. About three to four times per week, write brief blog messages using bulleted lists, links, and quotes from important sources. If you are careful to write using the keywords that are most closely associated with your cause, search engines will take your content and use it to bring the people who are most interested in your subject right to your blog.

Below is a list of activities you are already doing that could help you become a sought-after blogger.

- *You already make presentations.* Break up your presentation content into short blog posts. Blogging can also help you shape your new presentations by giving you an outlet to draft new concepts and phrases.
- *You already have many conversations.* Blog about what you are talking about. You don't have to name names; talk about principles and practices. Blogging also helps you become more natural, confident, and concise in your conversations with potential donors. Often, it isn't a presentation to a group of people that closes the deal—it is a seemingly incidental conversation in the elevator with an important decision-maker that does! Blogging helps you think of interesting things to talk about in advance.
- *You are always writing something.* Repurpose some of what you write in e-mails, news releases, and articles as content for your blog. As you blog more frequently, you will become more practiced at putting your case into written words. Blogging is a way to practice good business writing.
- *You are already answering questions and handling objections.* Put the answers to your most asked questions on your blog. It's easy to do; just walk through the most common objections you get in your advocacy presentations in the form of brief blog posts. By posting answers on blogs, you can also help those who find you on the internet who might have questions but were afraid to ask.
- *You are already working to improve your leadership skills.* Talk about what you are learning and reading about in your blog. As a nonprofit guerrilla, you are constantly reading and reviewing the latest products, books, and websites that are related to your cause. What many don't know is

that you can use the research you already are doing to position yourself as a thought leader in your area of consulting to your clients. When you read something, write out a short review about it and post it on your blog. People will associate your leadership lessons with you and your organization.

- *You already are staying up-to-date with current events.* Talk about what you are learning from news, research, and data about your topic. The same principle applies to news articles, blog posts from other organization leaders, and those handy websites you find on the web. You can unpack a few of the pros and cons about the issues and resources in your chosen nonprofit field in a blog post and get readership on your blog, too. It is likely your comments will be placed in search engines near the content you cite in your blog.

- *You are already advertising.* One of the big surprises about blogging is the fact that blogging brings much more traffic to your nonprofit's site if you host your blog on your organization's domain. You may think that when you post an article on your blog that the traffic from that post lasts only the few days it appears on the main page of your blog. But all your blog posts will turn into keyword-rich search engine food that will stay around for a long time after you initially post it. Your blog post will be attracting people for as long as you have it on your site because search engines catalog what you write and present it in search results.

    The best part of search engine traffic is that it is very targeted. People who type in a URL and come to your site take a potluck chance that you have something there they want to see. But not with search engines, when people come to your site from an internet search, they are looking for exactly what you are talking about.

Since all the work of writing the post is done, it's like having a free internet advertisement that showcases your organization out on the web for as long as you want it there. Getting search engine traffic is free. Of course, you can pay companies to list your site and even sponsor advertisements in search engine results. But if you regularly blog on the topics that are most relevant to your clients' needs, you will be placed highly in search engine results for the keywords in your posts. That's like getting free advertising every time you write a blog post.

■ *You already are doing public relations.* A blog is a great way to go public with your cause. In a way, having a blog is like having a PR agent that gets you published in print, web, and even radio and TV. How can that happen? As you blog, you can create content that is suitable to be used for articles and talking points for use in other media. After you have written them, it's only a matter of submitting them in the right places and to the right people. Networking! Some bloggers take content from their blogs right into the mainstream media, even appearing on national TV. A good blog post in the form of a 350- to 700-word article could make great content on a news or magazine website.

Here are a few ideas for getting your blog content working for you in other media:

■ Turn a series of blog posts into a free e-book your site visitors can download. Send a copy of the e-book with a news release to reporters.

■ Write in the format of the magazines and websites you want to target with your articles. That way your style will be a fit for their media.

- Bulleted lists make great radio call-in show talking points. Write up a short blurb for each point and send them to show producers.
- Do you have any news? Put together a news release and post it to your blog as you also submit it to editors.

> New generations of volunteers, donors, and clients don't just prefer to use social media, they demand it. Today's younger generation communicates with one another using social media and texting, not e-mail and snail mail.

CHAPTER 12

Guerrilla Social Media

GUERRILLAS KNOW A GOOD DEAL WHEN THEY SEE ONE. And social media is a very good deal for guerrillas because they focus on reaching individuals instead of merely selling their ideas to markets. With a little time, energy, and imagination, nonprofit guerrillas deepen relationships with their clients and supporters and increase the frequency of exposure of their message to the people they want to reach by using social media. The results speak for themselves.

It is ironic that while most nonprofits are focused on evoking change, as a group they tend to be the least likely to embrace change in the form of new communication media. Some nonprofits treat social media as if it were a social disease that needs to be eliminated from within their organization. Nonguerrilla nonprofit tech support offices fearfully block social media websites. Executive nonprofit boards create policies that forbid their staff to use social media like Facebook, MySpace, Twitter, YouTube, etc. at work. While it makes sense to limit the number of distractions (or temptations) your organization's employees need to deal with, to completely close the door to the use of social media is an over-adjustment.

Yes, there are distractions and there is potential for employee abuse of social media. However, these same distractions also pertain to the use of telephones, e-mail, expense accounts, use of time, and dozens of other things. Ultimately your organization's success is up to the integrity of your staff to hold themselves accountable for fulfilling your nonprofit's mission. Your organization's inability to trust your people to do the right thing with social media might negatively impact their morale. Guerrillas are willing to take the chance because they see the great the benefits of social media marketing.

Don't make the mistake of thinking your target audience thinks like you do about social media. Some nonprofits have an imaginary profile of their target audience in their heads. To these people, social media is mostly about wasting time. They imagine their nonprofit staff will possibly become a crew of lazy slackers if they allow them access to these sites at work. They think websites like Facebook can't reach their target audience because the target doesn't use them. The people who forbid the use of social media are usually also people who don't personally use social media themselves.

For the record, the people who use social media like Facebook are not all young people. The largest group (43 percent) are

18 to 25, but other segments are rapidly increasing on the network. When you add all the users over 26 years old together, you see that 45 percent of users are not that young. A full fourth of Facebook users are over 35. Only about 12 percent are teens. Young adults are still a rapidly growing segment now using Facebook, but those aged 55 and older are growing very rapidly too. Women are the fastest growing gender on the network. Facebook says women now outnumber men in every age group on Facebook, making up 56 percent of all users. Add these facts together and you see that older women 55 and up are quickly getting into social media. According to demographic data from Facebook in 2009, 55-year-old women users increased by 175 percent in the first quarter of that year. What do you call the fastest growing segment on Facebook? More than likely you'd call her "Mom" or "Grandma." Women age 55 and older also happen to be the same people who engage in philanthropic and volunteer endeavors in the greatest numbers. Organizations that block the use of Facebook may be cutting themselves off from the exact kind of people they want to reach. When nonprofit leaders say they don't have time for social media, they are unwittingly closing the door to great nonprofit marketing opportunities.

Messages Spread Fast on Social Media

Another reason your organization should consider using social media is because social media is designed to spread information through relationship networks quickly. It works on the same principle of Six Degrees of Separation. The Six Degrees principle states that people are so interconnected with one another by human social relationship networks that no person is ever more than six people connections from any other person on earth. Some researchers believe because of the popular use of social media, people are now separated by only three degrees. If you work in a health-related nonprofit, you already know how quickly a virus can spread. Now, think about the benefit of spreading your organization's ideas like a virus around the world. Your nonprofit can't afford to neglect a network that powerful. If the people you want to reach most are just three steps away from you, your message could get to them very rapidly on social media. You can raise awareness, mobilize people, and evoke change if you make your message compatible with the way social networks work. Below are ways you can increase the viability of your outreach on social networks.

Ten Ways to Master Nonprofit Guerrilla Social Media

1. *Message.* For your message to have any impact for your cause, it has to make people act. As in all advertising, a funny or interesting video, even if it becomes a very popular online phenomenon, if it doesn't get people to take action, it is useless to your nonprofit.
2. *Meme.* The message of your viral outreach needs to be easy to grasp without explanation and easy to pass on to others.
3. *Meeting.* Find the media that your target audience likes to use and go where the people are. Media researchers estimate 60 percent of adults belong to a social network, but most only belong to one. Spread your virus in a variety of networks.
4. *Manage.* Funnel the contacts you make in social media toward your website or blog. Make your website the second tier of your social media strategy. The third tier is people registering with your site. Mobilize the people who sign up on your site to take action and help spread the message.
5. *Material.* Give people the content they need to pass on your viral marketing. Provide assets for your audience

to make their own videos, allow them to put their picture in an e-card, anything that helps to put them into the storyline and send to their contacts.

6. *Mobilize.* Make it easy to pass your content through word-of-mouse. Choose the video tools that allow you to embed your videos directly into Facebook, blogs, etc. Social bookmark tabs need to post your link and teaser copy into other sites.

7. *Medium.* Make your content a good match for the medium. Long videos will not be watched as much as shorter ones. Break up paragraphs in articles and write lead sentences remembering they may also serve as the teaser copy for the links when they are visible on other sites.

8. *Marketing.* Your content needs to have links back to your sites and copy that promotes your organization. Don't leave the "More Info" section blank; include good copy using your key words and links.

9. *Metrics.* Watch the statistics. Check not only how many people view, forward, or Tweet your content, also track how many click through and take the next step with your message.

10. *Momentum.* Start the ball rolling by forwarding your content to the networks of your intended target. Leave room in Tweet messages for people to "re-tweet" (RT) your messages. Prime the commenting by starting the first comment on links and posts you put in other networks. Push your virus into new networks until it takes off on its own.

Ready to Use Social Media?

Only you can judge if your organization is ready to use social media. Some organizations are hesitant to get involved because they fear losing control of their message. You don't lose control of your message with social media, you lose the illusion of control. You don't have control. New media have changed the face of communication forever. Gone are the days of one-way communication. The question is not if your organization will use social media, it is more a question of when. Your donors are looking for a more personalized relationship with your nonprofit. New generations of volunteers, donors, and clients don't just prefer to use social media, they demand it. Today's younger generation communicates with one another using social media and texting, not e-mail and snail mail. If you want to reach them with your message, you would be crazy to eliminate the option of using social media in your nonprofit's work.

Should your organization get started on social media now? Ask yourself a few questions. If you answer yes to most of them, it's time to take the plunge.

- Are you committed to keeping your profile updated with fresh content?
- Are you willing to be open and candid about the good and bad in your organization?
- Are you ready to relate to people no matter how receptive or antagonistic they are to your message?
- Are you willing to be patient when results don't happen overnight?
- Are you prepared to work hard to understand the people in your networks?
- Are you ready to reinvent your use of office time?
- Are you ready to listen and not only talk about yourself?
- Are you prepared to mix a little of your personal life with your nonprofit work?

Get Involved Firsthand

Don't put a young person in charge of your social media just because they seem to understand the medium. It may be easier for you to learn the medium than it is to teach them what took you years of experience in nonprofit relationships to learn. Some marketers delegate the social media marketing to out-source services. These services can be helpful in optimizing your social media marketing strategy for the short term, but over the long term, if you are not actively engaged in knowing and using your social networks, you will not learn as much about your audience as you can. In addition, you could set yourself up for embarrassment when you fail to recognize one of your most active social media contacts in a real world meeting. The bottom line for the social web is there are people in these networks and each of these people need to be personally impacted by the message of your nonprofit if your are going to be able to evoke community change or reach people with your important message.

Top Social Networks

There is a seemingly endless list of social media sites available for use in your nonprofit communications. It's hard to know where to start. Below we have provided a list of the top social networks. It is not necessary to use them all. In a way, social media are like direct mail address lists. Direct marketers say, "It's in the list," meaning your success depends on the list you use and the prospects on that list. The same principle applies to social media; pick the ones that are most popular with your target audience.

Here are 25 social media networks that make excellent guerrilla marketing weapons for nonprofit marketers.

1. Blogging

Guerrilla activity: Raise awareness for your cause by blogging. A blog post doesn't have to be very long; write about as much as you would in a brief e-mail. Tips lists bring readers, too. Make friends with other bloggers and the people who comment on your work. Blogging also increases traffic to your website.

Optimization tips: Host your blog on your organization's domain to build traffic to your site. Update regularly, two to three times per week, to build traffic. Use the tags and key words that will generate traffic and place well in search engines. Put them in the titles and in the body of your posts. Link to other blogs often. Answer and befriend people who comment.

2. Podcasting

Guerrilla activity: Create a regular podcast. It doesn't have to have high production values to create a following, and only needs to be a few minutes long. The flexibility of the MP3 format allows people to choose how they listen to your regular audio updates and increases the number of listeners.

Optimization tips: Permit listeners to subscribe through RSS feeds. Also post your content on iTunes and other podcast distribution sites.

3. Vimeo.com

Guerrilla activity: Host a regular video show. Live stream an event or telethon fundraiser. Network with like-minded people.

Optimization tips: Embed your videos in blog posts and on social networks and link to them in e-mail news and Twitter updates.

4. SlideShare.com

Guerrilla activity: You can create webinars making the case for your cause to thousands of people for free. Repurpose your PowerPoint presentations and documents from advocacy presentations.

Content can be easily embedded in other online media. Great guerrilla research tool, too.

Optimization tips: Use keywords in the titles of your posts. Complete the profile information with marketing-savvy content and favorite other users.

5. YouTube.com

Guerrilla activity: Get your message onto the largest network of video viewers on the internet by favoriting, posting videos regularly, or creating a video blog. Network with others who also post. YouTube videos easily embed in Facebook and blogs for faster viral marketing.

Optimization tips: Don't leave the "More Info" section of your videos empty. Use keywords, good copy, and links.

6. Facebook.com

Guerrilla activity: Increase the frequency of your exposure to audiences with the most potential to support you by participating in Facebook. Deepen relationships with individuals, share photos, and messages, learn their likes and interests. Start discussion groups and fan pages.

Optimization tips: Use the "Favorites" in the "Info" section of your profile as a means for networking. Each favorited item becomes a key phrase that produces a clickable query (you see it turns blue) of the network's database to show you like-minded people also on Facebook. Greet people on their birthdays.

7. MySpace.com

Guerrilla activity: MySpace helps you reach a more culturally and ethnically diverse audience. The site also makes it easy to find musicians and others in the arts. The site is popular with blue-collar segments, subcultural groups, folks who prefer to be outside the mainstream, and is widely used by teenagers as well.

Optimization tips: Show your appreciation when someone adds you to their friends by sending a thank you banner that also promotes your cause. Use the "Browse" feature to search for people in your area who fit your exact target profile using demographic data and zip codes.

8. Orkut.com

Guerrilla activity: Like Facebook and MySpace, works for all groups of people, but is especially popular in Latin America and with Hispanic audiences.

Optimization tips: Start building a network by allowing the site to scan your online e-mail address book. Browse communities to find groups of people you want to reach.

9. Twitter.com

Guerrilla activity: Sending 140-character updates throughout the day includes followers in the storyline of your nonprofit's work and increases the number of exposures the audience has to your brand. Easily find and follow leaders and create a following for your cause using Twellow.com. Very useful in mobilization already, Twitter has been employed in revolutions (Moldovan and Iranian elections).

Optimization tips: Use the 160 characters in the "Bio" section to talk about your nonprofit and include your link in your profile. Don't spam! Increase your clout by updating frequently, sharing links, "re-tweeting" messages, and using hash-tags # to follow (and lead) conversations. Follow people who follow you. People will follow you generally if you follow them.

10. LinkedIn.com

Guerrilla activity: This business-driven network helps you target professionals and entrepreneurs. You can ask questions and get answers from qualified experts, find new staff members, locate fusion partners, get introduced to powerful people—all the potential makes you dizzy!

Optimization tips: Connect with people by asking for introductions from your contacts. Putting "LION" as part of your name signals that you are an open networker and will add anyone who requests to your list.

11. Plaxo.com

Guerrilla activity: Another business network with professional contacts, fusion partners, and donors. This network is often used in tandem with the user's Outlook address book. Blends well with other social media feeds and has automated tools to help you network.

Optimization tips: When others in the network update their information, your address book will automatically update when you connect Plaxo to your Outlook address book. This helps you stay in touch with people as they move from place to place

12. Ning.com

Guerrilla activity: Create your own branded social networking site for your nonprofit on a network with thousands of existing profiles. Gives you a lot of control over the look of your network. You can keep your custom social networks separate by making some for advocacy and others for mobilization.

Optimization tips: Once you create your profile, you can use it as you join new networks on Ning. Large work groups can create private ad hoc networks on the site to manage projects or tasks. Use it as a sustainable behavior education and accountability tool.

13. NetworkforGood.com

Guerrilla activity: This site finds donors and brings them to you. Manage your profile on the network, quickly add tools to accept donations on your site, manage and send your fundraising e-mails. Get free fundraising tips also.

Optimization tips: Encourage your supporters to create badges that raise funds for your nonprofit and place them on their websites and profiles.

14. VolunteerMatch.com

Guerrilla activity: Like a dating site for nonprofit guerrillas and volunteers. Find energetic workers for your cause. List your nonprofit, get mobilization tips, and find fusion partners.

Optimization tips: Get featured in a "Nonprofit Spotlight" profile that tells the story of your organization with all your contact information and messaging. Upload your storytelling videos in the video section.

15. MeetUp.com

Guerrilla activity: Helps you act local in your global cause. Promote your local meetings to targeted audiences or find meetings where you can network with others. Identify the early adopters and most active members by setting up meetings and getting to know people who come.

Optimization tips: Experiment with starting your own meetings that promote your theme, educate, or recruit new supporters and volunteers. Join in attending groups that are most compatible with your mission or who need your input most.

16. Friendfeed.com

Guerrilla activity: Combines your social media feeds and gives you another way to find and follow people across various social media networks. You can also sort your friends by professional, personal, and favorite categories.

Optimization tips: Add all your social media feeds and follow all your social media contacts who also use Friendfeed. Then start to mingle and find new friends on your other networks.

17. SecondLife.com

Guerrilla activity:A virtual 3-D community that attempts to create a fantasy world similar to the real world online. The characters users create may be fantasy, but there are real people behind them.

Optimization tips: Your nonprofit can create a virtual location on the site and network with the international audience who comes to visit you.

18. Technorati.com

Guerrilla activity: Helps you know where your blog (and other blogs) ranks on the internet. Develop a profile for your blog and mingle with others in the blogosphere. As your blog gains awareness through the linking from other bloggers, your site gains in "Authority" and credibility with search engines.

Optimization tips: Start by claiming your own blog. Then proceed adding blogs to your favorites. Visit the top blogs and join in on the comments. Stick with relevant comments on the topics being discussed. Avoid overly promotional-type speak or spamming comment sections.

19. Delicious.com

Guerrilla activity: Connect with people by sharing internet bookmarks. Use bookmarking to help promote your websites and give credibility to them with search engines. Search the biggest collection of bookmarks as part of your guerrilla research.

Optimization tips: Be part of the community by adding bookmarks you like. Don't just bookmark your own blog's links—that's no fun! Go to the most powerful and relevant blogs and comment on them.

20. AllTop.com

Guerrilla activity: This aggregator of blogs by topic allows you to find people based on their interests and affinities. The site is arranged much like a web directory; each page lists the most relevant blogs at the top. Great for research and excellent for identifying the top social media mavens to add to your nonprofit's publicity contact list.

Optimization tips: Build your own listing of blogs and position yourself as a thought leader for your issues. Make contact with the best bloggers on your topic and relate to them as you would other media representatives and reporters.

21. Squidoo.com

Guerrilla activity: Created by guerrilla marketing mastermind Seth Godin, the site is designed for users to create and edit a page entirely dedicated to their agenda with content, links, etc. It is great for research, because lenses are sorted by topic like a web directory. Another good way to sort through the mass of information on the web and find people to interact with. Can also raise money for your nonprofit.

Optimization tips: You can earn money from your lens and become one of the nonprofits to which site users donate. Users designate an automatic 5 percent of their earnings to the charity of their choice and many users donate up to 100 percent of their share of earnings to nonprofits. Get the picture?

22. Digg.com

Guerrilla activity: This social bookmarking site can drive traffic to your website or blog. Members vote on links posted on the network. The more popular the post, the more traffic gained. If you get listed on the front page—buckle your seat belt!

Optimization tips: Become a power user member of the community and you can become a very powerful advocate for your cause.

23. Wikipedia.com

Guerrilla activity: This website is a comprehensive encyclopedia about everything, written and edited by users. It is useful for your guerrilla research, but also you can stay up-to-date on important topics of interest to your cause. When something new happens, it is often updated on the site within a few minutes.

Optimization tips: Don't try to market on the site—you will be kicked out as a user. You are there to make sure the information about your organization, personalities, and cause is balanced and accurate.

24. Amazon.com

Guerrilla activity: Your organization can find books and recordings and earn commissions from the associates program by using affiliate links. Gives you targeted access to people when you create reviews of all the relevant books in your topic. People looking for (or talking about) books on your organization's important topics are also potential prospects and partners.

Optimization tips: Little known or used by most is that you can create a customized "Real Name" profile with your organization's information and links that is visible when you review books or comment in the discussion forums. Amazon is consistently in the top 40 sites on the entire web. Why wouldn't you want to be seen there?

25. Widgets

Guerrilla activity: Useful fundraising and advertising widgets can be placed on your blog and on sites that care about your cause. All that is needed is to copy a section of HTML code into your website or blog. Widgets are a simple way to syndicate content, promote fundraising, and get prospects in your database.

Optimization tips: You can also program your own widgets that permit you to change promotional messages (and/or banners) on all your supporters' sites at once.

> As a nonprofit marketer, you need to understand people's needs to help them, but you can't understand the specific needs of all the people in your community. You can, however, understand the needs of a smaller group of people.

CHAPTER 13

Niche Marketing Guerrilla Style

W E'D LIKE TO DO YOU A FAVOR AND TELL YOU **something that will help you become more effective at achieving your nonprofit's mission. What we tell you will spare you the** danger of the greatest threat to your organizational planning and execution. Heeding what we say could determine the fate of your organization. Some who read what we say won't believe it. Others who read it will believe it, but won't act on it. Guerrillas will listen carefully and take action.

So here goes: You cannot be everything to everybody.

Let that simple statement soak in. If your organization is going to be effective, you will have to concentrate on a specific segment of people in a target market. You need to select and define your organization's niche. A niche is a narrow range of clearly defined products, programs, and services that is offered to a tightly focused group who share similar wants and needs. As a nonprofit marketer, you need to understand people's needs to help them, but you can't understand the specific needs of all the people in your community. You can, however, understand the needs of a smaller group of people. When you know who you are trying to reach and begin to understand their needs, your organization's offerings (and communication) can be presented in a way that speaks directly to their needs. If you speak to their needs, they will pay attention to your communication and not block it out. If you speak to their needs, they will respond to you.

Nonguerrillas dilute their effectiveness because they have trouble determining their focus. They have no niche. They tell themselves they can be all things to all people when they really can't. They respond to questions about their niche saying, "Our

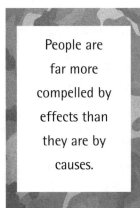

People are far more compelled by effects than they are by causes.

niche is everyone because everyone needs to hear our message." But "Everybody" is not a target audience. No organization can effectively serve everyone. Even messages that are intended for universal audiences have to be effectively shaped to fit different people because the one thing that people have in common is that they are all different. The only way you could reach all people with the same presentation and approach is if there were only one way of thinking, one universal radio station, one TV station, one language, one lifestyle, etc. You cannot be everything to everybody, but you can easily be something to somebody. The sooner you get that message, the faster you can start making an impact.

Make a Bigger Splash in a Small Pond

Take an example from the for-profit marketing world. A marketing consultant wanted to set up a marketing consulting business. He knew better than to try to reach everybody and get lost in the sea of other marketing consultants in the world. So he set to work looking for a smaller target he could reach. In his research, he discovered there were no marketing consultants dedicated to serving pool and spa dealers. He created his niche as a marketing consultant for pool and spa dealers. By narrowing his focus, he was able to learn a lot about the marketing needs of pool and spa dealers. His consulting business offered the marketing solutions they needed most. Because he was the only pool and spa marketing consultant, pool and spa dealers recognized him immediately as someone they needed to get to know. He got their attention. Word-of-mouth spread quickly in the industry, and he easily became a featured speaker at the pool and spa conventions. He started a pool and spa marketing e-mail newsletter and wrote articles about pool and spa marketing for pool and spa industry newsletters and magazines. He used his research and writings to produce a self-published book and training course which he sold to pool and spa dealers. He had more business than he could handle within the "small pond" (that's not just a pun) of the pool and spa industry.

Benefits of Having a Niche

The same principles the pool and spa marketing consultant learned can work for your nonprofit, too. Instead of trying to tread water in a sea of other nonprofits, you can learn the needs and make contact with a smaller group of people who are easier to reach. When you know your niche, your organization will become more effective at reaching people and they will become more responsive to your outreach. Here are a few other benefits of having a clearly defined niche:

- *Builds a stellar reputation for your organization.* When people in your target think of your organization, they will think of how well you fit their needs and how blessed they are in having contact with your nonprofit. Think of the Special Olympics. Ask anyone involved with Special Olympics, they will tell you they hold a deep reverence for the reputation of that organization. As they should.

- *Sets your organization apart from others.* If your organization is known for making a difference by doing a narrowly defined task, your nonprofit becomes the kind donors and volunteers notice and want to support. There are many kinds of housing development charities, but there is only one Habitat for Humanity.

- *Gives more access to the target audience.* When you become an expert in the needs of a concentrated group, doors start to open to deeper relationships in that community. A nonprofit museum for the blind would interest the blind and others who serve the blind community. They would be more likely to recommend the blind-focused nonprofit and may even share data about their clients with a trusted blind museum organization.

- *Brings almost instant credibility.* Your knowledge of the community's needs and the credibility that comes from your reputation causes the target audience to trust you more readily. When your organization builds credibility in your niche, you could become the default authority about the group you serve. Marriage health counselors might be able to help couples of all kinds, but military couples may be more likely to listen to the advice of a military marriage counselor. When stress on the marriages of military couples makes the news, who will reporters call for an expert opinion?

- *Clarifies your tasks.* Instead of multiplying the number of things your organization does, you develop a sharp focus on a limited number of tasks and become a stronger organization. The keen focus leads you to become increasingly better at what you do. Who is better at rescuing Labrador Retrievers? A dog rescue nonprofit, or a Labrador Retriever Rescue? Since Labradors are the most popular breed of dogs, that nonprofit would help a lot of dogs.

To Which Niche Should You Switch?

Hopefully we have cured you of the nonsense thinking that your organization can meet the needs of everybody and helped you realize you need to determine your niche. Now, how do you find what your niche should be? Remember these questions from your three-sentence guerrilla mission statement: Who are you? What do you do? What difference does it make? Revisit them, this time thinking about how to determine your nonprofit's focus. Your niche tells people who you are and determines who you will reach. What you do and the difference you make in the lives of the people determines your positioning. Choose your niche, and you choose your future. If you don't know what your organization stands for in the minds of the people you want to reach, you will fall for anything that looks like an opportunity.

Here are a few issues to consider as you decide what niche is right for your organization.

- *Unique.* Can you stand out with the niche you select? Don't choose a niche that is already overloaded with competition; find one that is original. If you are the only one in your niche, you will be much more attractive to the people in the segment. Choose a niche that is big enough for you to serve but not one that is so large it attracts a flood of imitators.

- *Reachability.* Can you really find the people in the target audience? There is no purpose in choosing a unique target if you can't really connect with them. You may believe you can make a difference in the lives of a group of people you have identified in demographic research, but make sure you can actually spot them on the ground.

- *Substantial.* Is the segment large enough to justify the amount of focus you are putting on it? This is a tough call because there are a lot of important causes and needy people. Niche marketing helps nonprofits reach underserved communities by encouraging diversification between organizations. But if your target group isn't very large or significant in some other measurable way, it will be difficult to attract attention and support for your cause.

- *Responsiveness.* Do people in the niche want or need what you are offering? Marketing never works well when you are selling what you happen to be making. It only works when you are offering solutions people really need. Discover the needs of people and link your message to the solutions to those needs.

- *Believable.* Does what you offer sound plausible to the people in the segment? Can the cause be perceived as a real problem to them? Do you have enough expertise to do what you claim you can do? Is there a track record somewhere that shows you know how you could plausibly solve the problem? Can you articulate the process you will use to attain success? Do people think the product will actually work?

- *Sustainable impact.* Can you really change things? Ultimately, your cause needs to make a difference. Some organizations exist that make long-range plans and raise a lot of money initially, only to fizzle out and disappear because they can't create sustainability. When you can't demonstrate results, volunteers stop volunteering, funding dries up, and conflict in the organization heats up. Begin with clear, obtainable outcomes in mind.

- *Donor support.* Will donors get behind the cause? If what you are doing in your niche is perceived as an eccentric personal project, it will be difficult to find financial partners. To make your ideas work, you will need the generous support of many people. Make sure you have the foundation for financial support to get the job done. Is the problem large enough to attract people who will be loyal to the cause and support it? Even the most important ideas can fail if donors don't believe in them.

Niche marketing is the opposite of mass marketing. Don't stop with only refining your focus to a narrow audience. Keep your focus on offering a limited range of high-quality programs, products, and services. Don't expand the number of things your organization does; do what you do best. Know who you are and what your niche is and own that space in the marketplace. The chart below shows how niche markets compare to mass markets.

> Your niche is what you stand for in the minds of your prospects.

Niche markets are small, but they reap big results. Therefore, your organization should not try to serve more than a couple of niche markets. This helps focus your organization

Nonprofit General Market	Guerrilla Niche Example
Marriage Health Counselor	Military Marriage Health Counselor
Sports Leagues	Special Olympics
Ecology-Secure Landfills	Diaper Pollution Education and Prevention
Housing Development	Habitat for Humanity
Museum	Museum for the Blind
Dog Rescue	Labrador Retriever Rescue
Credit Union	Urban Check Cashing and Financial Counseling Service
Church	Overnight Factory Shift Workers' Fellowship
Youth Development	Latino Youth Preparatory Education
Health Care Services	Parish Nursing
Public Safety	Automobile Cell Phone Use Safety
Venture Philanthropy	Micro-enterprise Lending
Medical Crisis Family Support	Ronald McDonald House

and assists your volunteers and staff in cultivating more share of your customers.

Positioning

Positioning is what people think about when they think about your organization. Imagine your target audience with little file cabinets in their minds. Where will they file information about your nonprofit? Are you a large organization or a small one? Are you more focused on communities or policies? Do you work with children or adults? There are thousands of ways people might perceive your organization. Positioning is understanding and managing perceptions.

As you work out an understanding of your niche, your organization's positioning becomes clearer. Positioning is an attribute of what your nonprofit's identity is in the minds of the people you wish to reach. Your position is different from your brand. Your position is how people perceive you; your brand is what people experience from you. It is much easier to create a brand if you have clear positioning. Don't stop working on your niche until you understand your positioning. Without having an accurate understanding of where you are in the minds of your target and where you want to be (re-positioning), you can't set proper marketing goals. Write out a brief positioning statement that puts into words what your organization represents in the marketplace.

> Any marketer can make the case for their organization's needs, but if you understand the motives and psychology of the people you target, you can gain an edge on your competition and stand out in the marketplace

Let us pick with your brain a little. What kind of breakfast cereal would you eat if you wanted to be a champion? What kind of cereal is just for kids? What kind of cereal would you eat if you wanted to help your heart by lowering your cholesterol? If you are like most people, you would have said Wheaties, Trix, and Cheerios, respectively. But why do you think that way about these products? What got all those ideas about breakfast cereals into that brain of yours? Next time you go to the grocery store, walk down the cereal aisle. There is an intense guerrilla communication battle going on there. While the ingredients of cereals are mostly the same (wheat, corn, or rice), breakfast cereal marketing is quite varied. Study the entire aisle of cereals and you will see a practical demonstration of niche marketing and positioning. Cereal marketers compete for shelf space and the shopper's money with precise differentiation tactics. Look closely and you will see there are ten ways they compete: place, price, promotion, people, product, service, selection, quality, convenience, and speed. Your organization can have the same kind of powerful communication that cereal marketers have, minus the marshmallows, when you learn how to be associated in the minds of your target audience with your preferred attributes. You are competing for shelf space (and money) in the minds of your target audience after all.

Getting on the Same Page

Making an effort to understand how people perceive what you are saying when you communicate with them seems like a "no-brainer." But surprisingly, few organizations have a clear concept of how they are perceived by the people they hope to reach. They also have not taken time to outline how they wish to be perceived by the people they are targeting. Your organization may be sending mixed messages and reducing its effectiveness needlessly.

Here is an exercise to try with your nonprofit team. Ask the members of your organization's leadership to independently write down on a slip of paper five attributes that describe your organization. Also, ask them to write down five words that would describe what they feel the target audience thinks about the organization. Not only will the list be different between what the staff thinks and what they think the community thinks, chances are high no two team members will have the same words for either list. This is a great way to illustrate to your team the importance of getting your positioning together. When they make their two lists, they will be tacitly admitting they understand that the messages your organization is sending are not the same ones being received by the target audience. They will also be demonstrating how they are not on the same page with how they perceive the organization internally as a team. Imagine if you took a survey and got people in the community to make a list of five attributes about your nonprofit. You might have a real awakening. This shows how random nonprofits can be with their communication. They rarely intentionally think about what others are thinking, yet they are always trying to change people's perceptions. Go figure!

You can bet cereal marketing teams are on the same page about their products. And when tested, the marketplace is generally on the same page as well. This doesn't happen by accident. Positioning takes careful planning and concise communication. How do they do it? First, these marketers have researched how customers perceive their products. Secondly, they have meticulously worked to get all their marketing to portray their particular messages and product values. Thirdly, they have a keen understanding of who their competition is in the marketplace.

Your organization needs the benefit of having a tightly focused niche and clear understanding of your positioning. When you know who you are and what you are doing, you are a very dangerous competitor. Your potential for impact is enhanced when you are clear about your identity, too. Conversely, not knowing who you are and where you are going is dangerous to your dreams of making an impact for the greater good.

> The reason to use emotions is because mere
> facts won't motivate people
> to respond.

CHAPTER 14

Meeting Needs While Changing Minds

G UERRILLAS KNOW THE TRUTH THAT ESCAPES THE average nonprofit leader's awareness: People don't care about your organization or your cause as much as they care about themselves. That's why guerrillas develop strategies that appeal to their target audiences based on the benefits those people will receive and not on the features of their programs, products, services. While other organizations are trying to motivate people by describing their strategies, reporting distressing statistics, or making urgent fundraising appeals, guerrillas are linking their messages to solutions that meet people at the point of their needs and motivating them to take immediate action.

The economy today has given people the taste for the power they experience as consumers and has trained them to demand more choices, increased benefits, and value-added life-application in everything. The thought that this is a customer-driven society may grieve you. Despite how you feel about it, the reality still impacts how your nonprofit does its work. Customers expect to benefit from your organization and require more information about how you help them. In an ever-expanding world of "me too" nonprofits, what makes your organization stand out as unique are the benefits it brings to people. In the long run, this forced quest to provide benefits to customers accrues to the world's benefit, too, because the competition that now exists in the social sector ultimately increases programs and services to niche markets that may have otherwise been left underserved.

Your principal challenge as a nonprofit guerrilla marketer is to understand people and offer them what they need. This applies not only to the products, programs, and services you provide to your community, but also how you relate to volunteers, donors, staff, board members, etc. The information age has made this more feasible than it might have been in the past. You can use technology to learn much of what you need to know, if you take the time to do it. You can get inside the heads and hearts of your customers by e-mail, though texting, reading blog comments, taking surveys, conducting online focus groups, leading webinars, and initiating chat sessions. There are limitless learning opportunities available.

When working with your board and donors you may have to make the case for why you spend so much time trying to understand the needs of people. Raise awareness about the common mistake of focusing on the organization's perspective of the problem and the programs they have designed to solve it. Remind them not to forget to listen to their target audiences and to understand what is the most effective way to motivate people to take the required action that leads to change.

Benefits Instead of Features

Features are the specific things that a nonprofit does; benefits are the effects of what the nonprofit does. People are far more compelled to respond to the effects of your programs than they are to the programs themselves. Yet many organizations can't seem to stop themselves from talking most about what is least interesting to customers. On the flip side of every response is a reward for the person responding. Some non-profit marketers refer to this as a value exchange. The truth is, even when people are giving you money, or spending time volunteering, they are also getting a benefit in exchange. Sometimes the reward is intrinsic. The activity is its own reward, like when people experience art, theatre, or tasty food. Other times the reward is the result of the action, as when someone feels relief when finally free of an addiction. It would be wonderful to live in an emotionally intelligent world where all people were self-motivated to do the right things for their families, themselves, their communities, and the world. But the reality is your organization will most often have to think ahead of people and help them understand the benefits brought to them by your nonprofit.

It would be easy to motivate people to take action if all you had to do was announce the benefits and watch people immediately respond. But how can you motivate people to act when the action doesn't feel like it benefits them? What are the benefits of choosing to be a designated driver while all your friends are enjoying the party? How can you get people to adopt behaviors when the rewards are not for the individual, but instead accrued to society in general? Recycling isn't much fun. What is the payoff for the person saving all his plastic bottles? This is why it is all the more important to the nonprofit marketer to think ahead and map out the benefits obtained by people from their involvement or response. When you understand customers and know exactly how your organization leads people to rewarding experiences, you become very attractive to them.

Motives, Wants, and Needs

As we mentioned before, on the backside of every behavior is an attached reward. When you know what that reward benefit is to the people you want to reach and you use it in your communication, you are already miles ahead of your competition. Marketing communication is persuasive communication. If you want to motivate people through your marketing to take action, you'll need more than a few attention-getting propaganda tactics; you need to understand what makes people tick.

People Act Based on Motives

A motive is a person's inner desire to do or be something. Understanding motives is a prerequisite for finding the benefits people want. Any detective will tell you every act has a motive behind it. Motives often exist unconsciously to the individual. Motives cause people to recognize what they want and need. They know it when they see it. Before you start marketing, think about what motivates people inside. Motives can be positive or negative in nature:

Even when people are not overtly aware of them, motives play a role in decision making. Researchers say that 90 percent of

Negative Motives	Positive Motives
To remove a problem	To gratify senses
To avoid a problem	Intellectual stimulation
Dissatisfaction	Social approval
Depletion	To be truly spiritual

decisions are made on the subconscious level. Have you heard someone (or even yourself) say "Oh, I have heard of them, let's call them . . ." revealing that though they know nothing of the company, name recognition alone is sometimes reason enough to cause them to decide to do business with them. The unconscious mind plays a deep role in decision making.

People Crave Fulfillment of Their Wants

The next step toward understanding benefits is to grasp the wants people have. When something appears to satisfy a person's inner motives, it becomes a want. Just because someone wants something doesn't mean they will take action to get it. We all want things we can never have. As they say, the secret to happiness is not having what you want, it is wanting what you have. Benefits are what people want and need.

What else do people want?

- What is safe
- What makes them feel loved
- What makes them feel happy
- What makes them healthy
- What doesn't clash with who they see themselves to be
- What makes them wealthy
- What is easy

- What gives them purpose
- What is fun
- What tastes good
- What doesn't take too much of their time
- What takes the least amount of risk
- To avoid pain
- What others want
- What makes them popular

People Seek Based on Their Needs

Another part of understanding benefits is to discover what people need. When a person has a strong motive tied to a consciousness of what they want, they identify their needs and start looking for and paying attention to possible ways to satisfy them. The more basic to survival the need, the stronger the drive to find a solution. Perhaps you are familiar with Maslow's hierarchy of needs scale that ranks needs according in order of importance to the individual. It is hard to meet a higher numbered need on the scale when a lower numbered, more basic need is unmet. For example, from the scale we see why people who are hungry don't pay much attention to self-help seminars.

- Physical needs
- Security needs
- Social needs
- Esteem needs
- Self-actualization needs

Keep in mind also as you appeal to needs in your marketing that you understand benefits from the social perspective of your target audience. People first want benefits that help their families; secondly, they are attracted to what benefits them personally; third, they want what benefits their local community; and last, they are interested in what benefits the world.

Motives, Wants, and Needs in Action

Motives, wants, and needs interact together powerfully, causing people to take action. An individual's inner motives to be healthy and avoid social stigma causes them to awaken to the realization that they want the benefits of clean teeth, healthy gums, and fresh breath. This want sends them on a quest looking for toothpaste, toothbrushes, breath mints, floss, and dentists—anything that solves their problem. Their need gets them paying attention to marketing messages about the benefits they seek. Marketing that hits them at the point of their wants gets response. Notice, though, that people want the benefits of the products, not the features. They don't want toothpaste; they want clean teeth and fresh breath. Marketing that talks about the features of the toothbrush are far less compelling to them than marketing that talks about the desired results gained by using the particular toothbrush.

If people know they have a need, they don't wait around for marketers to tell them how to act—some take action themselves creatively. For example, if they are stuck somewhere with no toothbrush or toothpaste and realize they have dirty teeth, their motives could drive them to want to invent their own solution to their need for teeth cleaning by crafting their own makeshift toothbrush out of a napkin, using a little salt instead of toothpaste, with a piece of peppermint for a breath-freshening chaser. When you awaken people to problems you aren't equipped to help them solve, don't be surprised when they choose to create their own solutions.

Good branding is what people feel when they think of you.

On the other hand, marketing can create wants and needs. Way back in the 1800s deodorant marketers who understood people's inner motive to avoid social stigma alerted people that their body odor could be offensive to the people they want to impress. These guerrilla marketers gave the body odor problem an official-sounding name, "B.O." This caused people to wake up and smell that the solution to their newly perceived problem was using the deodorant the marketers were selling. Nowadays most people think of deodorant as a basic health need and include it in their morning routine. As a guerrilla social marketer, you could use marketing to get people to adopt even healthier habits. The better you are at discovering what motivates people, what they want, and what they need, the faster you will be able to mobilize them to act to get the benefits they want.

People Respond to Influence

Most folks like to think of themselves as independent thinkers and social free agents, but the truth is we like to be liked by other people and we listen to what others think more than we care to admit. Your target audience responds to your marketing messages after they filter them through their own social lenses of *roles*, *class*, and *culture*. Think about the ways these issues impact your presentation and approach to the people you want to reach:

- *Roles*. Social expectations impact how people respond to marketing. Organizations, groups, and institutions to which your target audience belong have an influence in how your customers make decisions. Also, roles include relationships such as best friend, spouse, father, mother, grandmother, etc.
- *Social class*. Most individuals relate to people who have similar lifestyles, values, economic status, occupations, interests, and behaviors. If their peers are against it, chances are slimmer your preferred target will pay attention to your message.

■ *Cultural influence.* Increasingly important as society become more diverse, cultural relevance is a vital part of your organization's outreach. Values, forms of expression, language, patterns of behavior all shape how individuals perceive your marketing.

While it is important to factor in the outside influences that impact your audience, you can take charge and use influence as a powerful weapon in your marketing as well. Psychologist Robert B. Cialdini explains the role of influence in his book *Influence: The Power of Persuasion* (Quill, 1984) and lists six weapons of influence. They are:

■ *Reciprocation.* When you give a gift to people, they feel obligated to return the favor by giving a positive response.
■ *Commitment and consistency.* When people sign a pledge or make a public statement about something, they feel obliged to remain consistent with it.
■ *Social proof.* When the people making claims about a subject are similar to the audience or recognizable to them, people tend to believe the assertions made.
■ *Liking.* People listen to others they like, or to people who are likable.
■ *Authority.* When an expert makes a claim, people more readily give credibility to what is said, even when the person's area of expertise is in another field.
■ *Scarcity.* When supplies are limited, or the cost of something is very high, it becomes more desirable.

People Decide Based on Emotions

Take a look around at effective nonprofit marketing, and you will see many good examples of emotional appeals. Conversely, some of the most ill-conceived nonprofit marketing also has the emotional approach. To move people, you have to connect with them emotionally, but how do you know what is a good approach and what is a bad one? Emotions are important to the human experience. Emotions are often the main reason why people do things. According to scientists, the brain is wired to respond to emotions faster than it responds to reasoning. Your brain and body respond thousands of times faster to something that is emotional than when you respond to something that is rational. For example, your body chemistry would react far more quickly to the person who makes a rude gesture to you on the street than you would to someone who walks up and mistakenly tells you something is Euclidean geometry when you know darn well it is non-Euclidean. People don't get worked up to act about facts as much as they do with emotions. So it is important to understand emotions. But emotions come in a variety of flavors, and knowing a lot about them before you use them in your marketing is a good idea. As you develop your emotional messaging, think how you can include feelings in explicit and implicit ways. A smiling face on a brochure communicates better and is more implicitly convincing than an explicit headline that says, "Our university will make you feel happy!"

Guerrillas get their edge in marketing by taking the guesswork out of how people will respond to their outreach through an understanding of psychology. Do a little cognitive behavioral therapy on your customers and think about how the feelings you use in your marketing will impact their response.

Sad, Mad, Scared Emotions

The chart below lists the range of emotions on the *Sad, Mad,* and *Scared* spectrum of feelings. The heading of each column lists the core emotional value of each feeling listed below it. Looking at the list of feelings, think about all the advertising campaigns you are familiar with from nonprofits that were

Sad	Mad	Scared
Guilty	Critical	Rejected
Ashamed	Hateful	Confused
Depressed	Raging	Helpless
Lonely	Angry	Submissive
Bored	Hostile	Insecure
Sleepy	Hurt	Anxious
Bashful	Skeptical	Bewildered
Stupid	Irritated	Discouraged
Miserable	Furious	Insignificant
Inadequate	Frustrated	Weak
Apathetic	Selfish	Embarrassed
Inferior	Jealous	Foolish

effective. Which emotion did they use? Also think about the ones you know of that were ineffective. The chances are high that more of the campaigns you can think of that leveraged emotions from the *Sad, Mad*, and *Scared* spectrum were among the less effective ones. Why is this? Because negative emotions tend to be avoided by people. Be careful in your use of negative emotions—people don't like to feel sad. Sadness makes them change channels, flip pages, toss brochures, and click on to other websites.

Using Fear Appeals

Fear can motivate people to act and is often necessary in health-related messages. Frankly, there are not many happy ways to say, "If you don't quit drinking and driving, you will eventually kill someone and/or go to jail." A person who has risky health behaviors needs to know they are in danger. It makes sense to sound the alarms. But when you awaken their fears of people, understand you often unleash unintended consequences. You may intend for people to take away a healthy caution from your message, but they could react in ways you did not anticipate. Look at the list of feelings again. You may intend to evoke one kind of feeling with your message, but people have the habit of deferring their feelings from one column to another when the intended emotion is too hard to face emotionally or socially.

People who have more self-esteem tend to take fear appeals at face value. People who have lower self esteem tend to replace a scared emotion for a sad one, or worse, a mad one. Using fear in your messaging could backfire on you. Your reasonable and valid fear message could inexplicably evoke shock, anger, mocking, or even despair.

Your major task may not be convincing your target audience that they need to change their behavior to avoid the risks involved; you may have to spend more of your efforts on building confidence that they have the ability to take the recommended steps to adopt the behavior. Not everyone who smokes cigarettes disregards the dangers associated with smoking. Many who smoke feel trapped, thinking quitting is too hard for them. They want to quit. They believe they should quit. They accept the scientific evidence that smoking could kill them. But they still smoke because they think they can't quit. Until they feel they can quit, fear appeals will only serve to increase a sense of despair about their situation.

Factors that determine if people will respond to a fear appeal as intended:

- Who is at immediate risk? People respond to threats to their family first, then threats to themselves, followed by community threats, and then global threats. The closer the threat to what is most important to them, the more seriously the threat is considered. How can you bring it home to them?

- Do they really believe the negative consequences can happen to them?

- How immediate is the threat? Longer range consequences get less urgent responses.

- Do they believe the likelihood is high the negative results will happen to them if they do not act as you tell them they should?

- Do they believe they have the ability (efficacy and resources) to take the recommended action for avoiding the negative consequence?

- Are they confident enough to take the recommended action?

- Is the action they need to take easy to understand?

- Can they act immediately while they are experiencing the fear? The longer the delay between decision and action, the less likely they are to follow through.

Joyful, Powerful, Peaceful Feelings

It's hard to mess up with marketing appeals using positive feelings. People are attracted to positive vibes, smiles, and success. Aren't you? You don't have to turn all your marketing messages into happy talk, but look at the list below and think about how many appealing messages you could create that would get people's attention. If you evoke good feelings with people, they jump on board much faster than they do with negative emotions.

Joyful	Powerful	Peaceful
Excited	Respected	Content
Energetic	Proud	Thoughtful
Playful	Appreciated	Intimate
Creative	Hopeful	Loving
Aware	Important	Trusting
Sexy	Faithful	Nurturing
Daring	Cheerful	Pensive
Fascinating	Satisfied	Relaxed
Stimulating	Valuable	Responsive
Amused	Worthwhile	Serene
Extravagant	Intelligent	Sentimental
Delightful	Confident	Thankful

People Justify Their Actions Based on Reason

Of course facts are not irrelevant to decision making. The facts need to be there because though people often act based on feelings, they tend to justify their actions based on facts and reason. For example, when asked why they engage in cardiovascular exercise, men rarely give the emotional reason, "Because I don't want to be fatter than the guys my wife used to date at my college reunion." And they are even less likely to give the scientific reason, "I wanted to involve the large muscles of my body in more relevant ways, thereby increasing metabolism and efficient distribution of oxygen in my bloodstream." They say, "I wanted to increase my endurance." The facts you give need to be centered on the benefits they bring to the individual.

When people make decisions, they go through a process. The last part of the process involves the left side of their brain. Whatever facts you give had better add up. Whoever claims your organization can do something will get scrutinized by the people who respond. A brain is a terrible thing to disgrace. Guerrillas never, ever use motives, wants, needs, influence, or emotions to mislead people. Guerrillas want a long-term relationship with their clients and supporters. Fooling people is a terrible start to a relationship.

Make a Benefits List

People are tuned in to benefits. Imagine them as having radio antennae coming out of their heads that receive benefit messages. Your job as a guerrilla nonprofit marketer is to become the station that broadcasts on their favorite channel, WIIFM— What's In It for Me? Your organization can learn to broadcast on their frequency by making a benefits list.

Host a discovery day. Gather the people in your organization together and talk about the values the organization brings to the community. It won't work well unless you include everyone in your organization. Bring in the entire staff, executives, top advocates, fusion partners, and at least one person from your target audience. Yes, bring in someone who represents the people you hope to reach. They will have insights everyone else will miss. Get out some butcher paper, markers, and tape so you can write the observations and ideas from your group on the wall. Explain the need for a benefits list, describe the issues discussed in this chapter, and get to work brainstorming a list of benefits from your nonprofit's work. What are the benefits you are most known for? What benefits are yet to be fulfilled, but are part of your strategic planning? What benefits does your organization provide that other organizations do not? Are there advantages that your competition has that you can also fulfill? Making a list of these issues will help your organization when it comes time for crafting compelling messages that communicate with people.

Any marketer can make the case for their own organization's needs, but if you understand the motives and psychology of the people you target, you can gain an edge on your competition and stand out in the marketplace when your organization shows the rewards for people's response to your marketing. Though it may take some time and might even make you blush, make the list as long as possible. Don't be shy; you need a comprehensive list of all the good things your nonprofit brings to the community. The list you create will become the tool you use to craft winning marketing messages. You may only focus on one or two of the items on your list in your marketing, but your list will become a valuable guerrilla marketing weapon and be used in many ways.

> A meme is your main benefit or behavioral message expressed visually or verbally in a way that conveys the entire idea.

CHAPTER 15

Expressing Your Organization's Unique Identity

YOU HEAR A LOT OF BUZZ FROM PEOPLE in the social sector these days about branding. It's the latest thing, but it is almost the last thing they really understand. We'd like to clear something up for you. Nobody outside your organization really cares about your nonprofit's brand. They care about themselves, and anything that doesn't appeal to their needs they will ignore, period. So let's get rid of two mistaken notions that a lot of people have about marketing a nonprofit's identity. First, it isn't just about grabbing people's attention and making them remember your brand's name. Secondly, for the record, branding isn't about slapping your logo on everything.

Branding is mostly about answering your customer's question, "So what does that have to do with me?" Your nonprofit's greatest identity marketing problem is not getting people's attention focused on your name, it is about tying your identity to

FROM THE FRONT LINES

NAME: Elaine Fogel

WEBSITE: SolutionsMC.net

"Nonprofit brands are different because they represent the organizations themselves. Every single touchpoint within a nonprofit has an effect on its brand—the person answering the phone, service delivery staff, CEO, fundraiser, cleanliness of its bathrooms, professionalism of its employees, and quality of its communications and visuals. Sometimes a poor experience at the most unexpected touchpoint can detrimentally affect an individual's desire to make a gift or become a member, and the organization will never know about it. Nonprofits that invest in building and maintaining their brands will reap the benefits in multiple ways, one of which is in generating more revenue. And the best part is that investing in the brand doesn't always require big bucks."

something they care about. People need to associate you and the things you do with something that resonates with their needs or they will forget your name as fast as they forgot what they had for breakfast last Monday.

What is in a name? Everything! Sometimes you hear people say, "I am not good with names, but I never forget a face." It sounds so polite, but what that often means is the people who say that are not sincerely engaged with others enough to care about their name. People rarely say, "I am not good with organizational names, but I never forget a good logo." You need to establish a name identity with people if you hope to influence them for your cause. How can people help spread the word about your organization or cause if they can't remember your name? How else are they going to remember you?

You can effectively communicate your organization's identity best when you have a memorable brand and a long-lasting and clearly understood theme line, and know how to launch a meme as an idea virus about your organization. Let's look at these below.

Creating a Memorable Brand

Branding is about proactively helping people know how to remember you. It is filling your organization's name with meaning in the minds of your intended audience. People have the psychological and emotional need to categorize things. They assign definitions to words and names. They classify organizations, programs, products, and services by grouping them in their minds by quality, taste, color, price, convenience, and scores of other ways. They rank and evaluate messages they hear and see. They even typecast kinds of behaviors. While it takes a while for the meaning of words to change in the dictionary, word and name meanings are not static in the real world. Words mean what people think they mean. People fill words with meaning and empower names with influence. What is an "Amazon," after all? Up until recently, she was a feisty ancient Greek warrior woman; now she's a ferocious book-selling competitor who could be putting your local bookstore out of business soon. What person would entertain the notion of encouraging their friends to "tweet" them only two years ago? The request would be meaningless. What does your nonprofit's name really mean to people? What should it mean?

If people in your target audience haven't made up their mind about what your organization means to them already, they will as soon as (or if) they pay attention to you. Don't leave it up to chance that they will assign the right meaning to your name. Wouldn't you rather participate in the process of how they label you in their minds? Will your organization blend into the background or stand out in the crowd when they notice you? Guerrillas only like camouflage on their book covers. They'd rather stand out from the crowd in everything else. Intentional branding helps your organization differentiate itself from all the other nonprofits that exist.

The way to stand out from the multitude of other nonprofits is to know exactly what benefits your organization brings to people. Your benefits list comes in handy at this point. Find the benefits that mean the most to your target audience and associate them with your name. Every brand is a promise that means benefits to the target audience. Good brands are emotional, too. They conjure up feelings about what your organization means to people. Branding is the gut feeling people get when they think of your organization. Your brand is only as strong as the emotions that are evoked when people consider you. Remember, people make

> It is not conformity that gets the attention of the people but rather variance.

decisions based on their feelings first, then logic. Tie your brand to what motivates people most, emotions and benefits.

Build an Identity, Not an Image

Guerrillas don't want to fabricate an organizational persona; they want to establish a valid reputation. Your reputation is one of your organization's most valuable assets. Your role as a nonprofit guerrilla is to be an accountable steward of your organization's name. Continually evaluate your branding and assess your nonprofit's name equity. Build on your reputation, don't build up a facade. Branding is not image management. If you want to create an illusion, then study magic. If you want to develop a brand, focus on establishing a stellar reputation based on honesty. Think about what you want your target audience to think about when they see your name or hear about your organization. What is the benefit you bring, and what makes it more desirable than all the other things that are clamoring for their attention?

Social marketing forefather Philip Kotler suggests using a fill-in-the-blank sentence like the one below to help plan brand messages for behavioral marketing.

We want [intended target audience] to see [desired healthy behavior] as [main benefit of healthy behavior] and more beneficial than [competitive unhealthy behavior].

This concept could easily be adapted by your team as you are developing a guerrilla marketing brand message for your nonprofit. How would you complete the blanks in the sentence?

We want [target audience] to see [name of your nonprofit] as the [position and niche] that helps [main benefit of your organization] in [targeted community].

Use the sentence you create as a starting point for a brand conversation in your nonprofit. Branding is a deep subject that needs to involve the entire organization. Include major stake-holders all along the way as you develop your branding. Don't get too far ahead, leaving them behind. Be careful not to let your internal discussions about branding turn into an organizational navel-gazing exercise. Nonprofits can get overfocused on their perspective so much that they leave out the point of view of their intended audience. Build your brand on your customer's needs, not just on your organization's aspirations. You want people to associate your organization with what is meaningful to them, not only on what is meaningful to you. Branding that is benefi-cial to people is invisible to customers. They notice their needs being met, not so much your messaging. Donors give because of what giving means to them. Volunteers are happy about the dif-ference they are making. The people you are helping see their lives being transformed. Communities notice the changes your organization is bringing about.

Tips for a good nonprofit brand

- Have an easy-to-pronounce name.
- Let your name define your organization's values.
- Have a unique name, not a sound-alike or bland name.
- Use colors, shapes, size, weight, symbols, copy, and mate-rials to make your brand stand out.
- Does your branding message resonate with your intended audience?
- Does it express your niche?
- Does it convey the meaning and message you intend?
- Is it real, or is it just a projection of what you wish you could be?
- Pretest your brand messaging.

Your brand becomes a platform for your organization to make an impact for your nonprofit's mission. Good news travels fast. When your organization is consistently related to positive benefits

BENEFITS OF HAVING A BRAND

- Presents your nonprofit as an organization that gets results.

- Identifies you with your niche.

- Gives you a recognizable identity in your community.

- Expresses your organization's values and personality.

- Associates your organization with your cause in the minds of target audiences.

- Saves you advertising money because your name becomes recognizable.

- Increases participation and "esprit de corps" among your supporters.

What to Watch Out for in Nonprofit Branding

- Becoming overly competitive with similar nonprofits. Compete against what is keeping people from making the right choices.

- Placing so much emphasis on enhancing your brand that you neglect your cause.

- Spending too much donor money on increasing the prestige of your brand.

you bring to the lives of the people with whom you connect, they will have trouble not talking about you positively to others.

Clearly Understood Theme Lines

A theme line is a brief sentence that expresses the spirit of your organization. Your theme line needs to be durable enough to last a hundred years or more. Guerrillas don't change their theme lines from year to year like an annual emphasis campaign. Your tag line needs to be tied to your organization's core values and mission. These are issues that don't change until you complete your task. Your theme line supports your brand message and underscores your organization's reputation. The theme becomes attractive to the people who support you because it encapsulates what they believe about your cause in a way that also helps them spread the word. Theme lines build impact for your organization over time. The more you use it, the greater the benefit to your organization.

Your theme line is not a boastful sentence, but it is a not-so-subtle truth that reminds people who you are and what you are doing. If your tag line is based on wishful thinking instead of honest reality, it will undermine you in your quest to accomplish your cause. Think of your theme line as the banner of truth you take into battle in your guerrilla marketing attack. You can create a tag line in only a few words. Try to get the gist of your three-sentence guerrilla mission statement into seven words or less. It is not as hard as it might sound to you. Some of the most effective organizations have discovered the power of a brief and clearly understood tag line.

A tag line is an excellent weapon in your guerrilla marketing arsenal. Put it on all your marketing materials. Your website, brochures, and advertisements can include your tag line. Sometimes a tag line even looks good as part of your logo. Don't stop

Organization	Theme Line
Red Cross	Change a life. Save a life.
Salvation Army	Doing the most good.
St. Jude Hospital	Finding Cures. Saving children.
Breast Cancer Research Foundation	Finding a cure for breast cancer.
March of Dimes	Saving babies, together.
Feeding America	Feeding America's hungry.
Goodwill	Let's go to work!
Easter Seals	Helping people with disabilities gain greater independence.
World Vision	You can help change everything for a child in need.
PTA	Solutions for America's education crisis.
Hands on Network	Volunteers changing lives through service.
Kids in Need	School supplies for the neediest schools.
National Park Foundation	Caring for our 391 parks.

when you have developed a clearly understood theme line, create a meme also.

A Meme Is an Idea Virus about Your Organization

Way back, at the beginning of history, Uba the caveman felt helpless for his hungry family, wondering how he could get food to feed them. Earlier, down at a nearby stream, Uba spent the entire day trying to grab the slippery fish swimming in the water using his bare hands. He couldn't catch a thing. Distraught about his

FROM THE FRONT LINES

NAME: Nancy Schwartz

WEBSITE: GettingAttention.org

"An effective tag line differentiates you from your competitors while expressing your organization's personality and adding consistency to your marketing and communications. And because it's positive, it generates a positive response from audiences.

When your tag line does work, it has the potential to become a perennial icon of your organization, lifting your brand from the commonplace to the unforgettable. Think *A mind is a terrible thing to waste*, from the United Negro College Fund.

And beware, nonprofit communicators. The absence of a tag line or the use of an ineffective one (and that's 72 percent of you) puts your nonprofit at a competitive disadvantage in soliciting funding, building your staff and base, and increasing use of your programs, services, and products."

situation, Uba sat down on a rock by the opening of a cave to rest and consider what he was going to do. Then, over his shoulder, Uba noticed that a beam of sunlight was streaming into the cave revealing something on the inside of the cave on the walls. As he entered the cave, looking at the wall, he had an epiphany. In a matter of seconds he knew what to do. He excitedly rushed back to the stream, confident he could now feed his family.

What did Uba see? On the wall of the cave, he saw a simple drawing of a figure of a caveman standing by a flowing stream of water spearing a fish with a sharpened stick. Uba saw the image and understood immediately how to give his family a tasty dinner.

That's only half the story. There is another cave dweller in the tale, Guerrilla Grog, the nonprofit marketer and community activist who made the cave paintings as a community service to other cavemen. He may have saved the entire tribe with his food-gathering education campaign. The simple behavior-changing message Uba saw was a meme created by Grog, the guerrilla social marketer.

You can get in touch with your inner Guerrilla Grog also by creating memes for your nonprofit organization. A meme (rhymes with theme) is a term for a form of communication that sails through people relationship networks like a hot knife going through butter. At first, you may find it hard to grasp what a meme is because the concept seems unfamiliar. The name sounds obscure, but memes are not complicated to understand. As you train yourself to spot them, it will eventually become difficult not to notice them. You are already an experienced meme-ologist, you just don't know it yet. People have been using memes since the prehistoric days of Uba and Grog.

Memes are:

- The lowest common denominator of an idea, a basic unit of communication.
- Extreme simplicity. Easily understandable in two seconds.
- Powerfully effective on the unconscious mind.
- Born through research.
- Mental software that motivates a behavior.
- Messages that quickly gain critical mass as people willingly spread them.

Memes are not the same as themes. A theme line is a set of words that summarizes what you stand for that you can use for ten years or forever. A meme is your main benefit or behavioral message expressed visually or verbally in a way that conveys the entire idea. Memes in social marketing have influenced people's behaviors in ways you no doubt will recognize. Here are a couple of successful memes to illustrate our point.

1. The United States Forest Service launched the now familiar meme "Only you can prevent forest fires" and the character Smokey the Bear in 1944. Since that time, awareness about fire prevention in America's forests has improved. In fact, it's hard to go camping without thinking about (and perhaps looking for) Smokey the Bear. If you happen to meet a real bear in the forest while camping, as you fall to the ground and pretend to be dead, you may still be thinking of naming him Smokey.

2. In 1980, the Crime Prevention Coalition of America organization developed McGruff the Crime Dog who said the meme, "Take a bite out of crime!" The campaign meme is still active in the minds of people today. McGruff appointed everyone who heard his message as community deputy crime watchdog. Now when many people see an unfamiliar person in their neighborhood, they unconsciously wonder if this will be their moment to bite crime in the backside.

Both these messages are no doubt familiar to you. Nobody has to explain to you what these memes mean. Both call you to take action to care for the world. Both the text and the cartoon characters themselves are memorable memes. We don't even have to show you the pictures of the characters, they are right there now on the frontal lobe of your mind. Memes are powerful communication that spread fast and free for the nonprofits that know how to launch them. Any organization can develop a cheesy slogan, but guerrillas know how to develop and launch a meme into the marketplace and get people buzzing their cause.

If you want to find the meme for your organization, the place to look is not in how clever you can be. It is being creative about understanding the wants, needs, and fears of your target audience. Creativity for art inspires people's souls. Guerrilla creativity inspires people to take action.

Don't Try to Be an Artist!

Nonguerrillas believe they can inspire people and move them with the quality of their artwork and the cleverness of their copy. But true guerrillas know better than to chase after the attention of people with art, because art is often poor at motivating people to act. Guerrillas are usually more skilled at moving people to act using creativity than even master artists who are very skilled at art. Why? Because most artists can't sell! For example, master artist Vincent Van Gogh was an inspiring artist but he was notoriously lousy at selling his work (something he left up to his brother Theodorus to do for him). Van Gogh's art might move you, but he (and his brother) had problems moving people to buy his art. Even now people often don't buy into the ideas of the artist; they buy the idea of buying the art. They don't often buy into the artists values as much as they invest in the market value of the artist's work. Your organization doesn't have the luxury of being a starving artist at the same time you are a hungry nonprofit. So don't become a slave to creative artistry that can't yield a response from the people you want to reach.

Why be concerned about selling in the nonprofit context? Nonguerrillas don't know that advocacy is a fancy word for marketing and marketing is a fancy word for selling. If you want to influence people, if you want to persuade people to change their behaviors, you are a marketer. All nonprofits are hawking something, behaviors, ideas, programs, services, products, etc. Put your creative efforts into developing a meme that gets a response.

You don't need to spend a lot of dollars getting a slogan written by an agency. The Nike "Just Do It" slogan is not a meme. Meanwhile, the National Institutes of Health's "Just Say No!" message is a meme. "Just do it" tells you to do something, but it is intentionally vague about what "it" is. It's a clever slogan. It was an excellent advertising campaign. The line is memorable to most people because of the millions of dollars spent creating advertising impressions on targeted audiences. But on the other hand, "Just say no" is just as well known to people and significantly less was spent on introducing that line to your brain. And furthermore, it tells you exactly what to do. You can take the Nike slogan and apply it to any context and hardly even think about the product. You can't do that with the "Just say no" message. Even when you use it as a joke, you know where the message came from. Memes are very economical. Memes don't always have to be used as promotional content either. The word "supersize" is a meme. The message is simple to understand. To make something super-anything is dramatic. The behavior suggested by the idea spreads as fast as the fast food spreads the backsides of those who eat it.

You can be a master artist and create powerful memes, but for them to work, you need to focus on selling the behavior you want. Professional country musician Dave Carroll did just that. He worked an entire year trying to get United Airlines to pay to fix his demolished Taylor guitar that was broken by careless United baggage handlers who threw it out of the luggage compartment of the plane and broke it into pieces on the tarmac at the airport in Chicago in 2008. Dave created a meme in the form of a country song, "United Breaks Guitars," that got 4,500,000 views on YouTube in the summer of 2009 just three weeks after it was posted. In the song, Carroll asks for and got the response he was looking for from the intended audience (United): "You broke it, you should fix it. You're liable, just admit it." In addition to solving his guitar woes, the song (and meme) helped draw attention to Carroll, spiking sales of his CDs, increasing his performance fees, and bringing in many lucrative offers. Behold the power of the meme.

Five places to look to find the creative idea for your meme.

1. Understand the problems faced by your target audience.
2. Look at ways your nonprofit solves their problems.
3. Study your benefits list.
4. Think about what is the inherent drama of your message.
5. The unique aspects of your nonprofit

Nonprofit Memes

Look at the memes in the chart on page 254 and learn from them. They focus on behaviors and getting people to take action. Just as action is the purpose of guerrilla marketing, a meme is at the heart of the action. The memes below focus on the desired action they want prospects to take.

Organization/Cause	Meme	Observation
Crime Prevention Coalition of America	McGruff the Crime Dog and line "Take a bite out of crime."	Turns everyone into an instant crime watch dog.
American Red Cross	The Red Cross symbol	A universal symbol adapted for an organization.
The Lance Armstrong Foundation	"Live Strong" message and yellow rubber wristbands	Motivates and inspires people on a very sensitive subject.
U.S. Department of Transportation	Crash Test Dummies	Only a dummy doesn't buckle up!
Partnership for a Drug-Free America	"This is your brain. This is your brain on drugs."	People may joke about it, but they talk about it and they usually agree with the message.
Big Brothers and Big Sisters of America	This simple message "Be a big brother" (or sister)	Great because the meme is also the name of the organization.
United Negro College Fund	"A mind is a terrible thing to waste."	What a powerful motivational message for donors, supporters, and the primary target audience.
Driver Safety	"Baby on Board" sign	Not a nonprofit organization, but effective and behavioral nonetheless.
SafePlace	SafePlace (name and icon)	Tells children fleeing abusive situations exactly what they need to know.
Meals on Wheels Association of America	"Meals on Wheels"	Dramatic message about getting food to hungry people, using wheels. Grog would be proud.

Organization/Cause	Meme	Observation
U.S. Department of Justice	"Amber Alert"	The story of Amber Hagerman, who was abducted and murdered in January of 1996, dramatizes the need for everyone to help find a recently missing child.
Salvation Army	Santa Claus and bell ringers in front of stores and on sidewalks	It's Christmas, time to give back.
Newman's Own Foundation	"Newman's Own" salad dressing and other food products	The concept of buying food products with the profits going to charity was taken to a whole new level. The meme is simple enough; keeps people talking and acting. The benefit exchange is tasty too!
Goodwill Industries	Goodwill Stores	Donate or buy things and help others. The name says it all.
Muscular Dystrophy Association	"Jerry's Kids"	Help Jerry Lewis, help MDA, help children.
Keep America Beautiful	The Weeping Indian	From the 1971 anti-littering campaign. An original meme and pioneering social marketing project
Various awareness advocacy groups.	Wearing awareness ribbons	Almost cliché now. Changing colors represent different causes (Yellow = troops, Pink = breast cancer, Black = mourning, etc.).

Organization/Cause	Meme	Observation
United States Forest Service	Smokey the Bear, "Only you can prevent forest fires"	The reasons for acting and the actions required hardly need to be explained.
Harvard School of Public Health's Center for Health Communication	"Designated Driver"	Impossible to miss the point of the message or the desired behavior.
Church fundraising	Passing the plate in church	You know what to do the second someone passes it to you.

CHAPTER 16

Cultivating Winning Relationships for Your Nonprofit

THE CEMENT THAT HOLDS EVERYTHING TOGETHER in nonprofit work is not the money you raise; it's not even your mission statement. What holds everything together is relationships. If you are not focused on cultivating good relationships, networking to involve more people in your organization won't help hold things together, it may just make things stickier. Nonguerrillas fail to understand the value of their relationships. Just as most businesses treat their customers, they ignore their contacts to death. They take people for granted because they are focused on their cause to the point that they are blinded to anything else. They are focused on what Bob Beaudine, author of the book *The Power of WHO: You Already Know Everyone You Need to Know* (Center Street, 2009), calls the "What" instead of the "Who." While seeking to accomplish their goals, Beaudine says, "Too many people start their dream search with a misstep. They focus on the 'What' (what they want) and neglect the 'Who' (those special friends or friends of friends who can help them)." It is as important for nonprofits to have a strategy for developing relationships as it is to have a plan for fundraising development.

In the for-profit sector, business deals yield profits that create the monetary capital that makes the economy function. In the nonprofit world, the collective civil and social effort of people creates the social capital that fuels the work of the social sector. Harvard professor Robert Putnam believes social capital is declining today because of changes in society. He says people are becoming increasingly disconnected from one another because they no longer participate in civic and social structures the way they used to in years past. In his book *Bowling Alone* (Simon and Shuster, 2000), Putnam observes that participation in societal groups like: PTA, churches, political parties, and even bowling leagues has disintegrated. He claims people don't bowl in leagues together as much anymore because they are less socially minded than they used to be and prefer to be on their own. Therefore, they are "bowling alone." He believes people may give money to nonprofit organizations, but they prefer not to participate actively in them because the power of people networks is in decline.

But contrary to what Dr. Putnam sees, social capital does not appear to be deteriorating today—quite the opposite seems to be true. Rather than being in decline, social and civic involvement seems to be experiencing revival recently. For example, social networking sites have brought people closer together to their long-lost friends, distant family members, high school and college alumni, global business colleagues, and even better—their kids. Facebook alone, with its 250 million users, has made the world a much smaller, more interconnected place. Watching the news for civic social capital, political involvement is on the rise among all generations. In the 2008 elections, a record 130 million people turned out to vote. If social capital is actually in decline, and people want to be left to *bowl alone*, the people in society don't seem to be aware of it. Baylor sociologist Dr. Rodney Stark says in his book *What Americans Really Believe*, (Baylor Press, 2008) that religious participation is not in decline. Rather, America has never been so active in church. In 1776 only 17 percent of the country belonged to a local congregation; today, 69 percent of Americans are affiliated with a church. Stark says if people are not involved in bowling leagues, it may merely be because they prefer to be involved with fantasy football leagues, where more than 35 million people participate. If social capital is actually on the rise, your organization can be among the first to understand how to take advantage of its power to make the world a better place by learning how to cultivate winning relationships. It would be a tragic mistake to act as if social capital is in decline in a period when it could be entering a golden age.

Making Connections

Nonguerrillas complain that people don't respond to outreach the way they used to in the past. But if the tactics that used to work for them are less effective now, it may be because people are changing what they expect from nonprofit organizations. People today want more two-way relationships and less one-way communications. The only thing that is needed for many nonprofits is to try another way of relating to people. The reason outreach isn't working for some is because organizations are not paying enough attention to the people they already know. Guerrillas know that if you spend more time thinking about who you already know than you do thinking about who you would like to know, you will find you have a sphere of influence that is more than powerful enough to accomplish your goals. It's not who you know as much as how well you know who you know. Instead of putting 100 percent of your efforts trying to identify new people with outreach, spend 10 percent on prospecting, 30 percent following up on the prospects you have in your database, and 60 percent of your efforts on assimilating and cultivating deeper relationships with the people who are already involved in your organization.

When you think of networking, don't think of electronic grids—think about people groups, kinship clans, colleagues, friends, mentors; think relationships. Nonguerrillas spend too much time thinking about how they can get to know the right people with the right amount of influence (or cash). But just as networking expert Bob Beaudine says, you already know all the people you need to know to succeed at what you hope to accomplish. If you already know everyone you need to know, then you are already in contact with the person of influence you need to know by virtue of your own existing network. There are more resources than anyone can handle available to those who know how to relate to their own networks. Each person you know is like a Rolodex of people contacts that are waiting to help you if you build your relationship with them. You are not only connected to the people in your network, you are connected to the people in your friends' networks. You can't see all the ways you are connected to other people, but that doesn't mean the connections are not accessible to you.

If you knew for certain that right now in your existing pool of contacts is the right person with the right connections that can help you do the most good, wouldn't you want to know how to connect with them? You could be talking to the exact person you need to meet in a matter of just a few connections through your existing friends. It is mostly a question of asking them to help you. This is possible because of the way relationships multiply across networks of people.

It has been suggested that there are only six degrees of separation between you and anyone else in the universe. Duncan J. Watts, author of *Six Degrees: The Science of a Connected Age* (W.W. Norton, 2003) says between e-mail, cell phones, satellites, friends, family, highways, and airports we are continuously surrounded and subjected to a world of networks. Imagine if you only had a network of 12 people you knew personally, if each of your 12 friends also had 12 other friends, then the number of potential contacts within your reach (through your friends) would expand out to 144 people. Continue to do the math and you will see that in just six degrees of distance from your original friends, your actual network would be almost 3 million people.

> It has been suggested that there are only six degrees of separation between you and anyone else in the universe. Researchers now claim it could be as small as three people.

- 1 X 12 = 12
- 12 X 12 = 144
- 144 X 12 = 1,728
- 1,728 X 12 = 20,736
- 20,736 X 12 = 248,832
- 248,832 X 12 = 2,985,984

People have far more relationships than just 12 friends. Think of the hundreds of friends and associates you may have who also have hundreds of friends. People are more connected to one another than they know. In the real world people have an average of 250 personal contacts. If there are six degrees of separation between all people, multiplying 250 connections to the sixth power would actually yield more than 244 trillion potential contacts—more people than exist. Talk about redundancy in networks! Recently, researchers for a French mobile phone company conducted an experiment that showed the degrees of separation between people is even smaller; they claim it could be as small as three degrees of relationships between people.

Thinking of networking this way, you realize you don't need to expand your network and find that next new person as much as you need to pay more attention to the network you already have. If you neglected just 12 of your friends or contacts, you would be shutting your connections off with at least 3 million people. All this points to the truth that time spent cultivating relationships is time well invested for the success of your nonprofit. The numbers make networking seem so easy, but it doesn't work as well in real life. Why aren't the people you have in your database of contacts already helping you accomplish your goals? The answer is simple. They don't want to. Or better, they don't trust you enough to help you because your relationship ties with them are too weak. People guard their own social capital as closely as any banker guards his monetary capital. People don't want to put all the invested effort they have put into their relationships on the line just to help someone they hardly know. The only way they will open up their Rolodex and connect you to the people in their network is for them to like you and trust you as a sincere friend. So your task as a guerrilla is to spend time and effort in getting better at loving people and cultivating good relationships with them. Loving people? This is charity work, after all.

What Do You Need to Know About People?

If you plan to implement the simple strategy of putting 10 percent of your efforts on outreach prospecting and 90 percent of your time cultivating better relationships with your new and existing contacts, you will be greatly aided by keeping a file of all your contacts and recording information about them in your database. Use whatever resources you have. Computer contact management software is the best, but even if you kept the information in a recipe file box, you would be doing more than most nonguerrillas do. Record details about your contacts to help you become a better friend to the people you know. Include the following data for each one:

- Contact information
- Family Information
- Education
- Background
- Special interests and hobbies
- Lifestyle
- Religious preference
- Social involvement
- Nature of your relationship with them
- How you came to know them
- Notes from all your contacts and communication with them

30 Networking Habits for Nonprofits

We have made the case that networking begins by strengthening your existing relationships, but you still need to spend about 10 percent of your efforts at finding new people. You shouldn't stop looking for new relationships, but you might as well stop if you are only going to ignore your contacts. Guerrillas are always looking for ways to make more impact on the bottom line. Just as guerrillas focus on profits and not sales, nonprofit guerrillas are focused on relationships instead of outreach. There is nothing wrong with reaching out as long as your emphasis is on the right things.

Here are 30 networking basics that will help you find, meet, and relate to new people.

1. Join clubs and associations.
2. Collect directories from agencies, companies, foundations.
3. Mingle at events and community gatherings.
4. Make personal contacts by e-mail, mail, or phone with people after you meet them.
5. Regularly schedule face-to-face meetings for coffee or lunch with new contacts.
6. Give speeches or lead workshops.
7. Contact the people you read about in articles, magazines, and books.
8. Give your contact information to people in the form of business cards, brochures, fliers, etc.
9. Submit articles to websites, blogs, and periodicals.
10. Join new gatherings of people you find listed in classified advertisements, meet-ups, and tweet-ups.
11. Give away something free in exchange for contact information.
12. Initiate conversations with people sitting near you when using public transportation.
13. Meet people from other organizations at conventions and conferences.
14. Regularly introduce yourself to people using your elevator speech.
15. Keep friendship on the agenda, not only your business, when talking to people.
16. Make eye contact and build a warm rapport with everyone.
17. Learn to be relaxed and confident in public settings.
18. Be emotionally engaging and have a sense of humor.
19. Don't dominate conversations; listen and be a conversationalist.

20. Get over your jitters and try not to appear nervous when meeting new people.
21. Know what you are talking about, keep your facts straight.
22. Be energetic when you talk and have good control of your voice.
23. Offer your business card in return when others offer theirs.
24. Make notes while a new contact is still fresh on your mind.
25. Edit your contacts and develop plans for follow-up later each day.
26. Have a long-range plan for staying in touch with all the people you meet.
27. Strive to remember names and personal details as much as possible.
28. Celebrate birthdays and other important dates with people.
29. Stay in touch by sending articles and useful information tailored to the interests of your contacts.
30. Keep records of your contacts and conversations so you can continue to learn about people.

What to Do About the Other Guys

Don't let the name fool you, guerrillas don't treat other organizations like they are adversaries who need to be conquered. Guerrilla marketing is about outsmarting and outmaneuvering the competition, but guerrillas are constantly doing reconnaissance looking for partners, tapping into people networks, and building winning relationships. If you value the individual relationships in your network, people you know will open their networks up to you. The same principle applies when networking with other organizations and companies. Guerrillas don't worry about competition, they think about creating fusion. Most nonprofits know about partnerships and sponsors. But when we speak about fusion partners we are not speaking about permanent or formal partnerships. Don't think marriage—think fling. If it works out, you have something great; if not, well, "You'll always have Paris!" We are not talking about seeking cooperate grants or donations either. Fusion marketing happens when two marketers are seeking the same audience yet have separate objectives. You don't have to create a contract, and probably won't need to get your trustees vote about your fusion partners. Fusion partners are ad hoc relationships. Some are long term, most are limited in scope.

Fusion partners say:

- I'll scratch your back if you will scratch mine.
- I will link to your website if you link to mine.
- I will give your business card to my clients if you give mine to your customers.
- We can host our event at the same time in the same location.

Fusion marketing isn't about bartering, it is about seeking the mutual success of your partners. Think about people who can help you get the word out that want your help getting their word out.

Make a Bigger Splash with Fusion Marketing

Nonprofit guerrilla Ken Surritte of WaterisLife.com leads a nonprofit that provides water purification filter straws to people in countries where clean water is hard to come by. His entire operation runs with one staff member (Ken) and three volunteers, yet through relationship-building and fusion partnerships, he is making a bigger splash with his pure water charity. Ken has all the usual strategies for raising funds and identifying sponsors that other nonprofits have, but he also is a fusion marketing genius. Guerrilla Ken found partners to help him brand his nonprofit to people who also reach his target. Partners help Ken reach his audience, and he helps them reach the media tying in their organization with the compelling story of helping children get access to clean water. Everyone wins with fusion marketing.

Here are some examples of Ken's fusion partnership successes.

- Jason Sadler, who founded iwearyourshirt.com, a company entirely built on one guerrilla marketing tactic, wearing a logo shirt in public, promoted the clean water charity by wearing a shirt with the nonprofit's name. Though Ken paid Jason to wear his logo shirt, Jason continued to talk about WaterisLife.com to audiences who came to hear his speeches about his business concept long after the promotion was over. Jason liked Ken so much, he even personally raised money within his own family members for the organization.

- Joel Comm, author of *Twitter Power: How to Dominate Your Market One Tweet at a Time* (Wiley, 2009), became a fusion partner with Ken. Joel is a well-known social media guru who invented the first celebrity-packed Twitter Tweet-a-thon fundraiser just to help Ken with his WaterisLife.com. Besides raising more than $20,000 in a few hours, Ken was putting his name in front of thousands of people in his targeted audience using fusion marketing, and he didn't spend a dime on promotion.

- Without using his advertising budget, Ken also connected with the NBA Chicago Bulls team, creating a fusion partnership website PureWaterStraw.com to promote access to clean water. Now the entire NBA is being challenged by players and teams to provide pure water solutions to needy children around the world.

There are many competitors who are not potential candidates for fusion marketing. Some of these have huge marketing budgets. You may not be able to outspend them, but you can compete with them in other ways with the help of your fusion marketing partners. Ken could never afford to pay the NBA to promote his nonprofit. He didn't have the budget to engage marketing gurus like Joel and Jason to help him, but through the power of sincere relationships and fusion marketing, it happened anyway.

Fusion marketing is co-marketing, or piggy-back marketing. There are multiple groups and individuals engaged in marketing to your target audience who would become excellent partners in marketing your organization. Not only are there fundraising partners available, there are partners to be found to help you in your advocacy and branding. For-profit guerrillas will also be your most willing and aggressive allies in helping your nonprofit with marketing.

Train your mind to see potential partners for fusion marketing:

- Consider other organizations and companies that also reach your audience.
- Expand relationships, seeing multiple opportunities.
- Build synergy with other marketing campaigns.
- Look for the "we" in winning.
- Demonstrate trust and learn to trust others.
- Share information with like-minded organizations.
- Though you are small, don't be afraid to think big and pitch ideas to larger organizations and companies.

> Proving you care is paying attention to the details. When things go wrong, see to it that the donor comes out on top.

CHAPTER 17

Seven Golden Rules for Fundraising Success

FOR NONGUERRILLAS, FUNDRAISING IS A MYSTERY that is about as unpredictable as the weather. One minute they are flooded with donations, the next they are in the midst of a serious drought. One day they are shoveling in an avalanche of money, the next month they are sending out the storm warnings and heading to their financial storm shelters. Guerrillas are not taken by surprise with the winds of financial change. They know they can become a fundraising force

> By touching on human emotions and acting out upon these Golden Rules, your organization will understand how to get maximum contributions for it's fundraising efforts.

of nature because they understand the rules of fundraising success and apply them in their development outreach. Just as there are rules in nature that can be used to predict the weather, there are rules in marketing that can take the guesswork out of fundraising. Guerrillas know the Golden Rules of fundraising success.

Fundraising success is not only about what you do to get people to give. It is what you do to make your nonprofit an organization worthy of receiving the support of people. For your cause to succeed, you need to find a lot of people who care about your work. You want the people who support you to do more than write checks, you want them to take ownership of the mission themselves. This can not happen until you are thinking from the perspective of your donors. The Golden Rules below will also play a part in guiding you as you develop your marketing materials. Success will require your time and effort, but as you practice and become more familiar with these rules, they will become second nature.

Rule 1: Know Your Donors

The basis of good fundraising is the treatment and cultivation of donors and the ability to ask them to support your organization in proportion to their ability to give. You must therefore know your donors as well as you possibly can. The foundation for having this kind of relationship is quality research and good information. Having a good knowledge of your donors and their contributing habits is key to persuading them to donate their money. When times get tough, they may tend to donate only their time, but it is up to you to keep them supporting your organization financially. This challenge is one you must overcome. 52 percent of nonprofits have their funding cut during a recession. The sad part about that fact is there is a much higher percentage increase in aid requests during this same difficult time period. Remember how we discussed in Chapter 5 that guerrillas focus on people? It will take time and imagination to figure out how to bridge that gap.

> On average 10,000 Baby Boomers will retire each day from 2010 until 2030. How will this example of "knowledge of donors" affect your organization's thinking and planning?

Individual donations are the backbone of nonprofit support. Ninety percent of most nonprofit funding comes from individuals. Grants, endowments, corporate gifts, and special fundraising events can never replace the amount of support that comes from individuals. Although the small amounts written on individual donors' checks seem insignificant compared to larger checks with lots of zeros on them from major sponsors and grantors, they do add up. Do not overlook the importance of these types of donors. That is why a donor list with much more information than names, addresses, and phone numbers is important. If you're thinking like a guerrilla, your list will have details about your donors' lifestyles such as where they eat, vacation, play, hobbies, achievements, favorite sports teams, and other small but important details. Can you imagine the time it takes to gather all that information? Well, you should, because it is part of paying the dues of being a guerrilla.

Once you have your donor list, you are ready to impress them with your knowledge and love of people. This interest in people will be evident in your marketing, and in the way you treat your donors. You will become a master communicator by listening (a guerrilla trait) and scratching below the surface to find the deeper connections that you both share. People want to know they are helping to bring about a positive change. They are not as concerned about everything your organization does as they are with what your organization does through them. People don't give because of who you are, they give because of who they are. They may generously donate money or volunteer their time, but deep down their prime interest is in seeing what impact they can make. This does not mean they are selfish, but they do want to feel important when assisting you and your cause.

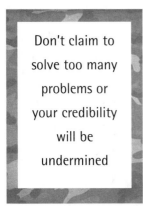

Don't claim to solve too many problems or your credibility will be undermined

Make them feel important by recognizing them at a social gathering. If your organization is in a large city, treat them to a sporting event and mention them over the Jumbotron or loudspeaker while they sit in a skybox. If you are not able to do that, then invite them to a dinner or cocktail party to mingle with other donors. This interaction will strengthen the reason why they gave and will make everyone feel good about what they did. Invite the media to take photos and possibly do a write-up in a local magazine or newspaper. Even handing out a plaque or award will show your donors and others that you care. Still too much for your organization's budget? It can be as simple as sending a card out on a holiday or birthday.

When you understand your donors well, you can look out for their interest in making an impact. The American Heart Association has a program in schools called Jump Rope for Heart. They partner up with large companies such as Subway and the NBA to offer incentives which in turn attract donors. They know that reaching out to even the youngest person is a smart move because they can get repeated donations year after year after year. Little Austin and Blake will ask mom, dad, grandma, neighbors, and anyone else for small donations so they can win tickets to a professional basketball game, wouldn't you? You may not be able to do these things with all your donors, but when you figure out the value of that donor over their lifetime, you will be more inclined to go out of your way to keep them donating. Knowledge of this rule is golden.

Use the worksheet on page 274 to see the long-term benefits of every donor.

Rule 2: Educate Your Donors

Nonguerrillas make the mistake of not helping donors understand the work they are doing. They figure what can a lay person really understand about their work? They may issue reports to their donors, but their supporters might not understand what the figures signify in relation to the stated mission of the organization. Guerrillas know the meaning of the adage "What people are not up on, they are down on." They make sure they educate their supporters, because an educated donor is a happy donor. It is tough for people to give their money to an organization when they have fears that the money may be spent unwisely. Some of your donors may have the mistaken notion that giving to your nonprofit is merely fueling a maintenance program that never really solves any problems. Who wants to give to an impersonal maintenance program? Guerrillas reassure their supporters about why giving to their organization is a smart move. Education calms fears and improves communication.

Education also builds trust and assures your supporters that all is on course. They trust you because you stay in touch with them and let them know what their donations have done. You send

THE VALUE OF A DONOR

The American Heart Association is a nonprofit that focuses on the value of donors. Their youth marketing campaign is aimed largely at elementary and middle schools. When they have a fundraiser at a school, they may get half the students to donate a minimum of $10 each. In a school with 1,000 students they can earn $5,000 per year. If for some reason the principal, physical education teacher, or PTA loses interest in their cause and stops assisting with fundraising, then the AHA will lose thousands of dollars per year needed for research and funding. In ten years they can lose up to $50,000 or more. That's why they send marketing directors out to the schools to keep communication and sense of purpose alive.

WORKSHEET

If you continue to provide good service and quality, how long will the donor contribute to your cause? _____

How much will this donor contribute to your organization per year? _____

Multiply the amount of money donated per year by the length of time this donor will contribute. _____

The result is the lifetime value of this donor. _____

This number should be engraved on a plaque to share with your staff and board members. It will help you focus on the critical elements of building up your organization.

brochures with colorful pictures and testimonials of how your organization changes lives. You reach out to them and keep the lines of communication open, not always asking for help, but showing the results of their support. Guerrillas work hard to stay in touch with donors because they know the result of their hard work is a base of supporters who give joyfully. Follow-up is an important part of your guerrilla marketing attack. If you want your organization to survive and thrive (especially during a recession), this is a must. Organizations that follow up with their donors within the first 48 hours of their giving and then again three to five weeks later create a unique opportunity for even deeper support. If you follow up with this type of intensity, you will be proving that you really care about your donors. This usually leads to strong relationships which can also lead to more referrals for you. You also eliminate the perceived risks of donating to your cause as mentioned earlier. You can't offer a money-back guarantee for donations, but you can offer peace of mind by showing your deep commitment to service. List the names of your current donors and the many others who have helped. Your reputation brings credibility, and credibility is free—so leverage it as much as you can.

Rule 3: Help Donors Find Personal Fulfillment

People want to make a difference. They are seeking personal fulfillment through supporting your cause. Nonprofits that are aware of the psychology of their supporters are far ahead of other organizations when it comes to attracting support. When your organization can find a way to help people solve their problem of finding fulfillment though charity work, they will be more willing to jump on board to help your cause. They support you because they can feel good about themselves while making the world a better place. The easy part for them is they only have to write a check. The hard part for you is coming up with a creative way to show the need for donations that also appeals to the perceived needs of the donor.

Let's say your organization is a youth tackle football league. What ways can you attract people to help your organization with your financial need? You have to think outside the box. Some examples of problems you are helping to solve could be, "lowering childhood obesity by letting the big boys play" or "keeping kids active in sports not gangs" or "bringing families together by building values." The list can go on and on. The point is you are providing messages of hope. You are making the public aware of a problem, and you are offering a solution. This way of thinking will help you create interest in people that may not have otherwise wanted to donate to your cause. If you can find a way to present to them a legitimate problem as well as a way to solve it, then you have come very close to winning the battle.

> Don't claim to solve too many problems or your credibility will be undermined.

Advertising expert Alvin Eicoff once stated, "Set forth the problem. Explain the solution. And then demonstrate why your specific product or service best provides that solution." He also said, "The first visual and audio elements of a commercial should state the problem clearly and concisely. The potential customer (donor) should feel a strong personal identification with the problem presented, reflexively nodding his or her head in acknowledgment." This concept can be applied to other parts of your marketing such as brochures, social networking, direct mailings, conferences, as well as a host of other weapons in your arsenal. Your donors will be more likely to contribute if they feel involved. Be assured that if you are solving a problem (particularly one that affects them), they will be more personally engaged with your mission. With involvement comes momentum, and that is the catalyst that propels your marketing.

Usually we do not go looking for problems, but rather problems find us. If that is the case, then half your work is already done for you—just pay attention to the needs at your front door. Spot the one problem that your organization can be positioned to solve with certainty and watch people come to you. Know your donors and their need for personal fulfillment, and link your message to solutions that are attractive to them. This rule is so important to your organization it's golden.

Rule 4: Build Trusting Donor Relationships

Can there be honesty in marketing? Guerrillas know the answer to that question is YES. But do the people you are asking to donate believe it? A recent national poll showed that a whopping 53 percent of Americans say they sense a "feeling of deception" about marketing. This distrust of marketing is also transferred to the outreach marketing conducted by nonprofits. Some organizations do exaggerate their results and overstate needs when trying to recruit support. Guerrillas are honest in all their marketing because they know that even if their marketing is 99 percent honest and 1 percent dishonest, that 1 percent will stand out in the minds of their target audience. All the marketing spin in the world will not make up for the smallest exaggeration of the truth. A reputation that took years to build could come crashing down in a matter of seconds if you're not careful. There is a very fine line between exaggeration and dishonesty, and once you cross it, it is very difficult, if not impossible, to regain the trust of your donors.

We know what you must be thinking. You just stepped up to bat and already there are two strikes against you thanks to a few seedy marketers. And you're exactly right. Too many others have fast-talked their way into getting what they want while leaving their donors disappointed. Their dishonesty was exposed, but the damage has been done. There is a huge gap for you to fill, and none of it is your fault. So what do you do? Examine every facet of your marketing closely. Is every sentence completely honest? Does the truth ring out from every word? Is your organization's theme truly believable or does it mimic the hyped tone other organizations use in their marketing? Can people see evidence of what you have done? What about your visuals? Are they fake looking? Are the models smiling in situations where people don't ordinarily smile? Be careful not to set off the disbelief alarms. Pretend the world's biggest cynic is sitting on your shoulder. Every time you create a marketing piece, listen to the cynic. He is there to make sure you stay on the straight and narrow path and to make sure you are following this golden rule.

Rule 5: Respect Your Donors

Most nonprofits say they care about their donors, but guerrilla marketers prove it. Your marketing can say all the right words and tell donors how important they are to you, but unless you take the concrete steps beyond those words they won't believe you. Guerrillas know that there's a world of difference between donor care and donor attention. Many companies lavish attention upon their donors, but only guerrillas excel at caring and knowing how to make them feel sincerely cared for.

Following is a list you can use to show your donors and prospects that you sincerely care.

- Prepare a written document outlining the principles of your service. This should come from the top of the organization, but everyone should know what it says and be ready to live up to it.

- Establish support systems that give clear instructions for gaining and maintaining service superiority. They help you to give more to donors by solving problems before they arise.
- Develop a precise measurement of superb customer service and reward employees who practice it consistently.
- Be certain that your passion for customer service runs rampant throughout your organization and not just at the top. Everyone should feel it.
- Do all that you must to instill in employees reverence for donors. They should see how this golden rule relates to your fundraising and your organization's future.
- Be genuinely committed to providing more customer service excellence than anyone else in the industry. This commitment must be so powerful that every one of your donors can sense it.
- Be sure that everyone in your organization who deals with donors pays very close attention to them. Each donor, or volunteer for that matter, should feel unique and special after they've contacted you or been contacted by you.
- Ask questions of your donors, then listen carefully to their answers. Ask them to expand upon their answers.
- Stay in touch with your donors. Do it with letters, postcards, e-mail, newsletters, phone calls, surveys, and, if you can, by attendance at trade shows and fundraising events.
- Nurture human bonds as well as a business bond with donors and prospects. Do favors for them. Educate them. Help them. Give gifts. Play favorites. Take them out to the ball game or the opera. Your donors deserve to be treated this special.
- Recognize that your donors have needs and expectations as well as you do. You've got to meet their needs and exceed their expectations. Always? Always.

- Share information with people on the front lines. The American Heart Association has a community board with members who meet regularly to talk about improving their service or meeting goals. Information sharing is easier than ever with the internet and other technology. Share information with donors and board members by having a website loaded with helpful data. More and more this is becoming mandatory.
- Because donors are humans, observe birthdays and anniversaries. Constant communication should be your goal.
- Consider holding "mixers" so volunteers and donors can get to know your employees, or the people they are helping. Mixers are breeding grounds for human bonds.
- Act on the knowledge that what donors value most are attention, dependability, promptness, and competence. They just love being referred to by their name. Don't you?

Proving you care is paying attention to the details. When things go wrong, see to it that the donor comes out on top. It is easy to appreciate a grateful donor, but your organization's character will shine brightly when you deal correctly with the donor who complains. Guerrillas know that paying close attention to a complaining donor can be an asset to their organization. Studies show that for every complaint you hear, there are 24 that you won't hear about. Be alert for consistent complaint patterns and make the necessary adjustments. Verbal apologies don't cost you anything and neither do written ones. Do all you can to eliminate complaints and you will be proving once again that you care about your donors. This golden rule tells you never to leave things up to fate.

Rule 6: Focus on Current Supporters

Why do you think that it costs five times as much to raise a donation from a new donor than from an existing one? The answer is easy . . . because the price is high to find a new donor while the price is free to find an existing one. Isn't it true that it is easier and less expensive to renew a magazine subscription than to attract a new subscriber? That is why it is so important to keep in touch with your current donors. This has the effect over time of constantly increasing donations while reducing your marketing investment. You already have a list of your donors. Go back to it often to update information on them. Keep communicating with them so when it's time to give, it will be easy for you to ask. Donations may start off low, but over time those repeat donors will give more as you develop that relationship. It does not come easy, but you are practicing great guerrilla marketing to help that average donor become a major contributor.

Your donor list will be there again when it comes time to call upon the donors of Christmas past. Those are people who contributed a few years ago, but for some reason stopped. Maybe they had a problem with your customer service, or perhaps they were struggling financially that year. The point is that there is an open door for you to revive that relationship; it will just take a little guerrilla creativity on your part. Investigate what they donated and what it was used for. What other activities or causes have they been involved in other than financial support? Did they give a reason for their absence? Once you have all this information, you will be able to approach them from the right direction. Call them up and present yourself as being new to the position. Thank them for what they have done in the past for the organization. Send them some updates and invite them back. You already know how to reassure your most involved donors, now it is time to show this group, too.

Keep in touch with current donors.

One other way to focus on current supporters is to have them focus on themselves.

You do this with a focus group of your most involved donors, but you could certainly try it with those who give the minimum as well. What you learn from donors will give you insight on why they give to your nonprofit organization. Simply ask the question "Why do you donate to our cause?" You may already know most of the answers, but be prepared for the one that you didn't know. This tactic embodies the spirit of guerrilla marketing because it relies upon imagination and energy instead of your bank account. When you do these things, repeat and referral giving are your just and generous rewards for sticking to this golden rule.

Rule 7: Make Giving Fun

You have a serious mission. The problems are real and you care about them. You want people to grasp the depth of the problems and take ownership of making the solutions happen. But that doesn't mean you can't have a little fun while raising money. It is no secret that your organization has to do something different to get the attention of donors. Nothing gets people's attention better than a little fun! Following is a list of the ABC's of Fun-Raising. As you are having fun, don't forget to take names of the people who sign up for the fun. These are people who can be approached later for more support.

The ABCs of Fun-Raising

- *Auctions.* Gather people to bid on art, jewelry, cars, antiques, baskets of food—almost anything. Have an old-fashioned down-home affair, or break out the black ties and tails. People love going to auctions and companies love giving away merchandise and services to sell at them because they also get the benefit of doing a little fusion marketing with your organization.

- *Boss for the day.* Let people bid on being boss for the day. Highest bidder wins. This is great at schools and can be used for principals, teachers, coaches, etc.
- *Car wash.* This works well for students as well as adults. Ask a gas station or office to let you use their facility. Ask for donations instead of setting a price.
- *Dress down days.* Businesses or private schools let their employees or students dress down for the day if they make a certain donation amount.
- *Event parking spaces.* Sell parking spaces for community events near your facility. Examples could be football games, carnivals, or even community yard sales.
- *Food at restaurants.* Many restaurants are willing to set up special days where they donate 5 or 10 percent of total food sales to your organization. Have volunteers on hand to explain what the donations are going toward. This works for restaurants as well because they get more customers on slower days.
- *Golf tournament.* Have your organization put together a golf tournament with the proceeds benefiting the charity of your choice.
- *Haunted house.* For Halloween, organize a haunted house and charge admission.
- *Ice cream social.* Plan one for employees, volunteers, friends, or the public. Ask for donations to attend.
- *Jail-n-bail.* Businesses can have employees "arrested" for a price. They sit at a makeshift jail until somebody "bails them out." This can also be used at school carnivals.
- *Kiss a pig.* Set a fundraising goal, and if that goal is met, have your principal, CEO, company president, or local celebrity "kiss a pig" in public. Lipstick for the pig is optional.
- *Long-distance runs.* You can add "a-thon" to just about any event and make it more fun and raise funds. Serious athletes

and amateurs love raising support from sponsors in a marathon or other long-distance run in honor of your cause. They also make excellent public relations events.

- *Money containers.* Let people canvass the community, filling custom-designed piggy banks, buckets, bins, or boxes with money for your organization.
- *NASCAR chance drawing.* Collect a variety of NASCAR items, autographs, pictures, memorabilia, and other promotional items and hold a chance drawing.
- *Open house.* A fitness center held an open house with a variety of free classes such as spinning, aerobics, and yoga. Donations were accepted.
- *Pledge drives.* Have a special event where people can sign up to support your organization. Host a formal dinner at a nice hotel and make the case for your organization. Or send people out with saddle bags asking for pledges. One side of the bag has blank donor cards; the other side will fill up with completed pledge cards in no time.
- *Questions for a buck.* One company raised money by having their boss charge donations for each question asked of him. Since he was constantly being asked questions, this made perfect sense. Word spread throughout the company about what he was doing and everyone continued asking questions and paying for it.
- *Recycle.* If your state gives refunds on returnables such as bottles or aluminum cans, then collect them and turn in for money. People like "going green."
- *Student/faculty basketball game.* Set up a benefit basketball game between students and faculty, or faculty from different schools, PTA parents, or even a local TV or radio team. Sell refreshments to collect even more donations.
- *TV chance drawing.* A youth football league raised money for equipment by selling tickets for a chance to win a flat-screen

TV and other prizes. All the prizes were donated from local businesses, and the tickets sold for $2 each or $5 for a book of three. The tickets were numbered and professional looking, making them more appealing.

■ *Ugly dog contest.* Get lots of pet owners involved in this. Choose a day when people can have a picture taken of their dog at the local pet store. Post the pictures for a couple weeks and charge donations for other customers to vote for the "ugliest dog." Donate the money raised to a pet charity and give the winner of the contest a gift certificate from the pet store.

■ *Vacation day chance drawing.* Have a drawing at a business for a vacation day. Get local hotels, timeshares, or one-day cruises to donate the gift in exchange for listening to their presentation.

■ *Wrap presents.* Have volunteers set up a booth at a local mall or department store around the holidays to wrap presents for donations.

■ *X-Men and other superheroes.* Put together a breakfast with superheroes, or even Santa or the Easter Bunny. Work with a restaurant or VFW post to use their space. Have someone in a costume and sell tickets. You can also have pictures taken with the children.

■ *Yard sales.* Clean out your attic, house, or garage, and raise money at the same time. Organize a community yard sale where a portion of the money is used to rent a space and then donate that amount to your charity.

■ *Zoo carnival.* Host a special petting zoo and carnival for the entire family. Charge a nominal fee for participation and use the event to educate potential new donors.

You don't want the cornerstone of your donations to hinge on fun events, but it certainly adds flavor and spice while attracting donations. Make sure you include these ideas in your marketing

FROM THE FRONT LINES

NAME: Marc Pitman

WEBSITE: FundraisingCoach.com

BOOK: *Ask Without Fear!* (Executive Books, 2008)

Fundraising isn't impossible. It can be an incredibly exciting adventure. Here is a simple plan I recommend to my clients. It can get you off to a good start and keep being used for years to come. To keep it easy, I encourage you to "Get R.E.A.L."

The first step is doing your RESEARCH—researching both your own fundraising goal and your prospects. I'm amazed at how few nonprofits really know how much they want to raise. Define it and use tools like GiftRangeCalculator.com to help you define your gift levels.

The second step is ENGAGE. I like to think of this as the dating part of the relationship. It's important to get to know your prospects before you "pop the question." This is a time to both get to know them and introduce them to your cause

Arguably the most important step is ASK. The number-one reason people don't give money to your cause is that they are not asked. If you've done the first two steps, this step will be quite fun. You'll already have the odds in your favor. You know that they are predisposed to saying "yes" and you'll have had time to shape the ask around their passions.

The final step is LOVE. I originally called this step Live/Like/Love. Whether the person says "yes" or "no," we can grow the relationship. And standard fundraising practice says we'll get 4 "no'"s for every 1 "yes."

I firmly believe fundraising is one of the best callings anyone could have! It truly is an "extreme sport!"

plan and calendar. You can also evaluate and analyze them later for their effectiveness. Follow this golden rule to engage in marketing that will amaze the public and motivate your donors.

Balanced Fundraising for Your Nonprofit

Another part of the big picture of development is to have a balanced view of fundraising. Nonguerrillas think of fundraising as a hated chore they have to do. They wait until the last minute (when things are the most urgent usually) to reach out and ask for support. Some work at fundraising like martyrs who must go alone. Others have such a small base of support, they are constantly scrambling for money and eventually end up neglecting their work. Very few nonprofits are started by people who love to ask people for money or by people who get a kick out of leading fundraising activities. They are started by people who care about a cause. Some mistakenly believed when they started the money would roll in almost automatically because the cause is important. When that doesn't happen they can become disappointed, even resentful toward people.

Guerrillas know money won't roll in automatically just because the cause is good; that's why they are active fundraisers. They manage to keep a cheerful disposition and are not desperate in their quest for raising money because they have a solid understanding about what it takes to keep their nonprofit support flowing constantly. If you are new to nonprofit work, here is a little guerrilla insider information to help you get a good start on raising enough money to keep your organization moving forward toward achieving your mission.

■ *Get over your fears of asking people to give money.* When you realize you are helping people find a more fulfilling life, you will come to find fundraising to be fun and exciting. Asking for money is as natural as asking someone to do something good for someone else.

■ *Don't be a Lone Ranger.* Your board members should help you actively in fundraising and development. In fact, that should be their main job. Work to appoint people who do not see their main task as supervising your work, but who see their role as being the chief fundraisers for your organization. It's a good idea to only appoint board members who also support the organization personally.

■ *Work to cultivate a comprehensive base of individual donors.* More than any event you could stage, more than any grant you could pursue, the individual donor is your most important supporter.

■ *Have multiple strategies for generating income.* Think of fundraising as establishing a diversified portfolio of financial support. On the next page we list other sources of income that can keep your nonprofit in the black.

Fundraising Type	Definition and Tip
Grant	A financial subsidy from an organization or company. Your organization will need to fit the criteria of the grantor, so research is your best friend. Start with your community first. The best grants are often locally funded. Grants are project oriented and are not used to fund the operational costs of running your nonprofit.
Foundation	An organization that manages grants, endowments, and other financial resources. Some are private, others are public. Depending on the group, you may find help in identifying the grants and endowments that are available for you cause.
Endowment	A financial fund that dedicates the proceeds generated from invested income to specific causes in perpetuity. Some of your wealthiest donors may want to set up an endowment for your organization.
Episodic Fundraiser	A special offering that goes over and above regular donations in honor of a person or during a holiday season.
Capital Campaign	Money raised for long-range projects or permanent buildings for your organization. Often you can work with development professionals to sell bonds that allows you to literally borrow the money from your supporters to build your building.
Planned Giving	Estate planning, wills, and trusts. Often foundations can work with your supporters to help them give money to you when their estates are settled upon death. People love to know they can leave a legacy behind that will make a difference.
Gifts in Kind	Companies and individuals can give you property or other valuable items which you can sell or use for the benefit of your organization.
Government Grant	The federal government has many grants available for nonprofits. Your organization needs to match the criteria for the grants exactly and be very diligent in keeping up with government requirements and paperwork.

Fundraising Type	Definition and Tip
Corporate Sponsor	Companies are increasingly looking for opportunities to do cause marketing. Businesses can give you merchandise, money, or even provide you with workers for your cause. Don't overlook the business sector when looking for money for your cause.
Federated Funds	Groups like United Way provide various levels of funding to organizations. Visit with representatives from the organizations to learn more about if your cause is a match for their support goals.
Product Sales	Nonprofits can sell products, they just don't sell products for profits. All the profits go to support the work of the organization. Your goods, services, and fees for programs can become a supplemental source of support to add to the money that comes from your base of individual donors.
Priority Needs	Make a list of your needs by project. Often donors want to support a specific project. Your priority needs list could include the purchase of equipment, the production of a new resource, or any other specific need.

> Make sure the work your organization does is as attractive as possible to potential volunteers.

CHAPTER 18

Seven Platinum Rules for Recruiting Volunteers

ASK ALMOST ANYONE AND THEY WILL TELL YOU it is impossible to run most nonprofit organizations without great volunteers. They are the driving force behind the programs, products, and services offered by effective organizations. It is true that founders, boards of directors, staff, and other important nonvolunteer positions often hold everything together, but where would they be without ground troops backing the cause? The quality of your volunteer recruiting program will determine the scope and impact of your organization, so it is important to have the highest quality recruiting program possible. Your nonprofit needs more than warm bodies filling the working positions, you need the very best—you need the Platinum Rules for Recruiting Volunteers.

Rule 1: Have a Clearly Defined Role for Each Volunteer Job

The first step toward a platinum-quality volunteer recruitment program is to have a clear understanding of how volunteers can help your organization accomplish its mission. Each volunteer job in your nonprofit needs a written job description with a list of qualifications candidates need to do the task. Make sure the work your organization does is as attractive as possible to potential volunteers. In guerrilla language, that means making the benefits of working with your organization obvious to the people you want to recruit. Where possible, quantify the impact made by each job in terms of numbers and measured results. Nobody wants to do work that is meaningless and underappreciated—especially volunteers. Volunteers want to do interesting work that makes a real impact for the greater good.

Having job descriptions and listing expectations may sound a little too much like the kind of thing a for-profit would do when hiring paid employees. You may wonder, will having high expectations make volunteer work sound too difficult and make it harder to find people? Where is the reward for taking on such hard work and submitting to high standards? You need to understand that volunteer work *is* paid work. People are not paid in money; the payoff is job

> Don't fail to understand the potential in all the people you know.

satisfaction, community impact, and appreciation from the organization. Volunteer work is very rewarding. Volunteers trade in their time, energy, and expertise for a feeling of purpose and a sense of making a positive influence on society.

There is also a cost to the volunteers that you should take into consideration. When people volunteer, they are giving up time that could be spent doing other things, like spending time with their families or earning money. Volunteers often pay for their own transportation, meals, and other expenses while working for your organization. Understand what the costs are, and make the benefits they receive in exchange for working for you outweigh their costs. If you treat volunteers like "unpaid staff" instead of cheap labor, you will find they will be far more interested and satisfied while working with your organization. Nonguerrillas undervalue the worth of volunteers and make volunteer work seem mundane. Guerrillas give their volunteers platinum-quality work to do by increasing the perceived value of each job.

> Studies report that the average cash value of a volunteer is $19.52 an hour.

Here are nine ways to add perceived value to volunteer jobs:

1. Give each job a name that communicates value.
2. Define the work being done with a written job description.
3. List expectations and work standards.
4. Communicate deadlines.
5. Require reporting and accountability.
6. Show how each job fits into your organizational structure.
7. Interview and appoint candidates.
8. Announce when volunteers take a position with your organization.
9. Evaluate volunteer partners and reward excellence.

Rule 2: Continually Strive to Increase Job Satisfaction for Volunteers

Volunteers may not be paid in cash, but you can give them a raise by increasing their work satisfaction. You can do this by helping them improve their skills with training and giving them opportunities for self-development. Nonguerrillas recruit volunteers, assign them tasks, and then ignore them. Organizations that take volunteers for granted have much higher turnover than nonprofits that work closely with volunteers and treat them like partners. Satisfaction at work is not only about money, even in for-profit companies. When people are asked to do meaningful work and feel they are engaged in something important, they are happy and more productive.

Here's how to increase job satisfaction for volunteers.

- Treat them like unpaid staff.
- Provide high-quality training experiences.
- Work with volunteers to pursue their own personal development and goal setting.
- Allow for flexible schedules and innovative approaches to work.
- Let them supervise the work of other volunteers.
- Increase responsibility and give greater decision-making power.

Rule 3: Understand How Volunteers Think

Another step toward a platinum-level volunteer recruitment program is to understand what keeps volunteers interested and to leverage that awareness to make working with your organization as fascinating as possible to them. Just as when people make purchase decisions, 90 percent of what goes into the decision to volunteer is subconscious. Why do people really volunteer? What makes them give up so much of themselves? Do you know why volunteers support your cause? You may know some of the obvious reasons why, but did you know that there is a slew of underlying reasons for how and why people contribute to organizations across the planet?

Nonguerrillas only understand about 10 percent of the reasons that make volunteering attractive to people. Guerrillas know about the rest of the motivational iceberg that is beneath the surface, and they use that understanding to deepen the interest of the people they want to recruit.

Here are 75 subconscious reasons people volunteer.

1. To find a personal mission in life
2. To give back
3. To make a difference
4. To change the world
5. To mobilize support
6. To be relevant
7. To belong to a greater cause
8. To legitimize financial support given to a charity
9. To experience spiritual renewal or new power
10. To express love toward mankind
11. To overcome fears
12. To seek the approval of others
13. To appreciate the blessings one has
14. To be patriotic
15. To be loyal to a cause
16. To sacrifice, go beyond one's self
17. To make right for wrongs committed in the past
18. To have made an impact before death
19. To turn away from worries and responsibilities at home to find inner peace
20. To be compassionate
21. To be able to boast to others
22. To express one's religious beliefs

23. To overcome guilt for wasting time, energy, or resources in the past
24. To go back to a battlefield with a purpose that is life-giving
25. To try to make use of a language learned in school
26. To learn some new things and grow intellectually
27. To be an expert on the subject matter related to the cause
28. To find one's self
29. To pretend to be somebody else
30. To be true to what one stands for
31. To see how one's core values hold up
32. To appreciate one's daily life back home more
33. To break with routines
34. To experience the thrill of being outside one's culture
35. To feel what it is like to be a philanthropist
36. To find solutions to problems back home
37. To have an experience to tell others about
38. To take a break from everyday activities of home and work—a temporary escape
39. To confirm one has made the right investments of one's time
40. To see firsthand something that might be historic
41. To see what the circumstances are in other places
42. To gauge resources needed to complete the cause
43. To assess the status of the cause
44. To spy on the "other side" of another cause
45. To get "outside the box"
46. To join the crowd
47. To impress other people at work
48. To have a more interesting life
49. To imitate others who have been models of behavior
50. To respond to the many calls and invitations to volunteer
51. To check the feasibility of being more deeply involved in a cause

52. To see if sustainable change really is possible
53. To believe in a cause more deeply
54. To experience hope by seeing people helped
55. To make one's own unique contribution
56. To see the rest of the country or world
57. To legitimize one's political views
58. To have a vacation with a purpose
59. To relieve tensions
60. To experience a "different world"
61. To have a controlled diversion of events, tastes, touch, etc.
62. To use one's imagination
63. To compare other ways of living with one's own background
64. To compete with other causes
65. To be passionate about something and feel good
66. To be amused by strange people, places, and customs
67. To spend quality time with friends, family, church members, etc.
68. To take good pictures and videos
69. To have great stories to tell back home
70. To have souvenirs of other places
71. To go to as many places as one can
72. To go more places than others do
73. To shop in places, ways, and for things that are not possible back home
74. To see beautiful things, places, people, etc.
75. To explore new ways of communicating

Rule 4: Don't Look for Instant Gratification

Volunteering doesn't come as second nature to everyone. For example, when Cali the cheerleader is asked by her cheer coach to sell cookie dough as a fundraiser, she is very excited about it.

One in three volunteers do not return.

However, her parents don't share her enthusiasm. They would rather have the option to "buy out" of the fundraising campaign, buying ten tubs of cookie dough themselves so they don't have to also volunteer their time. They figure if they have the money, it makes more sense for them just to give cash than to give of their time. They would rather not go with their daughter door to door using a sales pitch on their neighbors. The idea of going through the hassle of asking for purchases from colleagues around the office is not appealing to them at all either.

The point is, not everyone is cut out for volunteer work. It takes a special person with a platinum personality to give up their time and energy instead of just finding the easy way out and digging into their pockets. Don't become discouraged if your volunteer program doesn't have as broad appeal as your fundraising and development efforts do. You need to patiently master the skill of volunteer recruitment.

Guerrillas know that volunteer recruitment is another part of the marketing strategy they patiently develop for their organization. They use their list of 200 guerrilla marketing weapons and their winsome guerrilla personality to find and attract volunteers. Marketing does a lot of good things, but one thing it does not do is work fast. Develop a marketing plan that gets the message out about the tremendous benefits of working with your organization as a volunteer.

Rule 5: Go Out on a Limb

If you want to pick fruit, you can't only climb up the trunk of the tree—you have to get out on the ends of the branches because that is where the fruit grows. In volunteer recruitment, you have the same principle at work. You cannot stay around the office and find the volunteers you need, you have to get out to where the people are on the front lines and recruit them. If you are looking for more volunteers, talk to the people who already volunteer with your organization about their needs, interests, and other friends who might want to get involved. Nonguerrillas brainstorm about ways to attract volunteers without spending time with them. Your best volunteers might also be people who live in the communities you want to target. You will find your most ardent supporters and volunteers are the ones who are closest to the action. The people who stand to benefit most from your cause will be the ones who have the most interest in working with you. These people are also the ones who have the deepest network of relationships where it matters most. When looking for volunteers, be selective. Find the people who are the most qualified and who willingly see themselves as partners in the cause.

Rule 6: Put Your Guard Up

Nonprofits rely on the work of volunteers to get their job done. Quality control and training are far more important to nonprofits because of the importance of their work. That's why it is important to have the right people in the right role from the start. That is also the reason it is important to have standards for everything you do. Just as it is a good idea to have job descriptions for each job, it is also wise to have an operations manual or standards guide for the work that is led by volunteers. You must make sure that everyone who represents your organization does so by following the rules that are set forth before them.

How do you get people of different creeds, genders, ages, and sexes to work together without causing problems? Remove the barriers that come between your diverse groups by listening, communicating, and bringing about a sense of trust. Understand that with diversity comes many forms of skills, talents,

HOW GUERRILLAS OVERCOME VOLUNTEER PROGRAM MEDIOCRITY

- Overcome lack of inspiration with a clear vision and mission.

- Overcome volunteer dropout with increased satisfaction.

- Overcome inexperience with quality training.

- Overcome low confidence with encouragement.

- Overcome poor quality with high expectations.

- Overcome discouragement with appreciation.

- Overcome conflicts with patience and compassion.

- Overcome boredom with challenging opportunities.

- Overcome lack of excellence by listening to feedback.

- Overcome low accountability with support systems.

knowledge, and wisdom, all of which can be applied to the growth of your cause. A bad representative, be it a board member or volunteer, will cost you far more than a good one will earn for you. Keep in mind the delicate nature of your organization's reputation when you are using volunteers. It can take years to build it up and only seconds to destroy it. If you practice consistency and quality, many times those situations will not present themselves.

Here are some platinum quality standard volunteer practices that no nonprofit should be without.

- Know the difference between training people and making them sit through a lecture in the name of training.
- Teach skills and reward ideal behaviors.
- Measure and report the impact volunteers make on achieving the organization's mission.
- Help them improve their customer service skills.
- Give quality workers important assignments.
- Conduct background checks on workers who have contact with minors.

Rule 7: Make Volunteers Feel Appreciated

Besides giving to people in need, some nonprofits also give gifts to their volunteers. Nonguerrillas rarely give anything away. All they do is take. As a volunteer, wouldn't you be more willing to help a *giving* organization rather than one that is a *taker*? Guerrillas love to give and they know volunteers love to receive. A "giver" organization puts volunteer appreciation high on its list. Gifts intensify and strengthen the relationship between volunteers and the organizations they serve. Gifts work on almost anyone, no matter their age, sex, ethnic background, socioeconomic status, or any other differences.

Today there are many easy ways to give without breaking your budget. Some of the more popular gifts you may know about are T-shirts, cups, hats, calendars, clocks, and pens. These items are good for your organization because they fit almost any budget. One downside is the lack of space physically to advertise on them. As a guerrilla you should think outside the box when considering gifts for your volunteers. Think of gifts that somehow tie in with your organization's mission. Maybe you can give away pens that look like syringes with red ink if you are a blood bank, or plastic minifootballs if you are a youth football organization. Don't be afraid to include your nonprofit's name on the gift, along with website and contact information. Many volunteers are so giving, they like to give away the gifts they receive as gifts to friends as a way to start an advocacy conversation. Forty percent of people who receive these free gifts can remember your name six months later, and 31 percent can remember up to a year later.

Make sure you give away good quality items. No one wants a bag that rips after the first use or a desk clock that never works from day one. (That's one sure-fire way to lose those friends on Facebook.) Give gifts that show what a great job your volunteer or staffer has done. People love to be recognized by others, and you can do so easily with a T-shirt or even just a picture from an event they helped out with. Giving gifts is a win-win situation because you get to put the best foot of your organization forward, and at the same time offer some well deserved credit to your volunteers and employees. Even though your gifts are not extravagant, people will feel honored to get them. For your marketing to move from standing still to crossing the finish line, you need momentum. Free gifts are what start that momentum.

Once you have made a decision to give gifts, ask yourself these five questions:

1. How many people do I want to reach?
2. How much money is in my budget?
3. What message do I want printed?
4. What gift will be most useful to my volunteers?
5. Is the gift unique and desirable?

CHAPTER 19

Guerrilla Marketing Behavior Change

H ERE'S ANOTHER COUNTERINTUITIVE GUERRILLA marketing principle: While nonprofit leaders like to think of themselves as forward thinkers, they really need to learn to become backward thinkers. Guerrillas think backward, then forward. In direct marketing, when a guerrilla writes a postcard or sales letter, she writes her response device first. She does this so she is clear on what her readers are supposed to do. This is called "working backwards," and it helps you focus everything you do toward the response for which you are looking. It works in all forms of guerrilla strategy. Start by having a clear picture in your mind of the customer at the moment of decision. What is on the customer's mind? What are the steps that led to the decision to respond? What were the beliefs, desires, and motivational buttons that were pushed and caused them to decide?

Nonprofit guerrillas don't start at the beginning, they start at the end responses and outcomes they are looking for from their targeted audiences. They focus first on the actions they want people to adopt and they work their way backward to find where to start their behavior–changing campaigns. Everything they do is designed to get the desired response from their targeted audience. Customers are the starting and ending point of the guerrilla marketing circle.

Traditional marketing is based on experience and then judgment, which involves guesswork. Wrong guesses are too expensive for guerrillas, so guerrilla marketing is based on the laws of human behavior. In guerilla marketing, there's a little bit of Freudian marketing that understands the inner motives of the target audience. Also, the guerrilla's psychological approach has Skinnerian marketing implications in understanding what makes people change their behaviors. It is important to understand psychology because in marketing you are relating to people in ways that motivate them to act. In nonprofit marketing, you are changing people's minds, motivating them to adopt new behaviors, and building confidence to mobilize them to change the world. It doesn't take a Ph.D. to understand you can't do that if you don't understand why people think, feel, and act the way they do.

Guerrillas are not always looking backward. They also look forward. They help their preferred target visualize the benefits of life after they have adopted the new behavior. They make them aware of what feelings they will experience once they have made the commitment to the new way of living.

Education Is Not Enough

Nonguerrillas develop education, advocacy, and promotional programs with little thought about sustaining behavior change. They have many excellent strategies for changing beliefs and nearly unlimited strategies for education, but they lack tactics that alter how people behave. Because they have the ability to talk about change but have no model for changing behavior, they have limited effectiveness in evoking change with their media outreach campaigns.

Education alone doesn't change people. Your organization's educational programs, products, and services are not the most important things; they are only a means toward the end goal of changing behaviors. Researchers have shown repeatedly in studies that people who participate in education programs rarely change their behaviors, even when they understand why they need to change, and even when they feel positively disposed to change, if they are not encouraged to make a public commitment to a specific behavior.

Advocacy alone doesn't change people. Getting everyone to agree with you isn't the most important thing. Some nonprofits spend too much time trying to convert people to their way of thinking. They assume that if everyone had the right way of thinking, the world would be a better place. Imagine if everyone agreed with you, but nobody changed their actions. Would that change the world? Katya Andresen, author of *Robin Hood Marketing* (Jossey Bass, 2006) says, "We don't need to strive for a shared worldview; we need to have people take a specific action that advances our mission . . . They don't have to know everything; they simply need the information that is relevant to them."

Advertising outreach alone doesn't change people. Getting your message in front of the public isn't the most important thing. Many nonprofits mistakenly believe they can change the world with their

FROM THE FRONT LINES

NAME: Nedra Kline Weinreich

WEBSITE: Social–Marketing.com

BOOK: *Hands–On Social Marketing* (Sage, 1999)

"The field of social marketing is somewhat like Dr. Frankenstein's monster in the following ways:

- *It is made up of bits and pieces of many different disciplines.* These include health education, marketing/advertising, anthropology, and social psychology.

- *It has taken on a life of its own.* Over the past few decades, it has become recognized as a distinct discipline.

- *It often is misunderstood.* Many people incorrectly use the term to mean social media marketing or any type of marketing or advertising done by a health– or socially–oriented organization, no matter who the product benefits or how the program was developed.

But unlike Dr. Frankenstein, we can harness the strength of social marketing, using the best of all its component parts while carefully controlling its direction."

creative media strategies. But they are wasting their money when their media employs no behavior–changing call to action. They are limiting their effectiveness because their messages don't make the actions the audience needs to adopt desirable.

Education, advocacy, and promotion are only effective for transforming communities when they are supporting a clearly understood behavior–change strategy. Problems in nonprofit marketing stem from the misapplication of for–profit marketing tactics. Packaging behavior change is not the same as product packaging. Product marketing is narrowly focused on the behavior of buying. Nonprofits need to package all types of behaviors, beliefs, and attitudes, persuading targeted audiences to adopt them. When their educational programs, advocacy, and outreach don't work, nonguerrillas create new programs, redesign their advocacy strategies, and develop different advertising outreach campaigns. Instead of developing new programs, they need to think what behaviors need to happen to make the changes they are looking for to transpire, and develop a marketing strategy that is behavior–oriented.

Six Guerrilla Tactics for Behavior–Change Marketing

Social marketing is a form of marketing that is expressly designed for changing behaviors. The term "social marketing" was coined by Philip Kotler and Gerald Zaltman in a 1971 article for the *Journal of Marketing*, entitled "Social Marketing: An Approach to Planned Social Change." Kotler and Zaltman's ideas about using marketing techniques for social good led to the current definition of social marketing: "The use of marketing principles and techniques to influence a target audience to voluntarily accept, reject, modify, or abandon a behavior for the benefit of individuals, groups, or society as a whole."

While traditional marketers sell products and compete for customers with the goal of earning profits, social marketers sell behaviors, positioning them against competing unhealthy behaviors as more beneficial to individuals, groups, and society. Instead of profits, social marketers seek to impact positive social change. Social marketing is a unique form of marketing that is worth the effort to understand. We can't describe everything about social marketing in this chapter, but we can give you a head start toward making your nonprofit's marketing more behavior–changing. Here are six tactics you can use to add behavior change to your guerrilla marketing arsenal.

1. Define the Problem

Find the source of the problems that are causing the negative consequences in your community.

Go back to the real origins of your organization and think about the problems that inspired your nonprofit's beginnings. Why are you here? Where do you want to go? What does your organization want to accomplish? Read the first sentence in the Three–Sentence Guerrilla Mission Statement you developed in Chapter 4 to answer the question, "Why do you exist?" What is causing the negatives you are trying to overcome? Prescription without diagnosis is malpractice. You can't offer the solution until you know the sickness. What are the problems you are trying to solve? What are the present behaviors that are contributing to the problem? What are the behaviors that your target audience needs to adopt if your goals are to be achieved? How would you describe the social outcome your organization desires?

2. Determine the Behaviors

Identify the exact behaviors your target audience needs to adopt if the desired outcome is to happen.

Looking at the problem leads you to think about behaviors. What kind of behaviors from your target would change the status quo for the better? What are people now doing that needs to change? Telling people about the problem is not enough; you will need to show them what to do about it. What are the specific actions that will produce the outcomes you are looking for? Do you want people to:

- Pick up a new habit?
- Refrain from an activity?
- Change how they now do things?
- Abandon a false belief?
- Seek counseling?
- Make a commitment?
- Take leadership in their community?

Break down as many of the actions that are relevant to your outcomes as you can so you can address them one by one with your marketing strategies. If you know the nature of your problem well and have clearly identified the objective of your strategy, the behavioral goals should become easy to spot.

3. Describe the Target Audience

Segment the people you want to reach, identifying the ones who are closest to adopting the desired behaviors.

Get to know your target audience as deeply as you can so you can understand the opportunities to reach them with your strategy. Start with the groups that are easiest to get to adopt the desired behavior, then work your way to the tougher cases. Here are a few ways the people in your target audience may be similar to each other:

- Demographic similarities
- Locations
- Lifestyle
- Common behaviors that are counter–productive
- Attitudes about the desired behavior, both positive and negative
- Mistaken beliefs about the desired behavior
- People who are most likely to perform the desired behavior

Segmentation makes your work more manageable. You can reach more people more often when you have a smaller number of them. Also, narrowing your audience down into smaller groups makes it easier to get to know more about them.

4. Decide Your Approach

Select the behavior change philosophy that is the best fit for your goals.

You need a philosophy for your behavior change strategy. Keep the focus on outcomes and the behaviors that produce them. If you want to create sustainable behavior change, you need more than a sales mentality. Selling people on your ideas is not enough; you need the continued practice of the right behaviors if you hope to transform the world. Don't fall in love with your organization, your products, your programs, or services. Focus on impact.

Theories of Behavioral Change

Before you can create a behavior changing strategy, you will need a theory behind your approach. Approaches that work in one situation might not apply in another. Because social marketing is focused on more than a single behavior (i.e., buying), you will need to become proficient in the theories that work best for your target audience. Below we describe a few of the most common forms of behavior change theory. We don't have room to describe them in detail here. Guerrillas do their homework, so here are some springboards for further research.

Behavior Theory: Diffusion of Innovations
Origin: Everett Rogers
Basic Premise: There are five types of people who respond to innovations differently over time.

This theory states that people don't respond to new ideas all at the same rate. There is a time lag between when the first people respond and when the majority of people will adopt a new behavior. If you could plot the adoption of ideas on a timeline flowing from left to right, you would see there are five types of people: Innovators, Early Adopters, Early Majority, Late Majority, and Laggards. Innovators, about 2 percent of people, are the first to adopt an innovation. These people tend to be younger, avant guard risk–taking types. They set the trends that people follow. Early Adopters, approximately 13 percent of people, are the opinion leaders that take the ideas adopted by Innovators and evangelize them to the rest. Around 34 percent of people are Early Majority types who tend to be slower in the adoption process. The Late Majority, slower still, comprise another 34 percent of the population. Together, these two groups represent the mainstream of society. By the time the last of them have adopted a behavior or idea, almost everyone has. We say almost everyone, because the Laggards are the last 16 percent of the population to come around. It is up to the marketer to understand what type of person they are targeting with their behavior change strategies.

Guerrillas Tip: Influence between groups flows from left to right. Types are seldom influenced by people to the right of them on the continuum.

Behavior Theory: Social Norms Theory

Origin: H.W. Perkins and A.D. Berkowitz
Basic Premise: People are more likely to adopt a behavior they believe is normative.

These two researchers discovered their theory on the college campus. They found when students attend college, they tend to overestimate the amount of binge–drinking being done on campus. Because students think binge–drinking is the norm in college, they are at greater risk for engaging in the abuse of alcohol while at the university. When behavior–change marketing messages were developed to help students know that a much smaller percentage of college students are actually binge–drinkers, and that such drinking is not normative, they were able to significantly decrease the incidence of binge–drinking among the student population.

Guerrilla Tip: Use social proof in your behavior–change strategies.

Behavior Theory: Trans–Theoretical Model
Origin: James O. Prochaska
Basic Premise: People pass through six stages as they adopt a new behavior.

This model is based on a blending of psychological theories designed to help people overcome the bad habits that plague them. The theory states that individuals must go through six stages to change a habit or pick up a new behavior: Precontemplation, Contemplation, Preparation, Action, Maintenance, and Termination. At the Precontemplation stage, people are unaware there is a problem. Messages that assume they are engaged are ignored by them. When people begin to notice the problems, they are at the Contemplation stage. Many nonprofits work to get people to this stage, not realizing awareness of a problem is not enough. People need to get to the point where they are in the

Preparation stage. At this stage people are open and disposed to make a change, but they will not change until they are called to action. In the Action stage, people are making commitments to the new behavior. The next stage, Maintenance, needs to be sustained if they are going to get to the point where they Terminate the unhealthy behavior altogether. When engaging people who are not yet Contemplating the problem you are working to solve, use a step–by–step, longer range strategy rather than attempting to move them immediately to act.

Guerrilla Tip: Patience and understanding are vital in guerrilla behavior–change strategies.

Behavior Theory: Health Belief Model
Origin: Hochbaum, Rosenstock, and Kegels
Basic Premise: People's misperceptions can create barriers to behavior change.

Behavior–change messages are not only influenced by fact, they are shaped by the audience based on their perceived beliefs and abilities. This theory lists four types of perceived threat and net benefits: Perceived Susceptibility, Perceived Severity, Perceived Benefits, and Perceived Barriers. If a person doesn't believe the problem really will affect them, the low Perceived Susceptibility will make them less likely to take action. Also, problems with low Perceived Severity receive less response. Guerrillas will recognize the need to talk about the Perceived Benefits, and reduce the Perceived Barriers to adoption of the new behavior. A person's confidence in his or her ability to successfully perform an action also will determine how open they will be to adopt a new way of acting.

Guerrilla Tip: Research the perceptions of the people you want to reach.

5. Design the Strategy

Use the tools that are most effective at changing behaviors in your campaign.

Once you understand your problem and know the behaviors that will help evoke change, you are ready to start planning. Doug Mckinzie–Mohr and William Smith list seven community–based behavior change tools in their book *Fostering Sustainable Behavior* (New Society, 1999). Below, we summarize a few of our thoughts on each point.

- *Commitment.* Getting people to make a written commitment to adopt the new behavior can increase the effectiveness of your behavior–change strategy. When people make public commitments, they have a strong desire to be seen as consistent by others. No commitment means no accountability. When people commit to small things (like wearing a ribbon), they become far more open to making larger commitments later.
- *Prompts.* Find ways to remind your target audience of their commitments and about the desired behavior. Memes, taglines, rubber wristsbands, and awareness ribbons have been used in the past. What will you use?
- *Norms.* Involve the peers of the target audience and use social proofs in your campaign. When people believe a behavior is considered the norm, they are more likely to sustain the desirable activity.
- *Communication.* Use your media outreach as a supporting player in your strategy and not the entirety of your campaign. Advertising is a great tool for reminding people of something they have already heard about from another source.
- *Incentives.* If you can provide a benefit from the behavior,

people are far more likely to participate. For example, people may carpool just so they can use the HOV lanes and get to work faster. What can you offer that sweetens the deal when people adopt the behavior?

- *Removing barriers.* The harder something is, or the more inconvenient it is, the less likely it is that people will participate. What can you do to lower the perceived price of participating?

- *Design and evaluation of strategies.* Develop your outreach with a clear understanding of the people you want to reach using research. Guerrillas build in follow–up and evaluation in all their campaigns.

6. Develop Your Campaign

Create a behavior change campaign that uses all the elements of behavior change above.

Guerrillas create social change by keeping their focus on behaviors. All their organization's products, programs, services, advocacy, and outreach are targeted at getting people to adopt the changes in behaviors that accomplish their desired outcomes. Each behavior is treated as a "product" that is positioned as a benefit to the target audience. Everything is directed at getting people to adopt the new behaviors.

Here are some questions to help you develop your guerrilla behavior change strategy.

- Have you defined the problem you are working to solve?

- Have you defined the specific behaviors your target audience needs to adopt?

- Is there a clear understanding of the barriers to adopting the behaviors?

- Do you have a comprehensive list of all the benefits of adopting the desired behaviors?
- Is there a plan for evoking voluntary public commitments from your target audience?
- Do you have a process for encouraging support for people who adopt the behavior?
- Do you have a personal symbol for people to use or wear as a reminder of the commitment?
- Do you have a means to spotlight the people who are exhibiting the healthy behavior?
- Do you have a communication plan that promotes the commitment and benefits and reduces the perceived barriers?

> A marketing plan is created to be used as your road map to guide you toward successful marketing results; it is not meant to be a destination.

CHAPTER 20

Launching and Maintaining Your Marketing Attack

NOW YOU ARE READY TO PUT FINGERS TO KEYBOARD and create a marketing plan that expands awareness about your cause, increases recruitment of volunteers, mobilizes advocates, and raises more money. Three factors that will give your marketing plans the guerrilla's competitive edge: 1) how well you use the information you have gathered; 2) how thoughtful you are in selecting the right combination of weapons in your arsenal; and 3) how much you have allowed yourself to be inculcated with the take–action mind–set of the guerrilla. Look back on all you have learned that can be used to help you formulate a plan that maximizes results:

- You have eliminated your fears about marketing and now see how your organization benefits from an intentionally strategic approach to communications.
- You are crystal clear about your mission and vision.
- You know your competition better than they know themselves.
- You know your audience as well as you know your best friends.
- You know how your products, programs, and services appeal to your preferred targets.
- You know what behaviors will lead to the outcome that will change the world for the better.
- You are a networking and fusion–partnering machine.
- You know about the 200 guerrilla marketing weapons you can use to reach people.
- Your organization projects an identity that is both genuine and consistent.
- You have cultivated the personality traits of a guerrilla.
- You are ready to launch your attack!

Write a Marketing Plan in Just Seven Sentences

No doubt if you did your guerrilla level best so far, you have researched enough to write an entire marketing book—but we are not going to ask you to write a long–winded marketing plan like the nonguerrillas do. You can say everything you need to say in just seven sentences. Simple plans are more likely to be completed than complicated ones anyway. Your primary objectives in guerrilla marketing are to attract people, obtain customers, and keep them through winning relationships. A marketing plan is created to be used as your road map to guide you toward successful marketing results; it is not meant to be a destination. The goal is not to write a marketing plan just so you can check it off your to–do list. Everything you do in guerrilla marketing is intentional and driven by outcomes. Your marketing plan turns your mission and vision into reality by listing the actions you need to complete on a day–by–day basis until you have achieved your organization's dream. You don't need every single detail of every action transcribed; your plan only has to highlight your most important steps along the way toward your goals. When guerrilla marketers put their marketing planning on paper (and not just in an academic thesis), they create a powerful tool that helps them make community change possible.

1. *The first sentence states the purpose of your marketing.*
   Write a sentence about the actions you want people to take. What are you trying to do? What are the behaviors you want from people? If you are unclear on what you want out of your marketing, how do you expect your customer to know what to do? Guerrillas don't market by the seat of their pants; each marketing tactic has a measurable outcome in mind.
2. *The second sentence states the competitive advantage of the nonprofit.*
   What makes your offer a good deal to the target audience? Take out the benefits list you made earlier and look for the benefits that have the most appeal to your customers that also give your organization the most advantage over the competition.
3. *The third sentence describes the target audience.*

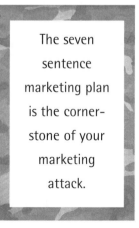

The seven sentence marketing plan is the cornerstone of your marketing attack.

Each marketing plan needs a separate target audience because you will need to know which marketing weapons and messages will reach them best. Talk to your audience with your marketing, don't talk to yourself. Nonguerrillas fall into the trap of doing marketing that has appeal internally within their organization but ends up being less appealing to their target audience. They are satisfied with seeing their messages out in the marketplace more than they are focused on reaching the target audience in ways that are relevant to them. That's why so much nonprofit marketing is filled with jargon and insider–speak that only makes sense to the already initiated. Too many nonprofits think they are their target audience.

4. *The fourth sentence lists the marketing weapons used in the attack.*

There are 200 guerrilla marketing weapons—you can't use them all. Pick at least 20 weapons to start with. Make sure you know how to leverage the power behind each weapon you use in your plan. Choose the media that are the best match for your target audience.

5. *The fifth sentence states your niche in the marketplace.*

Remember, the smaller the target, the bigger the bull's–eye. By choosing to specialize in a niche, you are not saying no to people so much as you are saying yes to more market share of the people you want to reach. You can dominate a smaller niche faster than you can carve out a share of an established, more competitive field. Guerrillas know it is easier to drill deeper into a vertical market, too.

6. *The sixth sentence expresses your identity.*

What is the reputation of your organization as it relates to the messages in your marketing plan? All your marketing needs to build on who you are and should look like who you are. What values do you stand for in the minds of your target audience? What will they think about your product? What will they think about you?

7. *The seventh sentence states your marketing budget.*

What marketing budget, you say? We understand that your organization doesn't have a wad of money to spend on marketing promotion—that's why you need guerrilla marketing. There is a lot you can do for free. But you can't do it all for free. In a tight economy, marketing is the single activity you can engage in that brings in more revenue to your organization. Don't be afraid to invest in the one thing that can turn your organization's situation around. Dedicate a consistent amount of money to marketing and you will see a return on your investment. Like any investment, the dividends build over time. How much should you dedicate? Many companies dedicate 4 percent, 10 percent, even 15 percent of their revenues to marketing. Only you know what is a fit for the culture of your organization.

Put all the sentences you write from the items above on paper with a marketing calendar for the next 12 to 18 months, and you have an excellent tool for getting your organization's marketing moving forward toward success. Most nonprofits have plenty of marketing activity, but too few have clearly defined purposes behind their marketing plans. Even fewer have written marketing plans.

The Analogy of the Parade

Looking at the marketing of most organizations is like standing on the sidewalk watching the Macy's Thanksgiving Day parade. Marketing promotions, events, and activities pass by like parade floats; some are more impressive in design than others, but the parade continues. The individual items in the parade may not be related to one another, but they are all entertaining in their own way. The parade goes by, float by float . . . or, rather, event by event, promotion by promotion. It's quite a spectacle to watch. Then, as the Santa Claus float appears (the end of the year), the marketer knows the parade is almost over until next year. No one seems to stop to ask what all the marketing activity parading by in the nonprofit's schedule has to do with the results on the bottom line. As long as the promotional items look good (or, at least, look better than last year's stuff), everyone is satisfied.

What nonprofit marketers need is a parade master who develops a theme for all the marketing they do and leverages the momentum from one marketing activity to the next with the organization's objectives always in mind. The parade master for your marketing plan is a guerrilla marketing calendar. Create a document with 52 lines, one for every week in the year. In five columns across the list write 1) number of the week; 2) thrust or emphasis for that week; 3) marketing weapons used; 4) budget for the week; and 5) results at the end of the week (i.e., responses, dollars, rating scale, etc.). Now all your marketing activity can be seen at a glance, and as a guerrilla, you can organize your parade of marketing actions into a guerrilla marketing victory march for your organization.

The 17 Secrets to Maintaining Your Marketing Attack

Below we list the concepts that can mean the difference between your success and failure as you launch your marketing attack. Getting started is half the battle, but the battle cannot be won if you give up the fight in the middle. These cornerstones of guerrilla marketing can carry you through even the most difficult situations. Each item will power charge your marketing and help you fulfill your organization's dreams.

1. *Commitment.* Even a mediocre marketing plan with commitment is more effective than a brilliant one with no commitment. Commitment is what makes good marketing happen.

2. *Investment.* Your organization's spending on marketing is not a mere expense; rather it is an investment that will yield a return. Thinking like a guerrilla is what makes your investment more sure to reap bountiful rewards.

3. *Consistency.* Your marketing will take a while to take effect. Stick with it and you will see results if you don't change your marketing, media, and identity. Consistency and repetition are keys to getting noticed by your target audience. Exercise great restraint before making changes.

4. *Confidence.* Trust is a valuable asset for your organization. People support organizations they believe in. If your clients give you a no–confidence vote, you won't be effective in anything you do.

5. *Patience.* Since marketing is an investment that yields dividends over time, you will need to be patient while you let it work. Many organizations change their marketing because they want overnight results. They never get as many results from making changes as they would from the big payoff they could receive through practicing patience.

6. *Assortment.* Guerrillas don't believe in using a single marketing weapon because they know a combination of weapons always works better.

7. *Convenience.* Make it easy on the people you do business with to work with you. Use processes that are less bureaucratic and they will respond to your outreach. It's not about you; it is about them, after all.

8. *Follow–up.* The real benefits in mobilization and fundraising happen after you have made the initial contact with people. Instead of ending when people first respond, with guerrillas things are only beginning.

9. *Amazement.* There are elements in the story of the work your organization does that may stun people. Make sure your marketing reflects these things. Marketing creativity is the truth made fascinating.

10. *Measurement.* You can double your results just by keeping track of your responses from people and adjusting to optimize your follow–up with them. The more you know what makes people respond, the better you can get them to repeat the behavior.

11. *Involvement.* The closer you are to the action, the better your marketing. Nonguerrillas who stay in their ivory towers are always at the mercy of the marketers on the front lines.

12. *Partnership.* Guerrillas are always looking for fusion marketing partnership opportunities for their nonprofits. When you help others succeed, doors open up for you also. It's not just good karma; it also saves you money and energy, and amplifies your outreach.

13. *Armament.* If you want to win the battle for the hearts and minds of your targeted community, you will need the right marketing tools to do it. The guerrilla's armaments are of the latest high–tech variety: computers, current software, social media, and cell phones. For the record, technology is not going away; if you have even a little Luddite in you, get the lead out.

14. *Consent.* Quite the opposite from what some people think, guerrillas do not force their marketing on unwilling parties. People actually anticipate communication from guerrillas because they get permission

from the people who receive their marketing materials. Nothing is gained by making a nuisance of yourself. Marketing to people who don't give permission is a waste of time.

15. *Content.* Guerrillas don't hype their products, services, and programs with misleading information or through overly slick design. Instead of offering style, they bring substance to their customers.

16. *Augmentation.* Good marketing happens in combinations. For example, guerrilla websites are more effective with offline promotions, freshly updated content, articles, webinars, instant messaging, and participation in discussion forums and social media. Guerrilla marketing weapons work in synergy with one another.

> There are one-way brains and two-way brains.
>
> One-way brains acquire loads of information but two-way brains take action on that information. Guerrillas have two-way brains.

17. *Implementation.* Guerrilla marketing is based on the take–action mind–set. You can have the most ingenious idea and most creative advertising strategy, but unless you are ready and willing to engage, you will not experience results.

How to Spy on Yourself and Improve Your Marketing

Guerrillas build feedback and evaluation into all their marketing plans. They are sticklers for using research and evaluation because they know it helps them learn what they are doing well and helps them identify areas that need improvement. It's a lot like spying on themselves. It's not unusual to find guerrillas starting pilot projects, testing direct mail copy, and asking customers for feedback. Site visits and secret shoppers also help guerrillas do self–espionage to learn how to make improvements.

Nonguerrillas don't want to use testing and evaluation. They are afraid they will learn something that will upset them (or their board of directors) and suggest that they need to change the way they do things. So rather than measure their effectiveness, they continue to do the same things over and over each year because they have always done them that way. If their programs don't yield the results they once produced, instead of seeking to make changes to increase responsiveness, they resolve to do what they have always done, only harder. Success gets trampled under the sacred cows of organizations that are afraid of feedback and evaluation.

One reason nonguerrillas don't like feedback is because they are not used to getting it. Actually, they get feedback; they just haven't accustomed themselves to watching for it and listening to it. When people stop supporting their organization, it doesn't occur to them to find out why. Year after year they keep records and write annual reports, but it never dawns on them to study their data and look for trends. When there is a decline in participation among a segment of the population, they assume people are no longer interested in their programs. They start looking for new programs that seem to be working in other parts of the country. No effort is made to research what are the current population and social trends among the declining segment in the field where they work.

> A guerrilla is flexible enough to know how to change plans when needed.

Most nonprofit organizations have more information on hand than they actually use in the form of the records they keep. Larger organizations are the worst culprits for not taking advantage of all the customer data they have. If your organization simply takes a look at your records, new ideas for improvement will become apparent. Guerrillas are keenly aware of what their customers like and don't like. If someone leaves, they find out why. They know what the public thinks of them because they ask in research. Guerrillas figure, why should leaders in their organization be the last to know when people like or dislike them? Getting evaluation and feedback doesn't intimidate guerrillas because they know feedback is not always negative. Researching the public perception toward your organization may reveal you have more opportunity to influence people than you think. You may know that people like your products and programs, but you may not know what they like about them or why they like it. Evaluation helps answer the questions that help nonprofits continually improve themselves.

Index